THE LONG OBEDIENCE

BY THE SAME AUTHOR

*Voices in the desert: Margaret and William Ballinger:
A biography* (Benedic Books, 1997)

Voorloper: Die lewe van Schalk Pienaar (Tafelberg, 2001)

*Prophet without honour: F.S. Malan: Afrikaner,
South African and Cape liberal* (Protea Book House, 2011)

*Iron in the soul: The leaders of the official parliamentary opposition
in South Africa, 1910–1993* (Protea Book House, 2017)

The opportunist: The political life of Oswald Pirow, 1915–1959
(Protea Book House, 2020)

THE LONG OBEDIENCE

The political career of Zach de Beer, 1953–1994

F.A. MOUTON

Protea Book House
Pretoria
2023

The long obedience
F.A. Mouton

First edition, first impression in 2023 by Protea Book House
PO Box 35110, Menlo Park, 0102
1067 Burnett Street, Hatfield, Pretoria
8 Minni Street, Clydesdale, Pretoria
info@proteaboekhuis.co.za
www.proteaboekhuis.com

EDITOR: Danél Hanekom
PROOFREADER: Carmen Hansen-Kruger
COVER AND BOOK DESIGN: Hanli Deysel
COVER IMAGE: Richard Cutler
SET IN: 10 pt on 14 ZapfCalligraphy by Hanli Deysel

Gedruk deur *novus print*, 'n afdeling van Novus Holdings

ISBN: 978-1-4853-1449-3 (printed book)
ISBN: 978-1-4853-1450-9 (e-book)

Original text © 2023 F.A. Mouton
Published edition © 2023 Protea Book House

All rights reserved. No part of this book may be reproduced or transmitted in any form or by any electronic or mechanical means, be it photocopying, disk or tape recording, or any other system for information storage or retrieval, without the prior written permission of the publisher.

CONTENTS

Preface 7

CHAPTER 1	A student of the right type, *1928–1951*	13
CHAPTER 2	The United Party candidate, *1952–1953*	24
CHAPTER 3	The golden boy, *1953–1956*	34
CHAPTER 4	The Senate Plan, *1956–1958*	47
CHAPTER 5	Contemplating a smaller party that can speak with one voice, *1958–1959*	60
CHAPTER 6	The Progressive Party, *1959*	70
CHAPTER 7	The winds of change, *January–March 1960*	79
CHAPTER 8	Opposing the banning of the African National Congress and the Pan Africanist Congress, *March–December 1960*	87
CHAPTER 9	A session of petrified minds, *January–June 1961*	95
CHAPTER 10	A young man with a great future behind him, *August–December 1961*	108
CHAPTER 11	To be shaped by defeat, *1962–1966*	116
CHAPTER 12	The Progressive Party as a propagator of modernity, *1967–1970*	127
CHAPTER 13	The comeback, *1971–1977*	136
CHAPTER 14	Member for Parktown, *1977*	147
CHAPTER 15	Impatience with parliament, *1978–1979*	155
CHAPTER 16	Farewell to parliament, *1979–1980*	165
CHAPTER 17	You cannot do good business in a rotten society, *1980–1985*	173
CHAPTER 18	Meeting the African National Congress leadership, *1985*	181
CHAPTER 19	A shaken and demoralised party, *1986–1987*	187

CHAPTER 20	The leadership of a battered political party, *1988–1989*	198
CHAPTER 21	Parliament and the Democratic Party, *January–September 1989*	210
CHAPTER 22	The shattering of the political mould, *September 1989–February 1990*	223
CHAPTER 23	A new political mould, *February–August 1990*	234
CHAPTER 24	Party leader, *September–December 1990*	243
CHAPTER 25	A kind of political concussion, *1991*	253
CHAPTER 26	The Liberal crusader, *1992*	261
CHAPTER 27	The marginalisation of the Democratic Party, *January–June 1993*	270
CHAPTER 28	Fighting for survival, *July–December 1993*	277
CHAPTER 29	A gruelling campaign, *January–April 1994*	287
CHAPTER 30	The near annihilation of the Democratic Party, *April 1994*	296
CHAPTER 31	Resignation and retirement, *1994–1999*	304

Epilogue 318
Bibliography 321
Index 328

PREFACE

Politics is a merciless business that does not reward prudence, vision or far-sightedness unless accompanied by short-term success. History can afford to take a kinder view.

D. Meleady, *John Redmond. The national leader* (Padstow, 2014), p. 9

"There should be a long obedience in the same direction, there thereby results, and has always resulted in the long run, something which has made life worth living" was Zach de Beer's version of a quote from Friedrich Nietzsche which he wrote down and gave to Dene Smuts when she was elected as the Democratic Party's parliamentary representative for Groote Schuur in September 1989. It was his way to remind her that liberal convictions in the apartheid state "were forged in adversity. Because there was no profit and there were no rewards in being liberal."[1] The long-term reward would be a liberal democratic South Africa, and this could only be achieved by telling the truth and by sticking to one's liberal principles.

"The long obedience" to liberal principles applied to De Beer's political career. For decades, with little reward, he opposed apartheid in and out of parliament. In 1950, as a student leader, he opposed the banning of the Communist Party, and as a Progressive Party member of parliament he championed the gradual extension of political rights to the black majority. In 1960 he opposed the outlawing of the African National Congress and the Pan Africanist Congress. This was a courageous action that would cost him his parliamentary seat in the 1961 general elections and condemned him to many years in the political wilderness. With the revival of the Progressives he was elected to parliament in 1977, but resigned

---

1 D. Smuts, *Patriots & parasites. South Africa and the struggle to evade history* (Rondebosch, 2016), p. 322.

in 1980 to focus on his business career. In 1988, he returned as leader of the battered and demoralised Progressive Federal Party, and from 1989 was co-leader of the newly founded Democratic Party, and from 1990 the sole leader.

During the darkest oppressive years of the apartheid state, he played a crucial role in keeping liberal democratic ideals alive. In doing so, he made a significant contribution to convince whites to accept constitutional reforms, helping to pave the way for President F.W. de Klerk's dramatic announcement of 2 February 1990 that signified the end of the apartheid state. And yet, in South Africa's first democratic parliamentary election of April 1994, De Beer as leader of the Democratic Party found himself accused of collaborating with racial oppression and exploitation for serving as a liberal in the apartheid state's parliament. Against the worst possible odds, he led the Democratic Party with its lack of party structures and money – while trapped between the competing National Party, African National Congress and the Inkatha Freedom Party – to a crushing defeat, securing only 1,7 per cent of the vote. The party's poor performance ended De Beer's political career, since he resigned as party leader as well as a parliamentarian. In the new South Africa, De Beer has become merely a historical footnote as the leader that had led his party to a near annihilating defeat in the country's first fully democratic election.

The desire to write this political biography dates back to 19 April 1994 while I attended an electoral information meeting for University of South Africa (Unisa) students in the Senate Hall. The leaders or senior leadership figures of the various parties contesting the election were invited to address the students. These leaders, including Marthinus van Schalkwyk of the National Party, were listened to in respectful silence until De Beer came to explain the policies of the Democratic Party. The students were outraged when he stated that as a liberal, he had always opposed apartheid. When he mentioned that he was one of a handful of Progressive Party parliamentarians who had been courageous enough in 1960 to vote against the outlawing of the African National Congress and the Pan Africanist Congress they erupted in contemptuous jeering. It struck me that the students had no knowledge or understanding of the role of liberalism in opposing apartheid. This study is an attempt to explain the complexity and ambiguity of being a white liberal in a period of intolerance and oppression, and to evaluate De Beer's political achievements.

Apart from the Covid pandemic that led to archives being closed, it was a challenge to write this political biography as De Beer made no real effort to keep any of his papers. He told his daughter, Wendy de Beer Furniss, several times that he hadn't kept papers as he felt he either had to keep everything, or else there wasn't much point in it. By 1990/91 he had some boxes of papers stored in an empty flat adjacent to the one he lived in in Clifton, but in a plumbing-related flood quite a lot of the documents were ruined. Some of the remaining papers, about seven or eight boxes full, containing texts of numerous speeches, and draft articles for newspapers and magazines, as well as newspaper clippings and a few personal documents, were packed up and taken to the Netherlands when he was appointed as the South African ambassador. From there it was shipped to Wendy in London.[2] Fortunately, Wendy kept the letters he had written to her over the years and they provide important insights into his political career.

Disappointingly, the United Party archive at Unisa produced nothing more than newspaper clippings even though he was a prominent member of the party. The Progressive Party papers in this archive were equally disappointing. When the national head office of the Progressive Federal Party went through its documents in 1981 with a view to sending them to the archives at Unisa, files found of De Beer were not seen as suitable archival material, as they were seemingly too personal, and they were returned to him.[3] It is possible that these files were destroyed in the Clifton flat flood. Fortunately, the Progressive Federal Party/Democratic

---

2   Correspondence with Wendy de Beer Furniss, 13 March 2021.
3   University of South Africa (hereafter Unisa) archives, Progressive Federal Party papers, File 32.3, J. Selfe – Zach de Beer, 25 May 1981.

Party collection at the University of the Witwatersrand provided important information on De Beer's role in the administration, finances and policy making of these parties. The uncatalogued papers of Max Borkum, a former prominent Progressive Party activist, at the University of the Witwatersrand has private letters by De Beer on party activities. At the Brenthurst Library, the H.F. Oppenheimer papers contain several letters to Harry Oppenheimer, his mentor and friend, as well as to Pieter de Kock, a close friend, who was Oppenheimer's personal assistant in the late 1950s. To Oppenheimer and De Kock he confided his personal worries, problems and ambitions. The archival collections of contemporary politicians such as J.G.N. Strauss, Douglas Mitchell, Van Zyl Slabbert, Helen Suzman, Sir De Villiers Graaff, and Joyce and Frank Waring also provided information on De Beer's political career.

I was unable to consult the papers of Harry Lawrence and Donald Molteno as the Jagger Library at the University of Cape Town was gutted in a fire on 18 April 2021. Although the archival collections in the basement were undamaged, the reading room had been destroyed.[4] Fortunately, these collections deal with a part of De Beer's career that has been used extensively in historical works written on the early years of the Progressive Party.

Hansard, the published debates of the House of Assembly, was extensively used and provided an important insight into the political thought of De Beer. Furthermore, I was in the privileged position that I could interview De Beer's children Wendy, Debbie, and Zach. Wendy interviewed her mother Maureen on my behalf. Another important source was Mienke Bain, De Beer's personal assistant between 1988 and 1994. I also interviewed or corresponded with several former Progressive and Democratic Party politicians such as Dennis Worrall, Wynand Malan, Tony Leon, Peter Soal, Douglas Gibson, Ken Andrew, James Selfe, David Gant, Peter Gastrow, Robin Carlisle, and Dr Pieter Mulder, a former mem-

---

4 In July 2022 I was informed by Clive Kirkwood, archivist for special collections, that there is no timeframe for the reopening of the reading room.

ber of the Conservative Party. Sadly, more than 60 years after the founding of the Progressive Party in 1959, all the Progressives of De Beer's generation are deceased.

In 1986, as a doctoral student researching the political career of Margaret Ballinger, former leader of the Liberal Party, I interviewed or corresponded with Colin Eglin, Ray Swart, Helen Suzman, Jan Steytler, Walter Stanford, Oscar Wollheim and Zach de Beer. Today, many years later, I was able to use these interviews to create the political environment in which the Progressive Party was formed in 1959 and understand Ballinger's attitude to her fellow liberals. However, listening to the recording of my interview with De Beer, I could not help but regret that I did not ask him more about his own career.

In attempting this political biography, I followed the example set by W.K. Hancock, the highly respected Australian biographer of the South African statesman Jan Smuts. He argued that the chief danger for a biographer was that he would distort the historical record by making him his subject's advocate.[5] As a liberal and a former supporter of the Progressive Federal Party and Democratic Party, I could not be impartial about De Beer, but was determined to be honest and candid. At all costs I wanted to avoid a eulogistic biography or an apologia, and attempted to portray him honestly and candidly.

During my research and writing I owe much to Wendy for her support and patience in dealing with my never-ending queries, and for providing me with scanned copies of photographs, cartoons and documents with the support of her husband Graham. I am grateful to all the staff of the many archives and libraries I visited for their assistance. I am particularly indebted to Marieta Buys and Busi Mofu of the University of Stellenbosch, Henry Liebenberg of the University of South Africa, Jennifer Kimble and Sally MacRoberts of the Brenthurst Library, Gabriel Mohale of the William Cullen Library at the University of the Witwatersrand, and Dr Paul Murray of the Bishops Diocesan College archive.

---

5   W.K. Hancock, *Professing history* (Sydney, 1976), p. 61.

A special word of thanks to Anton Ehlers and Jan-Jan Joubert for assisting me with my research. My gratitude also goes to Danél Hanekom, my editor and friend, for her assistance and patience in making this book readable. Finally, a word of thanks to Aline. Without her love and support this book would not have been possible.

F.A. Mouton
PRETORIA

CHAPTER 1
A student of the right type
1928–1951

At the two memorial services for Zacharias (Zach) Johannes de Beer in Cape Town on 31 May, and in Johannesburg on 3 June 1999, he was praised as a conviction liberal. Compared to so many of his fellow liberals in the apartheid era, his sense of duty and justice to all regardless of their colour or race in an ultraconservative and racist society was not the product of a Damascene conversion or the gradual development as an adult, but dated back to his childhood.

De Beer was born on 11 October 1928 as the second of four children of Jean Isobel (McCrae) and Zacharias Johannes (Ray) de Beer in Aberdeen House, 20 Victoria Road in Woodstock, Cape Town where his parents lived at the time. He was named after his grandfather, Zacharias Johannes – known as Zack to his friends – who was born in 1856 in the Paarl, and after his studies at Stellenbosch became a teacher at Paarl Gimnasium in 1878. For the period between 1880 and 1882 he was headmaster of the school. In 1883 he returned to Stellenbosch to qualify as a Dutch Reformed Church (DRC) minister. His first congregation was in George in 1887, and from 1895 to 1923 when poor health forced him to retire, he was a much loved minister in Papendorp in Cape Town, which eventually became Woodstock. Shortly before his death on 13 August 1929, he had baptised his namesake grandson.[1] A hallmark of Reverend De Beer's career was his love for travel – he visited Europe, America and Palestine – and for church music. Before his ordination he was

---

1 Sheilah Macrae Lloyd, "Remembrance of time past. Childhood days" (Unpublished memoirs of De Beer's sister in the possession of Wendy de Beer Furniss), *Die Burger*, 14 August 1929.

the organist of the Paarl congregation. This was a love his grandson shared.²

Ray de Beer was a highly respected medical doctor with a practice in Woodstock. He lived with the principle that the individual must be of service to his community and country. According to his obituary in the *South African Medical Journal* (16 May 1953), he had a large working-class practice in Woodstock with "a reputation for honest-to-goodness doctoring". He would tend to poor patients, especially in the coloured suburb of District Six, without expecting payment. His dedication to his patients made him a much-loved character in Woodstock.³ De Beer adored his warm, charming and principled father. When talking to his own children about their grandfather, he would often become very emotional.⁴

Jean de Beer was from Inverness, Scotland, where her father was the stationmaster. To De Beer's amusement, his mother had Scottish nationalist predilections and believed that the most worthwhile political event of the twentieth century was the stealing of the Stone of Scone by young nationalists from Westminster Abbey in 1950.⁵ According to her granddaughter Wendy, she was "quite a forceful character".⁶ While studying art at Edinburgh University she met Ray. After his graduation in 1918 he returned to Cape Town and she arrived in South Africa in 1923. They married shortly after. This led to some unhappiness in the De Beer family as Jean's mother-in-law wanted her son to marry an Afrikaner.

Because of Jean's inability to speak Afrikaans, the home language of the De Beer family was English. As she could not cope with her son's Afrikaans names, she duly called him Ian, which her

---

2 https://www.gemeentegeskiedenis.co.za/de-beer-zacharias-johannes/ (Accessed on 25 May 2022.); Interview with Wendy de Beer Furniss, 24 May 2022.
3 S. Gastrow, *Who's who in South African politics*, No. 3 (Johannesburg, 1992), pp. 47–48.
4 Interview with Wendy de Beer Furniss, 16 April 2020.
5 Z259, Z. de Beer, "Confessions of an old Cape liberal". (In the possession of Wendy de Beer Furniss.)
6 Correspondence with Wendy de Beer Furniss, 29 May 2020.

husband grudgingly accepted. Their son was less accepting, and in his late teens rebelled and insisted on being called Zach like his grandfather.[7] Through his father, the extended De Beer family, and with the help of their domestic servant in the kitchen, Zach was fluent in Afrikaans.[8] He was proud of his Afrikaner identity.

De Beer was raised in a warm and loving family, and an affluent one in a time of economic hardship, with the assistance of white nannies. This affluence was reflected in him visiting his Scottish family with his mother in 1938. Growing up during the Great Depression, he would have memories of rows of white men digging trenches with picks and shovels, and with a distinguished old man looking like General Hertzog working in the garden.[9] He attended Bishops Diocesan College in Rondebosch from 1936 to 1945 where he was known as De Beer II as there was another De Beer pupil. Standing at five foot eleven and a half inches, he was athletic, and as a member of the first teams in cricket and rugby was awarded school colours in 1945. One of his teammates and a close friend was Clive van Ryneveld, who would play rugby for England and cricket for South Africa.

De Beer also excelled off the sports fields as a house prefect for Ogilvie House, a day-boy house. In 1945 he was a member of the Ten Club, a society comprising the top ten academics in the senior year. He was also a member of the Foreign Affairs Society. That he showed an early interest in politics was reflected in him being the secretary of the College's Debating Society. On 27 October 1945, in the wake of the nuclear attack on Hiroshima, he debated the topic "That in the opinion of this House, technical advances are a danger to mankind". The proposer of the motion, M.P. Rydon, pointed out the dangers of modern weapons of war and that the enormous mass of money spent on such things could well be used

---

7 Sheilah Macrae Lloyd, "Remembrance of time past. Childhood days" (Unpublished memoirs of De Beer's sister in the possession of Wendy de Beer Furniss.)
8 Interview with D. Cox, 13 April 2020.
9 Z290, Speech at an architectural dinner, 5 October 1985. (In the possession of Wendy de Beer Furniss.)

for better purposes, such as the abolition of slums. De Beer, in seconding the motion, compared the present-day world and the potentialities which it has to a child with a bottle of arsenic. He was loudly cheered, and the motion was carried with a vote of one.[10]

De Beer matriculated in 1945 with a first-class pass with distinctions in English, Latin, Mathematics & Physics. In addition, he won the College's first prize in the Louis Esselen Afrikaans Speech Competition. Furthermore, he shared the Hands Essay award, with an essay on Christianity in the modern world. The report of the Literary Society in the *Diocesan School Magazine*, (Vol. XXX, December 1945) described it as a provocative one:

> As cold was the absence of heat, so, he maintained, was the evil of the absence of good. The world had now reached a crisis where its only salvation was in Christianity. The choice was between Christianity and hell.

As an adult his religiosity would fade, but he never lost his determination to fight for good against evil.

He was also a committee member of the Play-Reading Circle. A legacy of his time at Bishops was his love for Afrikaans poetry. His daughter Wendy remembers him reciting poems of Eugène Marais for her and her siblings when they were growing up. With his retirement he had to downsize his library in Saxonwold, Johannesburg, considerably, but took his poetry collections of N.P. van Wyk Louw (1956), *Nuwe verse*; Eugène Marais, *Versamelde gedigte* (1957); and Adam Small, *Kitaar my kruis* (1962) with him when he moved to a smaller flat in Cape Town. He especially enjoyed the poems of G.K. Chesterton. When a close friend, Andrew Savage, former Progressive Federal Party MP for Walmer, died in July 1990, he could, after being unable to find the poem, recall part of Chesterton's "The rolling English road" – although not completely accurately – to laud Savage's courage while facing a long

---

10 I am grateful to Dr Paul Murray, School Archivist, Bishops Diocesan College, for providing me with the information on De Beer's school career.

and debilitating illness.[11] Poetry would pepper his parliamentary speeches.

In 1946 De Beer went to study medicine at the University of Cape Town (UCT). By then his interest in politics was aroused by World War II. He always had a particularly clear vision of being taken to a war fundraising evening and belting out "There'll always be an England"' at the top of his voice. But more importantly, the assault of Nazism on human dignity left him with the perception that racism was wrong.[12] De Beer attributed his own deeply held liberal principles to his father who exemplified classical liberal ideals and was a life-long subscriber to the left-wing *New Statesman*. (Ironically, Ray's younger brother Dan, a DRC minister and Secretary of the Transvaal synod's General Commission for Public Morals, became one of South Africa's leading ultraconservative public figures. He would become known as "Hunter of Sins" and "Mr Morals".[13] However, he would be a much-loved uncle of De Beer and his siblings, including his younger brother Donald, who became a Catholic priest and a leading figure in the Catholic community. In 1992 the Pope made him a domestic prelate with the title of Monsignor.[14]) Although Ray was not actively involved in party politics, it was regularly discussed at home, fuelling his son's interest.[15] Through these discussions he became aware of the political career of the Afrikaner liberal Senator F. S. Malan who died on 31 December 1941. In an interview with the *Financial Mail* (25 April 1980) De Beer made it clear that much of his political thinking had been influenced by Malan who saw the need to reconcile the aspirations of Afrikaner nationalism and black nationalism.

---

11 Correspondence with Wendy de Beer Furniss, 16 December 2020 and 3 August 2022; De Beer – Errol Moorcroft and Rory Riordan, 25 July 1990. (In the possession of Wendy de Beer Furniss.)
12 Z259, Z. de Beer, "Confessions of an old Cape liberal". (In the possession of Wendy de Beer Furniss.)
13 C.J. Beyers, J.L. Basson (eds), *Dictionary of South African Biography*. Vol. V (Pretoria, 1987), pp. 165–166.
14 Interview with D. Cox, 13 April 2020: *The Southern Cross*, 30 July 2000.
15 *Finansies & Tegniek*, March 1985.

F.S. Malan was a fiery Afrikaner nationalist and the editor of *Ons Land*, the most influential Dutch newspaper in the Colony and mouthpiece of the Afrikaner Bond in the late 1890s. In April 1901, during the South African War, *Ons Land*'s criticism of the British military resulted in Malan being sentenced to one year in prison for the criminal libel of General John French. For Malan, prison was a road-to-Damascus experience as it made him aware of individual freedom and freed him from his racist views. After 1902 he would be a leading proponent of a common citizenship for South Africans of all races. At the National Convention (1908–1909), which framed the South Africa Bill, Malan appealed for a union with a general and non-racial-qualified franchise, based on a high qualification test. Malan believed that white survival would best be secured through the extension of equal political rights to all races. For him total racial segregation was unwise, impractical and unjust. The Convention rejected a general franchise, but Malan did secure the retention of the African and coloured franchise in the Cape. Malan used his influence as a cabinet minister in the governments of Louis Botha and Jan Smuts to moderate the rigours of racial segregation on black people, while he was an outspoken defender of the non-racial franchise in the Cape Province. In the 1924 general election Malan lost his parliamentary seat. Smuts had to use his influence to ensure that he was made a senator in 1927. Malan only remained in the Senate to defend the Cape franchise against attempts to remove it from the common voters' roll. In 1936, an emotional Malan fought to the bitter end against legislation which succeeded in placing black voters on a separate voters' roll.[16]

During his political career De Beer did his utmost to emulate the example set by Malan.

In May 1948, De Beer was stunned when the NP secured an unexpected narrow victory in the general election. "No one thought it was going to win and the NP was regarded as passé in English-speaking circles. Much of the controversy among my friends

---

16 For Malan's liberalism see F.A. Mouton, *Prophet without honour. F.S. Malan: Afrikaner, South African and Cape liberal* (Pretoria, 2011).

was about how good or bad communism was ..."[17] The United Party's (UP) defeat was a consequence of the NP becoming a mass nationalist movement because of Afrikaner opposition to the decision to side with Britain in World War II. White unease with rapid black urbanisation and the subsequent rise in crime was also a factor. The NP based its election campaign on apartheid, which aimed at stricter segregation on a territorial, political and social basis.

In power, the NP immediately applied legislation to separate black and white at all levels of society. Up to 1953, the fundamental pillars were enacted, for example, the Mixed Marriages Act of 1949 that made marriage between whites and non-whites illegal. The following year, an amendment to the Immorality Act banned sexual relations between whites and all people of colour, while the Population Registration Act of 1950 classified all South Africans according to race. The Group Areas Act of the same year brought about residential segregation based on colour. The Bantu Authorities Act of 1951 partly abolished elected local councils, as well as the Natives Representative Council[18] to be replaced by tribal authorities. Apart from regarding the NRC as a haven for communists, H.F. Verwoerd, the Minister of Native Affairs, justified its closure on the grounds that it failed to accommodate ethnic divisions among blacks. The Native Laws Amendment Act of 1952 allowed only black people, who had been born in urban areas and had lived there continuously for fifteen years, or who had worked continuously for the same employer for ten years, to live permanently in them. Visitors and work seekers were limited to a stay of seventy-two hours. Urbanised blacks were also deprived of permanent property rights in urban areas. The Abolition of Passes Act of 1952 tightened existing pass laws which controlled the movements of black workers. Pass books were replaced with reference

---

17 *Sunday Tribune*, 29 May 1988.
18 The Council was established in terms of the Natives Representative Act of 1936, providing for elected councillors to represent the interests of black people.

books containing personal details and reference to the person's race. Living and working in "white" areas were illegal without a reference book. The Bantu Education Act of 1953 stipulated that black education had to be compatible with African traditions and with the goal of serving their own communities.

The ideal was to create "good Bantus" instead of imitators of Western civilisation. The Separate Amenities Act of 1953 enforced social segregation, for example on beaches. The NP also entrenched economic apartheid. The Native Labour (Settlement of Disputes) Act of 1953 prohibited strikes by blacks and did not legally recognise black trade unions.

The implementation of apartheid politicised De Beer. His concerns about its racism and intolerance was bolstered by Dr T.B. (Tom) Davie, the newly appointed principal of UCT, an outspoken champion of academic freedom and a champion of the right of universities to appoint staff, and to enrol students, whatever their colour, race, or religion. Davie was a person who signified duty and service to his community and country. In World War I he had joined the Royal Flying Corps, and during the Rand Revolt of 1922, while serving with the Transvaal Scottish Regiment, he was seriously wounded. During World War II, as a pathologist, he organised the blood transfusion services in Britain. Davie's values and sense of duty had a lasting influence on De Beer. In 1959 in a parliamentary debate, he explained how the culture of tolerance and open-mindedness at UCT had shaped his political thought:

> It taught me many things and one of the most valuable things it taught me is not to attempt to force other people to conform with my will and with my ideas.[19]

As the leader of UCT's Liberal Association, he became involved in student politics. In 1949 he was elected to the Students' Representative Council, becoming its president in 1950. He used this position to improve the position of black students. On 11 Septem-

---

19 House of Assembly debates, 10/11 April 1959, Col. 3665.

ber 1950, the council accepted his motion that the university had to provide funding for the establishment of campus accommodation for black students.[20] His presidency of the student council led to his first public political action. Sheila van der Horst, acting chair of the Civil Rights League, invited him to address a protest meeting in the Cape Town City Hall to oppose the Suppression of Communism Bill.[21]

The Civil Rights League was formed to oppose the growing authoritarianism of the apartheid state – the notion that white domination could be permanently maintained by sacrificing the rule of law. This led to the Suppression of Communism Act of 1950 that outlawed the Communist Party. This Act provided government the powers to prohibit any organisation that encouraged communism. In effect, the Bill was a means to persecute organisations and individuals opposing apartheid, including liberals who were vehement opponents of communism. This made it possible for the government to expel three democratically elected parliamentarians, the native representatives Sam Kahn, Brian Bunting and Ray Alexander, from the House of Assembly for being communists.[22]

De Beer's involvement with the Civil Rights League led to his association with Donald Molteno who shaped the development of his liberal principles. He was an outspoken liberal who believed that South Africans irrespective of race should be eligible for the franchise. Between 1937 and 1948, he had served as a native representative in parliament. With his election at the age of 29, he was the youngest member of the House of Assembly where he made an impact as one of its best members. Edgar Brooks, who had served

---

20 UCT administrative archives, SRC minutes, Box 175, 11 September 1950. (I am grateful to Anton Ehlers for providing me with this information.)
21 University of the Witwatersrand (hereafter Wits), Helen Suzman papers, Mb2.33.1.12, S. van der Horst – H. Suzman, 27 May 1994.
22 In terms of the Natives Representative At of 1936 blacks in the Cape Province were removed from the common voters' roll, placed on a separate roll with the right to elect three white representatives to the House of Assembly.

with Molteno in parliament, described him as one of the "clearest, strongest and honest minds with which I have ever come into contact".[23] He was respected as one of the country's leading advocates and left parliament in 1948 to focus on his legal career at the Cape Town Bar, as well as to campaign for the maintenance of the rule of law.

De Beer's presidency of the student council had another lasting influence, that of meeting his fellow councillor Maureen Strauss, oldest child of J.G.N. Strauss, leader of the UP and the official opposition. Struck by his blue eyes, and his gift of the gab, she developed a relationship with him.[24] The fact that he as a fit and strong student protected with fellow students public meetings against thugs from the NP,[25] could only have raised Maureen's esteem of him as she had a close relationship with her father.[26]

De Beer was fortunate to graduate in 1951 as he survived a potentially serious collision with a tree after falling asleep behind the wheel of his vehicle. He escaped serious injury but had a lifelong scar on his upper lip.[27] How impressive a student he was, was reflected in a letter that Professor B.J. Ryrie, Dean of the Faculty of Medicine, wrote to Ray. He was full of praise for his son's examination results, as well as his record as a student, "he has been a student of the right type, taking his so useful part in the life and work of the university".[28] His high standing at UCT was reflected in him being awarded the Abe Bailey Memorial Scholarship to visit Britain.[29]

On 29 March 1952, while serving as an intern at Groote Schuur Hospital, De Beer and Maureen got married. More than 600 guests,

---

23 E. Brooks, *A South African pilgrimage* (Johannesburg, 1972), p.77.
24 Recording of Wendy's interview with her mother, Maureen de Beer, 1 May 2020.
25 Wits, Brian Hackland papers; Interview with Zach de Beer, 14 July 1980.
26 H. Collie, "The man who succeeded Smuts", *The Outspan*, 11 January 1952.
27 Interview with Wendy de Beer Furniss, 2 November 2021.
28 Prof. B.J. Ryrie – Ray de Beer, 5 November 1951. (Letter in the possession of Wendy de Beer Furniss.)
29 *The Cape Argus*, 22 January 1953.

including Brand van Zyl, the Governor-General, and cabinet ministers attended the ceremony in the Rondebosch DRC congregation. The reception was at Fernwood, the parliamentary sports club. Dr Davie proposed the toast.[30] Three children, Wendy (1954), Zach (1955) and Debbie (1958) were born from the marriage.

De Beer spoke English to Maureen as her home language was English and because Mrs Strauss could not speak Afrikaans. However, he spoke Afrikaans to his children and taught them Afrikaans songs such as "Suikerbossie" and "Sarie Marais". Wendy recalls that at the age of four, her father had given her an Afrikaans bible. They attended the local DRC Sunday school, and were enrolled at the Afrikaans-medium Groote Schuur Primary School. Wendy also recalls her father's joy when as a small girl she responded in Afrikaans, "Ek is sopnat" (I am soaking wet) after falling into the Fernwood swimming pool.[31]

---

30 *Cape Times*, 31 March 1952.
31 Interview with Wendy de Beer Furniss, 24 May 2022; Correspondence with Wendy de Beer Furniss, 3 August 2022.

CHAPTER 2
The United Party candidate
1952–1953

After completing his housemanship year at Groote Schuur Hospital, De Beer joined his father's practice in Woodstock. Established as a general practitioner, he became more involved in the UP. It was a party struggling to come to terms with its defeat in 1948, the death of J.C. Smuts in 1950, and the growing popularity of the NP's white supremacy stance amongst the conservative white electorate.

A crucial weakness of the official opposition was the unpopularity of Strauss in the UP's parliamentary caucus. Various factors made him unacceptable for many MPs. Some felt that he was a political liability as they believed that his unpopularity as the Minister of Agriculture in the Smuts government did much to lose the UP the 1948 election. However, his shy and reserved personality was the main source of misgivings. His aloofness was seen as coldness, self-centeredness and arrogance, flaunting the fact that he was more intelligent than his fellow MPs. It was especially his inability to suffer fools that alienated many. From the first day of his leadership Strauss not only had to deal with a resentful caucus, but also with relentless and merciless personal attacks on him by the NP and its supporting press. In addition, the UP was financially bankrupt with a decaying organisation, while it was deeply divided between conservatives and liberals.

The liberals, a small but vocal group in the party, were outspoken defenders of the rule of law, criticised aspects of the principle of segregation, and viewed the coloured franchise as an inalienable right to be defended to the end as the franchise was seen as a solution to South Africa's racial challenge. The 1853 constitution of the Cape Colony provided for a franchise with educational and age qualifications which placed no bar on colour and advocated the principle of equal rights for all "civilised" (Westernised and educated) men. At the National Convention of 1908–1910, the Transvaal, Orange Free State and Natal were opposed to the Cape franchise. This impasse led to a compromise in which the Cape franchise was accepted for that province and entrenched in the constitution, and could only be altered by a two-thirds majority vote of both houses of parliament sitting together. Membership of parliament was restricted to white men while the Cape provincial council would be open to men of all races.[1] For the NP with its social engineering the 45 000 coloured men on the common voters' roll in the Cape Province was ideologically unacceptable.

Prime Minister D.F. Malan made it clear that the constitutionally required two-thirds majority to remove coloureds from the common voters' roll would not deter him. On 8 March 1951, the NP introduced a Bill to place coloureds on a separate voters' roll to elect four white parliamentary representatives. The Bill was not introduced to a joint sitting of the House of Assembly and the Senate. The NP claimed that because of the constitutional developments giving South Africa dominion status in the 1930s the entrenched clauses no longer applied.

On 14 May 1951, parliament passed the Separate Representation of Voters Bill. Strauss played a leading role in initiating legal proceedings against the Act. This was against the wishes of some UP members as they feared that it would play into the hands of the NP in the coming general election.[2] In March 1952, the Appeal Court nullified the Separate Representation of Voters Act for ignoring the entrenched section of the constitution. The NP, arguing that the court decision invalidated parliamentary sovereignty, promptly passed the High Court of Parliament Bill which turned parlia-

---

1. L. Thompson, *The unification of South Africa 1902–1910* (Oxford, 1960), pp. 219, 223, 225.
2. D.M. Scher, "The disenfranchisement of the Coloured voters, 1948–1956" (D.Litt. et Phil. University of South Africa, 1983), pp. 188, 205, 236–237, 250–251.

ment into a high court to repeal the decision of the Appeal Court. The Bill was vehemently opposed by Strauss as an underhand attempt which smashed the constitution and damaged South Africa's image abroad.[3] On the insistence of Strauss, the UP again turned to the courts. On 27 August 1952, parliament constituted itself into a high court, the UP boycotted the meeting and declared the Separate Representation of Voters Act valid. Two days later the Cape Supreme Court, to the fury of the NP and most Afrikaners who were of the opinion that white survival was more important than the constitution, declared the High Court of Parliament Act invalid.[4]

The conservatives in the UP – personified by Douglas Mitchell, the autocratic and dynamic ultraconservative leader of the UP in Natal, the most influential wing of the party as it was the only province dominated by the party – were crude white supremacists, sharing the NP's racial prejudices.[5] Mitchell made it clear that he stood for white "baasskap" (dominance) – that the white man was the political boss and would remain so. And yet, the party's right wing supported Strauss's stance on the coloured vote. Mitchell, who could not speak Afrikaans, was a passionate defender of the language rights of the English-speaking community and the Commonwealth link with Britain. This played into Strauss's hand to defend the entrenched clauses. The NP's pro-German stance during World War II, and D.F. Malan's statement in 1948 that South Africa belonged to the Afrikaner and his efforts after 1948 to loosen ties with Britain, fuelled Mitchell's fear of an Afrikaner republic at the cost of the cultural rights of the English-speaking community and the Commonwealth link with Britain. Strauss hammered on the fact that if the NP could circumvent entrenched clauses on

---

3   House of Assembly debates, 22 April 1952, Col. 4136 and 5 May 1952, Col. 4925–4934.
4   A. Bekker, *Eben Dönges. Balansstaat. Historiese perspektief* (Stellenbosch, 2005), p. 75.
5   R. Swart, *Progressive odyssey. Towards a democratic South Africa* (Cape Town, 1991), pp. 31–32; J. Strangwayes-Booth, *A cricket in the thorn tree. Helen Suzman and the Progressive Party* (Johannesburg, 1976), p. 113.

the coloured franchise, it could do the same to the clause securing English as an official language. Mitchell became a staunch defender of the entrenched clauses, and a loyal supporter of Strauss.[6] At the same time he was determined to stamp out any liberalism in the UP. This fuelled the internecine warfare in the UP parliamentary caucus.

In February 1953, De Beer was approached to enter the nomination contest to select the UP candidate for the Maitland constituency in the upcoming general election of 15 April 1953. The constituency was created out of parts from the existing Salt River, Mowbray and Malmesbury constituencies and included the suburbs of Observatory, Milnerton, Rugby, Brooklyn and Maitland, and had 12 445 voters of whom 514 were coloureds. This constituency was the most unpredictable one in the coming election as it included a significant number of working-class Afrikaners. De Beer was initially surprised to be approached as there was an entrenched culture in the UP of a lengthy political apprenticeship. It was the norm that a political career would start in a city or town council before progressing to the provincial council and then to parliament. H.M. Timothy, his nomination rival, had been the provincial councillor for Salt River since 1949.

On entering the Maitland contest De Beer was certain that he would be nominated.[7] He had the advantage of having family associations with the constituency as he was born and raised in Woodstock where he also had his medical practice. In addition, his father was highly regarded and trusted in the area. His candidature was bolstered by his abilities as a public speaker while his appearance – athletic and blessed with the good looks of a film star – was bolstered by his intelligence and charm. The *Cape Times* (14 March 1953) was gushing in its admiration:

---

6   Unisa, Douglas E. Mitchell papers, File 1.2.21, D. Mitchell – E.E. Sturges, 18 March 1954.
7   Recording of Wendy's interview with her mother, Maureen de Beer, 26 April 2020.

Off the platform he has the easy, friendly manner of a man who likes people for their own sake – and he manages to bring this personality on to the platform and add to it a touch of seriousness. ... Everything about Zac de Beer is quick – above all, the swift and unhesitating manner he has of answering questions at public meetings.

His Afrikaner identity in a constituency with a large number of Afrikaner voters strengthened his candidature. The English-speaking Timothy, a 45-year-old garage-owner in Salt River, lacked his young opponent's star quality to grab the public's imagination. De Beer was duly elected as the UP candidate for Maitland. At 24 he would be the youngest candidate in the election.

Colin Eglin, whom he knew from the Villagers Football Club team where they played rugby together, was appointed as his election agent. It would be the beginning of a lifelong close friendship and political alliance based on their shared political philosophy, mutual trust, understanding, support, common purpose and the fact that they enjoyed each other's company and sense of fun.[8] What made their relationship so unique was that they had radically different personalities with differences that would impact on their political careers. Eglin did not suffer fools lightly – and his classification of a fool was pretty harsh.[9] De Beer, on the other hand, had great personal warmth, charm, and suffered fools gladly. He also had what the *Optima* magazine's profile in the 1980s described as a "shield of reserve and near cynicism".[10] He would become more courteous the lower his opinion of a person.[11] According to legend he only once lost his temper when as a teenager he was involved in a punch-up.[12] He also had the human touch that he never had to be reintroduced to anyone after an initial meeting.[13] Such a memory

---

8 C. Eglin, *Crossing the borders of power. The memoirs of Colin Eglin* (Johannesburg, 2007), pp. 48, 58–59.
9 Correspondence with M. Silbert, 21 November 2013.
10 Undated clipping of *Optima* in the possession of Wendy de Beer Furniss.
11 Correspondence with D. Gibson, 31 March 2020.
12 *Sunday Times*, 24 July 1988.
13 Interview with P. Soal, 11 April 2020.

is a great gift for any politician. But his greatest power as a politician was his ability to convince those who listened to him at public appearances of the merits of his cause. He explained this ability in an interview with the *Sunday Times* on 24 July 1988:

> You've got to tell them something that's worth saying, that makes sense. People can be predisposed in favour of a person by his charm, but at the end of the day, when they vote, if they're responsible at all, they vote on the basis of some understanding of a problem and an offered solution.

De Beer entered the election with the goal to improve relations between Afrikaners and English speakers, a firm belief in the rule of law, the principle of free speech, political association, tolerance, and the continued right for coloured men in the Cape Province to be on the common voters' roll. He accepted what he termed as "the proven South African tradition of social segregation", but that economic integration between black and white people was a fact which made political integration essential.[14] Under the UP's "white leadership with justice" it was accepted that the majority of black people had not achieved the necessary educational qualifications to be voters, but that political rights would be gradually extended if they complied with certain Western civilisation standards. For present day values these are paternalistic and conservative views, but in 1953 De Beer was politically far to the left of the average UP member. This made him a subversive radical in the eyes of the apartheid state. The NP, optimistic of winning Maitland, immediately set out to attack him. *Die Burger*, the influential official mouthpiece of the NP in the Cape Province, condemned him as a dangerous liberal as he was a speaker at a Civil Rights League meeting near parliament that led to violent clashes with the police. Furthermore, it was claimed that he had only secured the nomination because he was the son-in-law of Strauss.[15]

---

14   Debates of parliament, 12 June 1990, Col. 11453.
15   *Die Burger*, 4 February 1953.

The NP fought the election on three planks – stricter racial segregation with apartheid, the dangers of communism, and the coloured franchise. The NP portrayed the UP under Strauss's leadership as weak on patriotism, security and the protection of "white civilization". He was accused of frustrating the "volkswil" (will of the Afrikaners), and the sovereignty of parliament for blocking the removal of the coloured franchise.[16] In addition, the NP used fear tactics, harping on the danger of being swamped by a growing coloured population, and that the white man would be doomed if the UP should win the election. Despite this onslaught, Strauss insisted that his party's focus had to be on the NP's contempt for the constitution. The UP contested the election with the slogan "Vote for the right to vote again".

De Beer's NP opponent was Louis Weichardt, a former leader of the virulent anti-Semitic and national-socialistic Greyshirts.[17] He became the party's candidate as Maitland had many blue-collar workers and he had a reputation as a champion of the rights of white workers. *Die Burger* went out of its way to keep his Nazi past out of the public domain. In its series of biographical sketches of NP parliamentary candidates, it merely mentioned in passing that he was the founder of the Greyshirts while playing up his expertise as a businessman.[18]

Weichardt fought an energetic campaign. By 20 March, he had addressed eleven public meetings, with six more planned ones. He also made a concerted effort to visit individual voters to convince them that De Beer was too young to be elected to parliament. That anyone voting for a "bogsnuiter" (a mere child) was asking for trouble.[19] He condemned him as being too liberal. Weichardt resorted to the NP's favourite tactic of accusing liberals of being communists. De Beer promptly shut down this smear with a libel

---

16 L. Korf, "D.F. Malan: A political biography" (D.Phil, University of Stellenbosch, 2010), p. 449.
17 M. Shain, *A perfect storm. Antisemitism in South Africa 1930–1948* (Johannesburg, 2015), pp. 53–56.
18 *Die Burger*, 28 March 1953.
19 House of Assembly debates, 14/15 August 1958, Col. 2323.

summons of £5000.²⁰ The defamation case ended in August with a letter of apology from Weichardt.²¹

To counter NP propaganda, De Beer attempted to meet as many individual voters as possible, and to address a succession of public meetings. His campaign had the glamour that Clive van Ryneveld, by then a popular Springbok cricketer, canvassed for him. His biggest challenge was the NP claim that the UP desired racial integration at the cost of whites. Visiting an elderly voter who sat with his manifesto in his hand, he was told that as he wanted to take the pensions of whites to give them to blacks, he would not get his vote. When a stunned De Beer pointed out that he does not even mention pensions in his manifesto, he discovered that the person could not read, and that a friend had summarised it for him. Nothing he said could change the old man's opinion.²² However, he found Weichardt an easy opponent.²³ It was not necessary to focus on his opponent's unsavoury political past since only eight years after World War II it was still fresh in the memory of Maitland's voters, of whom a number were war veterans. Instead he set out to enthuse voters with his ideas for a safe and prosperous future. Weichardt conceded to *Die Burger* (20 March 1953) that his opponent had succeeded in whipping up the enthusiasm and the energy of Maitland's younger voters.

De Beer's last public meeting was on 8 April in the Martin Adams Hall in the NP-supporting working class area of Ysterplaat. As it was packed with NP supporters, it was a rowdy one. Earlier that day *Die Burger* had published a cartoon with the leadership of the UP marching with a banner that the right to vote meant "the right to vote for Solly and Sem!", referring to the communist trade unionist Solly Sachs and Sam Kahn, the former communist MP. The NP hecklers would continuously yell as a choir, "Stem vir die reg

---

20 *Cape Times*, 14 March 1953; *Die Burger*, 20 March 1953.
21 D.M. Scher, "Louis T. Weichardt and the South African Greyshirt movement", *Kleio*, 1986, Vol. 18, p. 68.
22 *The Cape Argus*, 14 October 1961.
23 Recording of Wendy's interview with her mother, Maureen de Beer, 26 April 2020.

om weer te stem. Stem vir Solly and Sam." (Vote for the right to vote again. Vote for Solly and Sam.) To loud NP cheers, a woman banged a black and a white doll together, yelling that this was the UP's real goal: sex across the colour line. De Beer was also attacked for being part of a Civil Rights League meeting that had ended in a riot near parliament. He had the ability to deal with hecklers with consummate ease and was measured in his response. The meeting ended in a vote of confidence for the UP.

Later that evening, while driving home from the Ysterplaat meeting, Ray suffered a fatal stroke.[24] His father's integrity and sense of duty would remain with De Beer for the rest of his life. Another legacy was that Ray was only 60 years old, leaving his son with a sense of mortality that he would die young.[25] It was some consolation for De Beer that he was sure that Ray knew he would win in Maitland. Political observers did not share his confidence, viewing the constituency as too close to call. For them this uncertainty was evident in the applications for postal votes. The NP had lodged 596 applications to the 514 of the UP. That both parties viewed Maitland as winnable was reflected in the high polling percentage. Of the registered Maitland voters 92,4 per cent expressed their preference on polling day. Interest in the contest was so high that when the result was announced at 2:15 in the morning hundreds of people were waiting in a light drizzle outside the counting venue.

The UP won the seat with an unexpected comfortable majority of 2105 votes, 6447 to the 4342 of Weichardt. De Beer was hoisted shoulder-high amid the wild applause of his supporters.[26] The result was attributed to his youth and enthusiasm, qualities that had grabbed the public's imagination.

Nationally the NP secured a victory with a bigger majority. The reason for this was that Afrikaners formed 61 per cent of the total white population, but 66 per cent of the electorate, and

---

24 Eglin, *Crossing the borders of power*, p. 50.
25 Interview with Wendy de Beer Furniss, 16 April 2020.
26 *Cape Times*, 16 April 1953.

most of them were fervent NP supporters. Since the 1930s, young Afrikaners had become supporters of the NP by upbringing rather than reasoning. Through their parents, teachers, Afrikaans newspapers, the DRC and cultural events such as the Day of the Covenant, young Afrikaners were indoctrinated with the belief that to be a good and true Afrikaner you had to be a supporter of the NP. In this way a blind obedience to the party and the acceptance that its leaders knew what was good for the "volk" (the Afrikaner people) developed.

The UP won the popular vote by securing 610 268 votes to the NP's 598 357, but the first past the post electoral system and the weighting of the urban vote – urban seats had significantly more voters than rural ones – was to the advantage of the NP, as it won all the rural seats except those in Natal. Moreover, the increasing urbanisation of Afrikaners meant that the NP captured seven urban UP seats.[27] The election result had crushed the last remaining hope that the UP could ever regain political power. However, the liberal faction in the UP had been enlarged with the election of De Beer, Ray Swart, Helen Suzman, Jan Steytler, Owen Townley Williams, I.S. (Sakkies) Fourie and J.P. Cope, all outspoken opponents of apartheid.

---

27 W.B. White, "The United Party and the 1953 general election", *Historia* 36 (2), November 1991, p. 79.

CHAPTER 3
The golden boy
1953–1956

On 21 May, before the opening of the new parliamentary session, the UP parliamentary caucus met in Pretoria to discuss tactics and strategies. The caucus was an unhappy place, divided and low on confidence. The tension amongst the members was deepened by the fact that the English-language press, after lauding Strauss to the skies as a great leader, had turned on him. Bitterly disappointed by the defeat of 1953, the editors viewed him as too aloof and colourless to be an inspiring leader. They wanted to replace him with Sir De Villiers Graaff, the UP leader in the Cape Province, who was elected to parliament in 1948. Young, energetic, good looking and with a distinguished military record during World War II, he was seen as the person to save the struggling UP.

The defeat created an opportunity for some UP MPs, resentful of Strauss's autocratic leadership style and aloofness, to start a rebellion. During the caucus meeting Bailey Bekker, leader of the UP in the Transvaal, supported by Abraham Jonker, Frank Waring, Blaar Coetzee and Arthur Barlow, criticised Strauss for his management of the election and his stance on the coloured franchise. For them the party had done its best on the coloured franchise, but they felt that it was a lost cause that had cost the party votes and would continue to weaken the UP if Strauss persisted in opposing the NP.[1] In reality, their rebellion was motivated by political opportunism as De Beer explained to the historian David Scher:

> The Bekker Group certainly based their Palace revolution on the Coloured vote issue. As always in politics, this was to some extent

---
1 Swart, *Progressive odyssey*, pp. 19–21.

the occasion rather than the cause. These gentlemen had correctly diagnosed that the political tide was running in favour of the Nationalist party, and they wished to get themselves into a position on the political spectrum more conservative that of J.G.N. Strauss …²

Attempting to satisfy the two wings of the party, Strauss came up with a policy of "White leadership with just recognition of non-European aspirations".³ This stance satisfied neither wing of the party as the conservatives viewed it as too liberal, and for the liberals it was too vague and conservative. On the other hand, it left the UP open to accusations by the NP that it had no clear alternative policy to apartheid. When UP MPs criticised government policies in the House of Assembly, NP MPs would continuously interject "What is your policy?", making it difficult for the liberals to oppose the social engineering of apartheid.

De Beer found the party leadership aloof and unwelcoming. Douglas Mitchell was especially intolerant and bullied those who dared to differ with him. Clashing with him could damage your political prospects. Furthermore, it was expected of new backbenchers to serve a lengthy apprenticeship to prove their ability.⁴ This meant that the membership of committees – and crucially – debating opportunities in the House of Assembly were determined not by your abilities but by your seniority.

However, he found it uplifting to meet with the newly elected liberals. Suzman, MP for Houghton, who would be his parliamentary bench mate, quickly established herself as the most liberal member of the House. Fourie, MP for Germiston District and a former professor in economics at the University of the Free State as well as its rector, became a close friend. For De Beer he was a

---

2   Scher, "The disenfranchisement of the Coloured voters, 1948–1956", p. 387.
3   University of the Free State (hereafter UFS), Archive for Contemporary Affairs (hereafter ACA), J.G.N. Strauss collection, File 1/19/9/17/2, Vol. 4, Strauss's speech to the new parliamentary caucus after the 1953 election.
4   Swart, *Progressive odyssey*, pp. 31–33.

marvellous friend who broadened his knowledge of Afrikaner history, as well as his economic expertise.[5]

Ultimately, he found it exciting being a member of parliament, to be part of debates and to have coffee or lunch with old political veterans and to listen to their stories. He also experienced it as a slow and stately place where conventions were deeply held and carefully observed. The dignity of the House of Assembly was paramount. What struck him about his fellow MPs was that everyone knew something had to be done about the political rights for the black majority, but that the question did not present itself, and demanded urgent attention.[6] The NP MPs were high on self-confidence and self-righteousness that South Africa belonged to the Afrikaner. They continued with undiminished zeal to entrench Afrikaner power and white domination. With the cornerstones of the apartheid state set between 1948 and 1953, they were determined to use their increased majority to strengthen racial segregation and to remove the coloured franchise.

Facing this arrogant and hostile group, De Beer made his maiden speech on 30 July during the budget debate. Speaking alternately in Afrikaans and English, he highlighted the poverty of his Maitland constituents; that many of them were earning less than £40 a month and that their difficult situation was becoming more challenging. He emphasised that a lack of housing was the biggest problem facing Maitland, and that he differed with the government's contention that it was not responsible for urban housing. He argued that the state had to make itself responsible, as far as possible, for home ownership. The *Cape Times* (31 July 1953) under the heading "Housing needs of Maitland. Dr De Beer's plea in maiden speech" reported it as the leading speech of the day.

His fluent bilingualism, a highly regarded ability in the House, made him a backbencher to be taken note off. Schalk Pienaar, the parliamentary representative of *Die Burger*, a fiery Afrikaner nationalist with little time for the UP, admired his oratorical abilities

---

5   Wits, Hackland papers. Hackland's interview with De Beer, 14 July 1980.
6   *Sunday Times*, 5 February 1989.

and bilingualism. He noted that although De Beer's spoken English was better than his Afrikaans, he was one of the best Afrikaans speakers in the House.[7] De Beer also delivered all his speeches at public meetings in both official languages. He was so scrupulous in respecting the equal status of the two official languages that it was joked that he made use of stopwatch precision to allocate speaking time to each.[8] Even in opposition strongholds with hardly any Afrikaner voters, he delivered parts of his speeches in Afrikaans.[9] As a result the NP-supporting Afrikaans press, who could be very selective in their definition of who qualified as an Afrikaner, viewed him as one.

De Beer's status as a medical practitioner meant that the party whips expected him to focus on the medical and social portfolios, and he was appointed as the secretary of the Health and Social Welfare Committee in the UP caucus. During the Health budget debate, he congratulated the government on the substantial rise in the allocation to combat tuberculosis but urged that an even larger sum had to be allocated.[10] It made sense that the UP wanted to benefit from his medical expertise, but the obligation to focus merely on health issues was a source of frustration for him. Unhappy with his limited debating opportunities, he raised his frustrations with his father-in-law with whom he had a close relationship. They had regular walks on the beach to discuss issues. He urged Strauss to make more use of the talented intake of new backbenchers to support his leadership, and to give him more responsibility.

Strauss told Maureen that the problem was that the new intake of MPs was young and inexperienced, and that to give Zach more responsibility would harm him, as he would only be seen as Strauss's son-in-law. He had to secure his achievements on his own terms.[11]

---

7   *Die Burger*, 30 September 1961.
8   Profile of Zach de Beer in *Optima*, no date. (In the possession of Wendy de Beer Furniss.)
9   *Rapport*, 14 April 1974.
10 *Cape Times*, 11 September 1953.
11 Recording of Wendy's interview with her mother, Maureen de Beer, 26 April 2020.

As a result, De Beer was an observer when Malan, determined to exploit the divisions in the UP to get rid of the coloured franchise, introduced a new Bill on 14 July to a joint sitting of both houses of parliament to remove coloured voters from the common voters' roll. Despite the divisions in his own party, Strauss made it clear that he would oppose the Bill. By then the attempts by the Bekker group to reach a compromise with the NP on the issue had led to their expulsion from the UP. On 16 September, despite the support of the UP rebels, the NP still failed with 16 votes to secure the required two-thirds majority in the joint sitting of both houses.

Despite his limited speaking opportunities, De Beer felt that he had learned a lot in his first parliamentary session, and he had made his mark. His charm, combined with his sporting abilities – he played for the parliamentary cricket team and would become its captain in 1956 – made him popular amongst his fellow MPs. After the end of the session, he enjoyed the obligation for young backbenchers to spend weeks on the road to address public meetings in Karoo towns and hamlets. He felt that this benefitted him as he developed a knowledge of South Africa and its people.[12] Visiting these small predominately Afrikaner settlements made him fully aware of the strengths, desires, foibles, weaknesses and anxieties of Afrikaners. Many years later at his memorial service, Harry Oppenheimer highlighted the love and empathy De Beer had had for his fellow Afrikaners. This empathy was the result of his affection for his ultraconservative uncle Dan, but especially the Afrikaners he met during these rural meetings. He shared the sentiments that the Afrikaner poet N.P. van Wyk Louw expressed in his influential book *Liberale nasionalisme*:

> 'n Mens het 'n volk lief, nie omdat hy heerlik is nie en die beste volk op aarde is nie; jy het hom lief om sy ellende. (One does not love one's own people for being the most delightful or for being the best people on earth, but for their misery.)[13]

---

12   Wits, Hackland papers. Hackland's interview with De Beer, 14 July 1980.
13   N.P. van Wyk Louw, *Liberale nasionalisme* (Cape Town, 1958), p. 22.

Meeting these ordinary Afrikaners, most of them devout Christians with a desire that their survival in Africa had to be based on justice, filled him with empathy and the realisation that it was a worthwhile challenge to convince them to prevent a future race revolution that could destroy them. For many years De Beer and René de Villiers, liberal editor of *The Star*, had a standing joke, that by the way of greeting they would ask each other "Staan jy nog by die volk?" (Are you still standing by the volk?).[14] This was more than a joke as it reflected the essence of De Beer's liberalism to bring about gradual constitutional reform to save his fellow Afrikaners – who were mostly unwilling to listen to his message – from self-destruction.

The obligation to address rural political meetings led to his friendship with Harry Oppenheimer, UP MP for Kimberley, and son of the mining magnate Ernest Oppenheimer and heir to the Anglo-American Corporation (AAC). He and Oppenheimer were asked to address a UP meeting in the small rural town of Porterville.

De Beer was startled when Oppenheimer asked him for a lift explaining that he (Oppenheimer) did not have a suitable car; meaning that he did not think it appropriate to arrive at a political meeting in his expensive Rolls Bentley. De Beer drove them to Porterville in what Oppenheimer's biographer described as a "student-style jalopy".

On their way back to Cape Town the two stopped for dinner at a hotel. At De Beer's memorial service Oppenheimer recounted that although he was nearly twice his age, he was struck by his young companion's wisdom, gravitas and what a delightful and entertaining companion he was. That evening was the start of a lifelong personal and political friendship.[15] Oppenheimer would be a crucial factor in De Beer's life as he would be a mentor in both

---

14 Z259, "Confessions of an old liberal". (In the possession of Wendy de Beer Furniss.)
15 A. Hocking, *Oppenheimer and son* (Cape Town, 1973), pp. 304–305; Recording of the memorial service at the Johannesburg Country Club, 3 June 1999. (In the possession of Wendy de Beer Furniss.)

his political and financial career. The latter would always turn to him for advice and encouragement.

De Beer's sociability also led to a close friendship with Harry Lawrence, a highly respected and popular former minister in the Smuts government. He was a leading moderate in the UP caucus and was regarded by all as an outstanding parliamentarian. This friendship started with a political visit to the Eastern Cape. While staying in the East London Club, they had drunk far too much after dinner. The next morning De Beer was asked to attend to a pale and trembling Lawrence, who explained he was subject to a virus which attacked his digestive system. He prescribed him bed rest and a harmless chalky mixture. On returning to the club at lunch time, he found a recovered Lawrence eagerly awaiting his advice whether he might risk having a drink with his lunch. In 1986, De Beer described his response in a speech to the Food and Wine Society:

> For once, my good biblical education did not desert me, and I was able to give him the answer he wanted by quoting the first epistle to Timothy, chapter 5 verse 23 which reads: "Drink no longer water, but use a little wine for thy stomach's sake and thine often infirmities."

Thus was a great friendship cemented.[16]

For the 1954 parliamentary session De Beer remained relegated to health issues and participated in debates on the Medical, Dental, and Pharmacy Amendment Bill as well as the Railway Sick Fund. The closest he came to a contentious issue was during the debate on the Part Appropriation Bill when he raised the lack of housing for urban black people whose numbers were on the increase as a result of the country's industrial development. This shortage, according to him, had to be addressed as it was at the root of race relations in South Africa.[17] As in the previous years, most of the

---

16 Z270, Address to the Food and Wine Society, 18 August 1986. (In the possession of Wendy de Beer Furniss.)
17 *Cape Times*, 19 February 1954.

parliamentary session was taken up by the NP's onslaught on the coloured franchise. This led to a volatile atmosphere in parliament with bitter clashes between the two parties as well as with the Speaker who made no attempt to conceal his antipathy to the UP. Lawrence was suspended from the House for seven days after an argument with the Speaker. An outraged Strauss and the entire UP then marched out of the House. It was the first mass walkout in the history of South Africa's parliament. A few days later Strauss introduced a motion of censure in the Speaker.[18]

In June 1954, Strauss vetoed Malan's proposal of a free vote when all MPs could vote according to their conscience on the coloured franchise. Only thirteen votes short of a two-thirds majority, Malan had hoped to attract the support of conservative UP MPs and senators in a joint sitting of both houses of parliament. By rejecting a free vote, Strauss deprived Malan of a two-third majority with nine votes.

Eben Dönges, a senior government minister, accused the UP of committing a crime against the future of white South Africa by refusing to vote for the removal of the coloured franchise.[19] Strauss's stance cost his party dearly in the provincial election of 18 August 1954. The NP hammered on the threat of the coloured franchise for Afrikaner survival and captured 12 UP seats.[20] Malan retired from politics in October 1954 and was replaced by the hardliner J.G. Strijdom, popularly known as the "Lion of the north", who was determined to settle the coloured franchise issue.

In the 1955 parliamentary session De Beer was given more debating opportunities and he participated in the Natives (Urban Areas) Amendment Bill, popularly known as the "Locations in the Sky Bill". (The purpose of the Bill was to prevent domestic servants from living in flats in white designated urban areas, especially in Johannesburg.) He expressed his concern on the poor housing conditions of black people and that it was impossible to have a 100

---

18   J. Lawrence, *Harry Lawrence* (Cape Town, 1978), p. 228.
19   Bekker, *Eben Dönges*, pp. 78–79, 81.
20   Scher, "The disenfranchisement of the Coloured voters", p. 511.

per cent application of the principle of residential segregation in cities.²¹ But as a junior backbencher it remained his task to participate in debates the frontbenchers viewed as too trivial to attract their attention, for example the control of the Italian wood-boring beetle.

The Minister of Agriculture, P.K. le Roux, stated that beetle control would be relaxed as it was impossible to eradicate the pest. De Beer addressed the House as if he was participating in a debate on the highest constitutional matter. He thundered that one of the government's highest duties to its citizens was to provide economic security and stability, and an important part of that function was to try and protect reasonable investment. The ordinary person's house was generally the only investment ever made by him, and the government did not do enough to protect these homes against the threat of the Italian beetle. It was an effective speech that was prominently reported in the *Cape Times* (16 March) and raised his public profile. On 19 April, he participated in a mainstream issue by castigating the government for going out of its way to crush the alleged threat of communism, while making no effort to encourage liberal-democratic ideals amongst black people.²²

In May 1955, the struggle over the coloured franchise came to a boiling point when Strijdom in a cynical manipulation of the constitution introduced the Senate Bill to manufacture a two-thirds majority for the removal of the coloured vote. The Bill set out to enlarge the upper house from 48 to 89 members, and to pack it with NP nominees. On 17 May, De Beer as one of a panel of speakers addressed a protest meeting of 4000 people in the Cape Town City Hall. He launched an emotional attack on the Bill for destroying parliamentary rule as the country would be governed not by its chosen representatives but by nominated NP officials. To prevent this blot on South Africa's name, he appealed to Afrikaners and NP supporters to reject the Bill.²³ The parliamentary debate started on

---

21 *Cape Times*, 11 February 1955.
22 Debatte van die Volksraad, 19 April 1955, Col. 4422.
23 *Cape Times*, 18 May 1955.

26 May and lasted for 29 continuous hours. Every one of the UP MPs, apart from V.G. Fenner-Solomon, the party whip, participated. De Beer entered the proceedings on 27 April and condemned the Bill as constitutional prostitution that besmirched the name of South Africa. He also condemned the NP for smearing those who opposed the Bill as unpatriotic.[24]

With the passing of the Senate Bill, a dispute erupted in the UP over the reluctance of Strauss to commit the UP to restoring the coloureds to the common voters' roll after the NP had removed them. He felt unable to do so as he feared that it would estrange Mitchell, who was opposed to any such action.[25] For Dr Bernard Friedman, the liberal MP for Hillbrow, Strauss's stance was one of opportunism, lack of principle and a breach of faith. Under his guidance six liberal MPs threatened to resign if he could not give a categorical assurance. De Beer was not one of them as he was in an invidious position with his father-in-law.[26] In 1981 he informed the historian David Scher that it was such a difficult time for him that "the thought certainly did cross my mind that I have to leave the party".[27] A compromise was reached when Strauss declared that the UP on return to power would set out to right the grave injustice done to the coloureds in the best way open to the party and in a form which would serve the interest of the country as a whole.

Friedman, however, refused to accept the compromise and resigned from the party and parliament to fight a by-election in September 1955. Louis Steenkamp, a leading UP right-winger, narrowly defeated him. The saga left the liberals, who had supported Strauss in his struggles against the conservatives, deeply disappointed. Suzman concluded that he was the type of leader who chose to placate his enemies at the expense of his friends.[28] Disillusioned with Strauss, the liberals became receptive to the idea

---

24 Debatte van die Volksraad, 26/27 May 1955, Col. 6980–6989.
25 Strangwayes-Booth, *A cricket in a thorn tree*, pp. 99–100.
26 R. Swart, *Progressive odyssey*, p. 35.
27 Scher, "The disenfranchisement of the Coloured voters 1948–1956", p. 569.
28 Suzman, *In no uncertain terms*, pp. 21, 38.

of replacing him with Graaff. Out of loyalty to his father-in-law, De Beer did not openly identify with the liberal group. He was categorised as a moderate in the party caucus, but according to Ray Swart, MP for Zululand, there was no doubt about where his sympathies lay.[29]

By the 1956 session, De Beer had an established reputation as an outstanding speaker, and he played a prominent role in parliamentary debates. On 1 February, he vehemently opposed the Industrial Conciliation Bill that provided a system of job reservation which protected the interests of whites and entrenched the black people at the bottom of the economic ladder as a fascist measure. The Bill interfered with basic human freedoms and could only create new opportunities for administrative chaos and interracial rivalry.[30] The *Cape Times* (2 February 1956) gave his speech extensive coverage and praised it as one of the lucid ones of the day. In February the government introduced the South Africa Act Amendment Bill, which removed from the constitution the two-thirds majority clause entrenching the voting rights of coloured voters. In a volatile atmosphere with sharp clashes between the UP and NP, the joint sitting of both houses passed the Bill with 174 votes to 68, eight more than the required two-thirds majority. This allowed any legislation on the voting rights of the coloureds to be passed by parliament with an ordinary majority.

A few days later on 1 March, De Beer addressed a public meeting in Port Elizabeth. He was at his political and analytical best and the *Eastern Province Herald* in a detailed report pointed out that the chairman praised him as a rising young statesman. A few days later, J.B. Anderson of Walmer wrote to the editor to complain about the report of the meeting:

> Your report of the United Party meeting addressed by Dr Z.J. de Beer gives no idea at all of the impression created by that astounding

---

29 Swart, *Progressive Odyssey*, 35; Strangwayes-Booth, *A cricket in the thorn tree*, pp. 100, 135.
30 House of Assembly debates, 1 February 1956, Col. 772–782.

young man of 28. In my time I have attended many political meetings and I have heard some outstanding speeches, but I have never listened to anything finer than Dr De Beer's address.[31]

Anderson articulated what many political observers felt – that De Beer was the UP's golden boy with a bright future ahead of him. He bolstered his reputation with his opposition to the Separate Representation of Voters Amendment Bill, which barred coloureds from sitting in the Cape provincial council. (The South African constitution of 1910 granted the right to black people and coloureds to be elected to the provincial council as they had this right in the Cape Colonial parliament. One black man, W.B. Rubusana, and two coloureds, W.B. Rubusana and S. Reagon, were elected to the provincial council.) In terms of this legislation, only whites could represent coloureds in the Cape provincial council. De Beer condemned the Bill as a serious deprivation of rights, for coloured people were being told that they could never have an effective say in the government of the country. He ended his speech on a ringing note that history will judge the NP.[32]

For the overwhelming majority of Afrikaners there was no doubt that history was on their side and they emotionally lauded Strijdom as a hero and a saviour. High on its victory on the coloured franchise, the NP set out on 13 June to tighten racial segregation with the Population Registration Amendment Bill which provided for an amendment that if "a person who looks like a native wishes to be classified in any other race group, the onus is on him to prove that he is not a native". This meant that people who have lived as coloureds may be reclassified as black if they could not prove that they were coloured.

De Beer told the House that basic human rights were the cornerstone of the Western civilisation and that the NP with its crude racism, and search for votes with black-peril tactics, trampled on these rights. He expressed his disgust with the "stud book" of the

---

31 *Eastern Province Herald*, 5 March 1956.
32 House of Assembly debates, 18 April 1956, Col. 3889–3895.

apartheid state and appealed to the humanity of the government not to resort to crude racial categories as it led to human suffering.[33] His appeal was in vain.

---

33 House of Assembly debates, 13 June 1956, Col. 7814–7819.

CHAPTER 4
The Senate Plan
1956–1958

Eager to counter the destructive effects of apartheid, De Beer collaborated closely with Oppenheimer to develop the so-called Senate Plan. This plan originated with Oppenheimer, who felt that the two houses of parliament should share power equally. The Senate had to be reconstituted to be like that of the USA, empowered to block any abuse of power by the House of Assembly. He also implored that the Senate should consist of representatives of all people, elected by qualified voters of all racial groups. Feeling that he needed the advice of constitutional experts, Oppenheimer visited Britain, asking De Beer to accompany him when he attended the Duke of Edinburgh's Commonwealth Study Conference in Oxford.[1] Oppenheimer retained the services of leading constitutional experts, namely Prof. K.C. Wheane of Oxford University, and Sir Ivor Jennings, Master of Trinity College, Cambridge. Out of this initiative developed the Senate Plan.

A Senate that would have the power to block legislation which affected the fundamental rights of all South Africans and would consist of 12 black and coloured senators elected on separate voters' rolls, 33 senators elected by the white electorate, and five nominated senators. No proposal could pass the Senate if it did not have the support of the majority of white representatives. On the other hand, no proposal opposed by the coloured and black representatives could pass if it did not have the support of two-thirds of the white representatives.[2] Oppenheimer's intention with the plan was to put a measure of real political power into the hands

---

1 *Impact*, May 1980.
2 Hocking, *Oppenheimer and son*, p. 311.

of black people so as to make the implementation of racial legislation to which all blacks objected impossible without a really big majority of whites. Furthermore, it would provide constitutional checks and balances that would prevent a future black majority to be used for sectional ends. This Senate would help to create a constitution that would be a "Deed of Partnership" between the various communities in South Africa.[3]

To convince the UP to support his plan, Oppenheimer portrayed it as a constitutional move and not a fundamental change in the party's race policy. Behind the scenes he used his considerable charm to win over leading figures in the party such as Strauss, Bill Horak, the Secretary-General of the party, and Jack Higgerty, the Chief Whip in the parliamentary caucus. Horak and Higgerty, according to Oppenheimer, were not shocked with the idea that coloured and black people were represented by their own people in the Senate. However, Strauss was nervous about the effect on UP supporters and the electorate in general, fearing that the country would be shocked by the proposal. He wanted to hold the plan back until after the next general election. However, Oppenheimer wanted it to be part of the UP's election campaign. He asked De Beer to help him develop arguments to win over support for the plan in and outside the party. For example, he was of the opinion that the Senate Plan would do justice to the black majority while at the same time guaranteeing the continuance of white leadership.

De Beer was urged to have discussions with friendly newspaper editors as well as influential UP MPs such as Sidney Waterson, the MP for Constantia and a former member of the Smuts government.[4] On the back of the letter of 6 September 1956 he received from Oppenheimer, he wrote that the Senate Plan was good politics, and that they had to push for direct representation for coloured and black people. But he emphasised that they had to be willing

---

3 J.H. Oppenheimer – Graaff, 23 October 1956. (In the possession of Wendy de Beer Furniss.)
4 J.H. Oppenheimer – De Beer, 6 and 17 September 1956. (In the possession of Wendy de Beer Furniss.)

to accept indirect representation if compelled to do so. However, in capital letters he wrote that the "DOOR MAY NOT BE CLOSED ON COMMON ROLL". For him, the real political Rubicon was the common voters' roll for all South Africans.

Seeing Graaff as the coming man in the UP, Oppenheimer set out to win him over to the Senate Plan.[5] It made sense to cultivate him, as the stress attached to the long and gruelling struggle over the coloured franchise had undermined Strauss's health. In October 1956, he became ill with jaundice. On medical advice he took three months' overseas leave to recuperate. This meant that he would miss the national congress held in Bloemfontein in November, as well as the first weeks of the 1957 parliamentary session.

For Mitchell and the other provincial leaders Strauss's insistence on a three-month break was an indication that he could not carry the burden of the leadership, and they advised him to resign. He agreed to sign a letter written for him by Horak in which he stated his willingness to continue as leader, but he gave the congress a free choice on the matter of his leadership.[6] He left for the French Riviera on 16 November 1956.

The evening of 20 November, De Beer, who was in Bloemfontein for the start of the conference the next day, was informed of the UP's Central Executive Committee's decision that his father-in-law should be replaced and that it would be recommended to the conference. Graaff asked him to rush to Johannesburg to convey the news to his mother-in-law before she read about it in a newspaper the next morning.[7] It was a message that could have been conveyed with a telephone call, and it was an effort by Graaff to save him from an embarrassing situation in which he would have to vote on the future of his father-in-law.

With Eglin accompanying him, they drove all night to Johannes-

---

5 The Brenthurst Library, H.F. Oppenheimer papers, OPP/HFO/J1 (10), Graaff – Oppenheimer, 11 October 1956.

6 Unisa, UPA, W.A. Kleynhans papers, J.G.N. Strauss's letter to the 20th national congress of the UP, 14 November 1956.

7 De Beer – Strauss, 25 November 1956 (Letter in the possession of Wendy de Beer Furniss.)

burg in a vehicle provided by Oppenheimer. They arrived at the Strauss home minutes before the delivery of the *Rand Daily Mail*.[8]

While De Beer was catching up with some sleep, Strauss's letter, accompanied by two medical reports, was read to the conference. The four provincial leaders then addressed the delegates with the message that it was in the interest of the party that Strauss had to be replaced. The 500 delegates, with only nine opposing votes, including two MPs, Fourie and R.A.F. Trollip, voted for the motion to elect a new leader. Except for Fourie, the liberals did nothing to defend Strauss. Graaff was then unanimously elected leader with the enthusiastic support of both wings of the party.[9] De Beer arrived with a gracious letter of congratulations from Mrs Strauss to Graaff, which was read to the conference. He then had the difficult task of writing to his father-in-law to explain what had happened at the conference, and why he supported the change of leadership:

> Not that it is of any great importance, I feel that you should know my personal attitude. I think that the right thing has been done. I have spoken to you on this and related topics before, and you know that my view has always been that I would rather serve under you than under Graaff or any other obvious alternative. But over the past six months I have gradually become convinced that the state of your health was very largely the direct consequence of your job, and that a vicious circle would be set up which would make it quite impossible for you to carry on. ... I am certain that it was best for the party, for you and for him that Div should have been elected when he was. Needless to say, I refused to discuss the issue beforehand, but these were my views.[10]

He ended the letter by urging his father-in-law to remain in

---

8 Eglin, *Crossing the borders of power*, p. 55; *Die Burger*, 26 November 1955.
9 S.L. Barnard, "Die verkiesing van Sir De Villiers Graaff as leier van die Verenigde Party", *Joernaal vir Eietydse Geskiedenis*, 5 (1) December 1980, p. 42.
10 De Beer – Strauss, 25 November 1956. (Letter in the possession of Wendy de Beer Furniss.)

parliament. However, Strauss resigned from parliament in May 1957 and faded from the political scene. He remained on a good footing with his son-in-law.

Graaff's election as UP leader led to euphoria in the party and the English-medium press. He was, however, saddled with expectations he could never fulfil as he had numerous shortcomings as a politician. His war record, charm and good looks hid the reality that he had no political acumen and lacked ruthlessness to lead and unify a divided party.[11] He loathed confrontation, whether in dealing with internal disputes in the UP, or in crossing swords with the NP. He relied on his charm to conciliate. Ultimately, he was out of his depth as a politician, void of any political ideas on how to cope with apartheid. However, in 1956 De Beer had a close relationship with him and viewed him as left of centre in the party. He saw potential in Graaff.[12]

For his part, Graaff regarded him as a close confidant. It was a relationship that had its roots in Ray de Beer tending to Graaff's dying mother,[13] but moreover, it was based on his appreciation of De Beer's intellect and ability. For the new UP leader, he was a talent to be nurtured for a future leadership position in the party. In the party De Beer was seen as one of Graaff's "blue-eyed" boys.[14] For his part, De Beer felt that he could influence Graaff to support more liberal policies.[15] Ultimately, he underestimated Graaff's innate conservatism. He also quickly became aware of Graaff's inability to make up his mind. Years later he ruefully pointed out that Graaff was a man of great attributes, but a man who always had difficulty making up his mind on a clear line, while Mitchell was a man of very little attributes who never had difficulty making up his mind.[16]

---

11 *Die Burger*, 12 September 1959.
12 Wits, Hackland papers. Hackland's interview with De Beer, 14 July 1980.
13 D. Graaff, *Div looks back. The memoirs of Sir De Villiers Graaff* (Cape Town, 1993), pp. 139, 162.
14 Strangwayes-Booth, *A cricket in the thorn tree*, p. 138.
15 B. Wilson, *A time of innocence* (Bergvlei, 1991), pp. 242, 290, 316.
16 Wits, Hackland papers. Hackland's interview with De Beer, 14 July 1980.

Graaff's conservatism meant that the UP would be unable to adapt to a changing South Africa in which the black majority became increasingly radical, and the government more oppressive. The African National Congress (ANC), the leading political organisation for black people, organised resistance to the apartheid state. The early 1950s was a period in which the ANC's leaders moved closer to communists and their ideas of mass action. This led to the Defiance Campaign of June to December 1952 in which the ANC in alliance with the South African Indian Congress (SAIC) contravened apartheid laws with a massive display of passive resistance. Blacks were urged to ignore the use of passbooks and to use public amenities reserved for whites. Unrelenting repression by the government led to the campaign being called off, but the Defiance Campaign brought the ANC publicity that increased its membership and started a culture of mass confrontation against the apartheid state.

In October 1953, the alliance of the ANC and the SAIC was extended with the founding of the Congress of Democrats (COD), a radical white left-wing organisation that campaigned for equality and justice for all South Africans. Although the COD was a small movement, it played an influential role in the Congress Alliance, especially in drawing up the Freedom Charter. The Charter was accepted by the Congress of the People, a mass meeting of anti-apartheid organisations at Kliptown, near Johannesburg, in 1955, and committed the ANC to a multiracial and social democratic future South Africa.

For the NP, the confrontational stance of the ANC was part of a conspiracy inspired by the international communism movement to overthrow the state by violence. In December 1956, the government arrested and charged 156 anti-apartheid activists – including L.B. Lee-Warden, the COD native representative for the Western Cape – of plotting to violently overthrow the government and to replace it with a Soviet-style state. The result was a lengthy legal process that dragged on for years.

In the 1957 parliamentary session, issues were debated with the focus on the coming general election of 1958. To raise the UP's profile, De Beer seconded the private motion of V.P. Pocock, veteran UP MP for Sunnyside, that the government should consider the desirability of instituting a compulsory contributory pension scheme for all adult whites. In addition, the motion requested that a pension scheme and family allowances for black people be considered. De Beer reminded the government that the state had to provide social security for the people. To prevent such a scheme from becoming a burden to the state it had to be a contributory one.[17]

However, he felt that his main task was to oppose the NP's relentless efforts to segregate black and white people, and to warn the electorate that apartheid was impractical. During the budget debate, he warned that the government's focus on "separate development" for black people in the rural "native reserves" ignored the political and economic future of the urbanised black person.[18] As regards the Separate University Education Bill, which established the principle of apartheid in tertiary education, he was outraged that legislation could prescribe that a lecturer would be guilty of an offence if he criticised the government in the course of his duties. For him, this conformed to a totalitarian pattern, namely thought control, and he felt strongly that the government could not allow institutions, which propagated or taught ideas in conflict with its policies, to remain in existence.[19] The Bill passed the second reading and was then referred to a select committee which evolved into a commission of inquiry. As a member of the DRC, he vehemently opposed the Native Laws Amendment Bill, an attempt to prohibit all gatherings at which white and black people were present, including church services. For him the crux of the matter was ecclesiastical freedom.[20]

He also led the UP's attack on the government's Nursing

---

17 *Cape Times*, 23 February 1957.
18 *Cape Times*, 28 March 1957.
19 *Cape Times*, 30 May 1957.
20 House of Assembly debates, 1 May 1957, Col. 5153.

Amendment Bill. For the Minister of Health, Marais Viljoen, the Bill was a necessity to prevent the dangers of racial mixing in the South African Nursing Association and the Nursing Council. Since 1944, the number of non-white nurses had increased from 844 to 3099. Even more dangerous, according to the minister, was the fact that on the Witwatersrand black nurses had secured control of one of the branches of the Association. In terms of the Bill, black nurses would have no representation on the Nursing Council, and instead would be given advisory boards. However, the Bill made no provision for regular compulsory contact between these boards and the "white" body which made decisions on their behalf. In addition, black nurses would have to wear separate insignia, the outward symbol of their qualifications, although they secured the same professional qualifications as white nurses. For De Beer the Bill was mere "baasskap" as it deprived black nurses of their rights in their own professional association and gave them nothing in return.[21]

With his parliamentary performances De Beer was attracting national attention. This was evident in an article Aubrey Sussens wrote for *The Cape Argus* (16 May 1957) to identify up-and-coming backbenchers. For him, De Beer's speeches conveyed the impression of careful study and a clear mind skilfully employed, and he predicted that there was a seat for him in a future cabinet. That his influence in the UP was growing, was evident in his success to convince Graaff in July 1957 to appoint Van Ryneveld, his close friend and by then South African cricket captain, as the candidate for the safe UP seat of East London North.[22] This was some achievement as Van Ryneveld, although a sporting hero, had no political experience and was far more liberal in his political views than the average UP MP. His victory in a by-election in October strengthened the liberal group in the caucus.

However, De Beer's influence as well as that of Oppenheimer,

---

21 *Cape Times*, 12 June 1957.
22 C. van Ryneveld, *20th century all-rounder. Reminiscences and reflections of Clive van Ryneveld* (Cape Town, 2011), p. 138.

was not enough to convince Graaff to accept the original Senate Plan. When submitted to the various committees of the UP, the conservatives opposed any notion of direct parliamentary representation by coloureds and blacks. When the plan came up to the Central Executive, it was split evenly on this issue. Graaff as the chairman sided with the conservatives. The watered-down version of the Senate Plan – a Senate of 50 members of which four or five white senators were to be elected by coloureds, while blacks would elect six white representatives – was eventually submitted on 13 to 15 August 1957 to the UP's special election conference in Bloemfontein.

The conference started on a triumphant note for Graaff. According to the political correspondent of the *Rand Daily Mail* (14 August 1957), the cheers after his opening speech threatened to blow off the City Hall roof. This placed him in an unchallenged position on the policies of the party, especially as he viewed the task of the party "to entrench White political leadership" and promised that the UP was not seeking power to preside at the dissolution of the Western way of life in South Africa by handing over inordinate powers to those not fit to exercise them.[23] When the Senate Plan was discussed in a closed conference session, several liberals suggested that coloured and black people should elect their own representatives to the Senate, but this was rejected. Liberal delegates hoped that Oppenheimer would oppose the diluted plan, but he kept his peace. He instead put forward a motion that the electorate should support the UP as it was the party that stood for white unity, white leadership with justice, for freedom of dignity of the individual, and for government in the true spirit of democracy.[24]

The harsh reality for Oppenheimer and De Beer was that politically they had nowhere to go. The only alternative to the UP was the Liberal Party, a marginalised splinter party. Their hope was to convert Graaff to a more liberal line to oppose apartheid. For De

---

23 *Rand Daily Mail*, 16 August 1957.
24 Strangwayes-Booth, *Cricket in the thorn tree*, pp. 122–124, 294; *Rand Daily Mail*, 15 August 1957.

Beer the Senate Plan adopted by the conference was, despite its flaws, a way to extend political rights – limited, however, to black people – and a means to convince whites of the necessity to extend these rights.

On a personal level 1957 was a challenging year for De Beer. He was uncertain about his political future as Maitland, despite his comfortable victory in 1953, was not a safe seat. For the 1958 election, all parliamentary seats were to be adapted by the Delimitation Commission, and the NP was a master in gerrymandering constituencies in its own favour. In addition, his political career made it difficult to maintain his medical practice along with three partners. Apart from his politically enforced absence leading to tension in the partnership, it also meant a reduced income for him. By October 1957, he had to face the reality that if he wanted to secure any income as a medical practitioner, he had to reduce his political activities.

This was evident as he explained his financial predicament to his friend Pieter de Kock, the personal assistant of Harry Oppenheimer:

> Personally I require, if I continue in Parliament, an income of at least £600 outside my parliamentary salary. ... If I find that I cannot continue to practice I shall have to get it elsewhere or give up Politics as well as look for a job. ... You know very well what my friendship with Harry has meant to me. You know too with bitter reluctance I would become one of those who ask for favours. Since you have discussed the matter with him I would suggest that you show him this letter or tell him of its contents and leave the matter there until I can give further information.

He then added in a postscript, "Actually I am not as proud about accepting some assistance as the above makes it seem ..."[25] In the end all turned out well as Oppenheimer provided him with an

---

25 The Brenthurst Library, H.F. Oppenheimer papers, OPP/HFO/J32.1 (70), De Beer – De Kock, 10 October 1957.

allowance to continue with his political career and to maintain his medical practice.[26]

In the end the delimitation of constituencies worked in De Beer's favour as the NP wanted to create an additional Cape Town constituency to its own advantage. As a result, Maitland shed mainly NP voting areas to the newly created Bellville which would become one of the NP's safest seats. These new electoral borders made Maitland a UP electoral fortress. Other UP MPs were not so fortunate. The government's gerrymandering meant that Oppenheimer's safe Kimberley City was abolished and replaced by Kimberley South so that the NP would win in the next election. After delimitation, Graaff's Hottentots-Holland constituency bore no relation to the seat the UP had won in 1953. With its new boundaries the constituency stretched deep into NP-dominated rural southwestern Cape. The same process happened to Steytler in Queenstown, turning this once safe UP seat into a marginal one.

With the general election set for April 1958, there was a short parliamentary session between 17 January and 12 February. Eben Dönges, Minister of the Interior, used the opportunity to condemn the Senate Plan as a threat to white survival as it would provide a black parliamentary veto. While being continuously interrupted by NP interjections, De Beer defended and explained the plan to the House of Assembly. He pointed out that as whites would not voluntarily concede their political power, and while the NP's apartheid policy had no coherent plan for the permanent urbanised black people, the UP's proposed Senate would secure the fundamental rights of all South Africans.[27] He was so convincing that Jan de Klerk, Minister of Labour and Public Works and father of the future president, accused him of hiding the impracticality of the plan behind a smokescreen of eloquence. Ben Schoeman, the cantankerous Minister of Transport, was less tactful. Referring to De Beer's status as a medical doctor, he exclaimed, "It stinks so

---

26 The Brenthurst Library, H.F. Oppenheimer papers, OPP/HFO/J1 (51:54), De Beer – De Kock, 22 July 1958.
27 House of Assembly debates, 22 January 1958, Col. 107–109.

much that a doctor had to deal with it".[28] The debate was a warning that it would be a challenge to sell the Senate Plan to voters in the coming election, as it was so much more complex compared to the brutal simplicity of the NP's apartheid policy – strict racial segregation to ensure white dominance.

The NP's election strategy was a black peril one. For Strijdom the UP's Senate Plan was a dangerous threat to white supremacy as it would give blacks a stranglehold on whites and place civilization at their mercy.[29] The NP distributed a pamphlet "The UP's Senate Plan: A dagger into the heart of white South Africa" with the message that the UP was committing treason towards the white man.[30] De Beer defended his Maitland seat with the slogan of "Harmony and hope". He was confident of a victory as his NP opponent, F.J. van der Merwe, a farmer from Calvinia and the member for Beaufort West in the Cape provincial council, was seen as an imported outsider.[31] He also struggled to speak English and this made him an unattractive candidate for local English-speaking voters, who felt that as an Afrikaner he was placing the interests of the "volk" above theirs. In addition, De Beer benefitted from the fact that Graaff had a strong personal following in the Western Cape. Most UP supporters in Cape Town refused to believe NP propaganda that Graaff desired a black majority government.

With his victory in Maitland ensured, De Beer as one of the best bilingual orators in the UP, addressed 49 countrywide public meetings, making him second to Graaff as the most hard-working election speaker for the party.[32] In these meetings he warned that apartheid was a counsel of despair that would ruin South Africa. The only solution was the UP's policy of harmony by diluting sectionalism amongst Afrikaners and English speakers. This would be brought about by encouraging bilingualism with

---

28　House of Assembly debates, 22 January 1958, Col. 110.
29　*The Cape Argus*, 11 March 1958.
30　A.J. McConnachie, "The 1961 general election in the Republic of South Africa", (MA, University of South Africa, 1999), pp. 19–20.
31　*Die Burger*, 24 February 1958.
32　*The Cape Argus*, 14 April 1958.

the introduction of dual- and parallel-medium schools, and by encouraging interracial harmony between black and white people. He stressed that this did not mean that all South Africans could be treated as a homogenous group, "because the vast majority of our non-Whites have not reached the stage of development where they can exercise the full rights of responsible citizenship".[33] In his last meeting on the eve of the poll, he addressed 600 people in Mowbray, condemning the politics and tactics of the NP as the antithesis of the democratic principles that upheld and maintained Western civilization.[34]

On polling day De Beer retained his seat with an enlarged majority of 3174 votes, securing 6406 to the 3232 of Van der Merwe. Outside Maitland, the NP's black-peril tactics won over many Afrikaners who up till then had voted UP. The official opposition lost four seats to the NP, including Graaff's Hottentots-Holland. In Queenstown Steytler hung onto his seat with 13 votes. The one positive outcome of the election for De Beer was that his friend and ally, Eglin, was elected as the representative for Pinelands.

---

[33] Unisa, UPA, Sir De Villiers Graaff papers, Files of people, 193, Zach de Beer, "A message of harmony and hope".
[34] *The Cape Argus*, 15 April 1958.

CHAPTER 5
Contemplating a smaller party that can speak with one voice
1958–1959

After the election, Graaff secured the safe UP seat of Rondebosch, but his inability to hold on to the Hottentots-Holland constituency was proof for him that the electorate saw the UP as too liberal. He concluded that the Senate Plan was "more liberal than we could ever see the white electorate accept". He blamed the liberals for the party's poor performance:

> The real trouble was that so many of our liberal brethren had little experience of dealings with either platteland or blue-collar audiences. Virtually all of them represented safe seats and could never understand why other constituencies would not accept their ideas.[1]

Graaff was determined to strengthen the "centre-of-the-road" image of the UP.[2] To Ray Swart he made it clear that the party had gone as far to the left as its supporters would allow it, and he would not allow any move in a more liberal direction.[3] The election result also convinced Douglas Mitchell that the liberals had to be purged.[4] Behind the scenes the ultraconservative Vause Raw, MP for Durban Point, and a protégé of Mitchell, with the assistance of Klasie Viljoen, a Transvaal party organiser, prepared the groundwork to purge the liberals.[5] In parliament Graaff was

---

1 Graaff, *Div looks back*, p. 154.
2 S.L. Barnard and A.H. Marais, *Die Verenigde Party. Die groot eksperiment* (Durban, 1982), p. 105.
3 Swart, *Progressive odyssey*, p. 45.
4 T. Wilks, *Douglas Mitchell* (Durban, 1980), pp. 119–121.
5 Interview with Klasie Viljoen, 22 February 2011.

pushed further to the right as he lacked the ability to cope in a debate with the intellect and strong personality of Verwoerd, who had replaced Strijdom as prime minister following his death on 24 August 1958. Graaff, who respected Verwoerd's "outstanding mental ability", was intellectually no match for him, and susceptible to his charm.[6] Verwoerd was so convincing that even Suzman as a liberal, while listening to him in the House of Assembly, had to remind herself that apartheid was doomed to fail.[7]

Graaff's charm, and willingness to give the liberals a fair chance to put their case in the caucus, created the expectation that they could convert him to more enlightened policies. De Beer told Boris Wilson, the newly elected and outspoken liberal MP for Hospital, that together with Eglin, he was doing his utmost to influence Graaff to take a stronger stance against Verwoerd.[8] With the encouragement of Oppenheimer he also took a more liberal stance in the House of Assembly as he informed De Kock:

> I have gradually begun to cast myself in the role of the most militant liberal among the more prominent members of the party. I think this is right and in accordance of Harry's wishes, and in any case I enjoy it.[9]

He took this liberal attitude into a committee appointed by Graaff to examine party policy and the best way and means to propagate it. Nothing came of the exercise as the committee was so divided that it was unable to come to an agreement on what party policy was. Five of the six members recommended the eventual representation of blacks by blacks in parliament, but the sixth member, Raw, refused to accept it, and this threatened to split the party. The recommendation was then shelved.[10]

---

6   Graaff, *Div looks back*, p. 199.
7   Suzman, *In no uncertain terms*, pp. 65–66.
8   Wilson, *A time of innocence*, p. 290.
9   The Brenthurst Library, HHF Oppenheimer papers, OPP/HFO/J1 (51:46), De Beer – De Kock, 21 September 1958.
10 Strangwayes-Booth, *A cricket in the thorn tree*, pp. 131, 133, 135.

Apart from the internal struggle in the UP, De Beer increasingly played a leading role to oppose apartheid legislation in parliament. In August 1958, he was asked to wind up the UP's opposition to the Electoral Laws Amendment Bill. The NP with its sight on a possible referendum for a republic intended to reduce the voting age for whites from 21 to 18. After an all-night sitting, De Beer proclaimed that people between the age of 18 to 21 were immature and prone to strain and instability, and that this was reflected in this age group's high rate of suicides and motor-vehicle accidents. South Africa was a multiracial country with numerous problems, and these issues had to be discussed by people of maturity and who were capable of freeing their minds of emotions. He argued that the Bill brought parliament and politics into disrepute as it made the electorate less respectable and objective. "We are opposing the Bill to protect the freedom, the safety and the prosperity of all people."[11]

It is difficult to see that De Beer really believed in what he was arguing as he had been actively involved in politics before the age of 21. But he realised that the Bill would harm the UP at the ballot box as the NP had been using the school system to churn out young nationalists. During elections, it was a common sight to see students at Afrikaans universities marching in columns to the local polling booth to vote for the NP.

Still attempting to push the UP in a more liberal direction, De Beer conveyed his political vision during the Part Appropriation Bill; a vision that he would propagate for the rest of his political career. Speaking after Verwoerd, he made it clear that the apartheid state could not have its cake and eat it too. Either economic integration had to go, or political integration had to come, as there was no possibility of economic integration vanishing. The bottom line was that economic integration and the dependence on black labour made apartheid impossible. The choice was not apartheid or integration, but whether the various racial groups were going to quarrel or cooperate. A system had to be created whereby the voices of each racial group had to be heard, while no racial group

---

11 House of Assembly debates, 14/15 August 1958, Col. 2336.

should be in a position to take away the fundamental rights of another group. What was needed was a constitution providing a federal element, as well as constitutional protection of minorities, a system of checks and balances:

> I would urge hon. members, and in humility I would urge South Africa, to consider carefully whether it is not along this sort of road to cooperation by constitution that we can obtain the only ultimately peaceful solution for our problems in South Africa.[12]

In the wake of this speech which gave him considerable publicity he considered making himself available for the chairmanship of the UP in the Cape Province, the provincial leader of the party. However, in a party in which seniority was crucial in determining your position, he was only willing to do so if Graaff supported him.[13] Graaff felt he was too young and inexperienced and wanted Jack Connan, the veteran MP for Gardens and a leading conservative, for the post.[14] For him Connan's main qualification was that he was a "staunch party man". Although De Beer felt he was the favourite to win in a vote for the post, he did not want to alienate Graaff, and decided not to contest the election. At the last minute Connan refused to stand, making it possible for Steytler, who was also elected to parliament in 1953 but did not care about Graaff's opinion, to become the provincial leader.[15]

De Beer's timidity would have a profound influence on his career as Steytler's election made him the most senior figure amongst the liberals, and their de facto leader. He was a brave and principled person, but not in the same class as De Beer as a parliamentarian, public speaker, campaigner and administrator. De Beer, fully aware

---

12 House of Assembly debates, 18 September 1958, Col. 4182–4183.
13 The Brenthurst Library, H.H.F. Oppenheimer papers, OPP/HFO/J1 (51:46), De Beer – De Kock, 21 September 1958.
14 The Brenthurst Library, H.H.F. Oppenheimer papers, OPP/HFO/J1 (51:41), De Beer – De Kock, 26 September 1958; OPP/HFO/J1 (51:40), De Beer – De Kock, 2 October 1958.
15 Graaff, *Div looks back*, pp. 160–161.

of Steytler's shortcomings, would not find it easy to be his junior and this would strain their relationship with time.

Although the days in which it was expected of De Beer only to focus on medical affairs was long gone, he was occasionally required to provide some medical expertise. With the start of the 1959 parliamentary session, he seconded the private motion of Col. Shearer, UP MP for Pietermaritzburg City, calling on more state aid for the health services. He urged greater assistance to those with mental problems, as well as a bigger role for the state to provide medical aid.[16]

The rest of the parliamentary session was dominated by Verwoerd's Promotion of Bantu Self-Government Bill. The Bill abolished the system of white "native representation" in terms of the Representation of Natives Act of 1936 and provided guidelines for the development of self-government for eight separate black ethnic groups, the so-called Bantustans based on the reserves. Furthermore, it provided for the possible development of these ethnic units into self-governing states within the parameter of apartheid. Verwoerd's Bantustan vision deepened the divisions between the conservatives and the liberals in the UP caucus.[17] For Mitchell the Bill provided an opportunity to use black-peril tactics against the NP. To win back rural constituencies, he wanted to portray the NP as selling out the interests of whites by extending too much land and power to black people. Graaff's response was to reiterate the ideal of "white leadership of justice" with a UP government to increase the number of white native representation in the Senate, and to extend white native representation in the House of Assembly to all the provinces.

Against this background De Beer, Eglin and Lawrence, all regarded as moderates close to Graaff, became openly associated with the liberals in the caucus.[18] In April 1959, the three of them drew up a document titled "The irreducible memorandum" to set

---

16　House of Assembly debates, 13 February 1959, Col. 815.
17　Eglin, *Crossing the borders of power*, pp. 65–67.
18　Strangwayes-Booth, *A cricket in the thorn tree*, pp. 138–139.

out their political goals. They proposed that the UP should consult with truly representative leaders of the black majority, and should accept the principle of the extension of political rights. While the need for blacks on a common voters' roll was not to be explicitly advocated, the idea was that it must not be excluded as a future possibility – that "men of colour must not be indefinitely debarred from participating personally in the government of their country, as members of legislative bodies".[19]

De Beer did not participate in debates on the Promotion of Bantu Self-Government Bill, but in the discussion on the Part Appropriation Bill he set out to demolish the false sense of security created by the euphoria surrounding the Bantustan policy. Responding to a gloating Jan Haak, the NP MP for Bellville, about the strong economic growth in the apartheid state, he warned that the ideological prejudices of apartheid would systematically undermine this prosperity. He emphasised that eventually the country will have to reach out to the growing market of Africa, but warned that apartheid will close South Africa out of this market. Furthermore, the economy required an established and prosperous black urban population, but instead the government dreamt of removing them to some rural Bantustan. A growing economy was furthermore reliant on the cooperation and contentment of the black worker who was badly treated. For black people to contribute to South Africa they had to feel that they had a stake in the country. To do so, they had to have political expression, and the Bantustan policy could not represent urbanised black people. He further warned that in the rest of Africa a revolution of decolonialisation and modernity was taking place, and South Africa had to adapt to these changes, or this revolution would "trample us underfoot".[20]

To convince whites to oppose Verwoerd's social engineering, De Beer published, between 15 and 17 April 1959, three articles in *The Star* in which he condemned the Bantustan policy as "rank non-

---

19 McConnachie, "The 1961 general election in the Republic of South Africa", p. 160.
20 House of Assembly debates, 23 February 1959, Col. 1341–1352.

sense dressed up as statesmanship". He pointed out that South Africa had undergone an industrial revolution in the past 25 years with the move of black labour from the reserves, and that there would always be a large black population in so-called white urban areas. Clever arguments by Verwoerd could not conjure away these economic facts, while the Bantustan policy provided no political future to urbanised blacks. South Africa was and remained a multiracial country in which political rights could not in the long run be withheld from the black majority. With the Bantustan policy Verwoerd was asking for political trouble and creating a perfect seedbed for communism. Ultimately, the policy would not secure justice for blacks, or security for whites. The only alternative was a multiracial society that did not signify social integration but political and economic salvation in cooperation. This implied the extension of political rights to black people who have achieved Western civilization standards. He conceded that the fear of being swamped by the black majority was a sincere one for whites, and he proposed that the country did not have to adhere to the one-man, one-vote system:

> What South Africa requires is a system which will allow suitably qualified persons of all races to participate in the government that no race will dominate for its own racial benefit.[21]

Political power had to be divided between the various political groups. He proposed to do so by reconstituting the Senate on a communal basis and to endow it with sufficient power to check racist legislation. To counter white fears of swamping, he also encouraged increased white immigration to South Africa.

The Bantustan policy extended to the universities with the Extension of University Education Bill. In terms of the Bill, the universities of Cape Town and Witwatersrand were prohibited from accepting black students who would have to attend five ethnic rural colleges for Indian, Zulu, Sotho-Tswana and Xhosa students.

---

21 *The Star*, 17 April 1959.

Apart from the desire to have a strict separation between black and white, the government felt that black students at Wits and UCT were turned into opponents of apartheid by liberals. Furthermore, Verwoerd portrayed the Bill as beneficial to black students as they were a discriminated minority on the open campuses and were isolated from most of the universities social and sporting activities. De Beer was scathing in his opposition. In a 26-hour second-reading debate that went on through the night, he addressed the House after 07:00 on 11 April. He compared the apartheid state to the double-speak and double-thinking of the totalitarian state portrayed in George Orwell's *1984*: That the Extension of University Education Bill meant the opposite, namely the restriction of the rights of black people to attend universities of their choice, while the Promotion of Bantu Self-Government Bill took away their last remaining representation in parliament. Ultimately the Bill was an attempt to control the thought process of black people, negating the main aim of a university, an investment for greater cooperation and for the synthesis, the growth and the building of a greater culture.[22] He concluded with what the *Cape Times* (13 April 1959) described as "his psychological diagnoses of the Prime Minister and his policies":

> The Prime Minister's ideas of grandeur will drive him on until he and his party have direct control of every institution in South Africa, and his ideas of persecution will drive him on until there is no point left from which criticism of the Government can come.

The impact of his speech was diluted by the UP's refusal to explain whether it would allow blacks to become a majority on the campuses of the open universities, and whether they will allow white and black students to mix socially and on the sports fields. Graaff remained silent as he knew that it would be used against the UP in the coming provincial council elections in September. The NP mockingly rejected UP criticism as mere opportunism,

---

22 House of Assembly debates, 10 and 11 April 1959, Col. 3663–3673.

and as obstructing the government's attempts to enhance the opportunities of black students.[23]

Undaunted, De Beer expressed his disgust with apartheid during the budget debate of the Department of Interior Affairs. He once more attacked the Population Registration Act as an attack on the integrity of the human personality, that it was a crime and a shame.[24] That his condemnation of the flaws and inhumanity of apartheid was getting under the skin of NP MPs was evident in a debate on the racial conflicts between Indian shopkeepers and black people in Cato Manor, a slum outside Durban. While accusing the government of undermining and curtailing the basic institutions of the Western way of life, namely the church, courts, trade unions, universities, and parliament, an incensed J.H Abraham, NP MP for Groblersdal, interrupted his speech so incessantly that the Speaker ordered him to leave the chamber. On his way out he stuck his tongue out at De Beer.[25]

The 1959 parliamentary session was an unhappy one for the UP as Graaff was unable to provide an alternative to apartheid that was acceptable to the conservatives and the liberals. A frustrated De Beer and Eglin made it clear to Lawrence that they were contemplating a smaller party that could speak with one voice and that they were not too concerned whether they could win Graaff over.[26] This attitude was bolstered when Mitchell, as part of his effort to claim that the NP was doing too much for blacks, intended to introduce a resolution at the party's national congress in Bloemfontein on 12 and 13 August 1959 that the UP would oppose spending any more money on the purchase of land as promised by Hertzog in the Native Trust and Land Act of 1936.

In the words of the *Sunday Times* (16 August 1959) it was an attempt to "out-Nat the Nats". The purpose of the resolution was also to force the liberals, by then dubbed the "Progressives" by the press,

---

23 *Die Burger*, 13 April 1959.
24 *Cape Times*, 30 May 1959.
25 *Cape Times*, 1 July 1959.
26 Lawrence, *Harry Lawrence*, p. 243.

out of the party. On 31 July the *Rand Daily Mail* exposed the "get-rid-of-the-liberal" movement. An informant told the newspaper that "To get rid of these liberals would win us many votes". Helping Graaff to write his conference speech, De Beer did his utmost to get him to oppose Mitchell's resolution. On Graaff's request he prepared a memorandum to present the case against Mitchell's resolution. In this document he warned that the acceptance of the resolution could force him out of the party. The Friday before the congress started, he told Graaff:

> "De Villiers if you defeat the land resolution and you don't let them slam the door on the common roll then people like me will stay with you. We don't like it because we would rather have liberal advancement, but will put up with this." And he said, "Well Zach then it will be all right because I'm not going to let it pass. I'm going to defeat the land resolution. And as to the common roll for blacks, I may let them give the door a bit of a push, but I won't let them slam it."

This assurance by Graaff led to him writing to Oppenheimer the night before the conference to inform him that there would be no split in the party.[27]

---

27 Wits, Brian Hackland papers. Hackland's interview with De Beer, 14 July 1980.

CHAPTER 6
The Progressive Party
1959

The national conference started with Graaff opposing the Bantustan policy, proclaiming that the "abrogation of White leadership over even a part of South Africa would place Western civilization throughout the country in jeopardy".[1] This set the tone for the conference as in the debate on a common voters' roll for blacks and whites there was an all-out onslaught on the liberals. The result was a vote that slammed the door on the ideal of a common voters' roll.

On the 13th the debate on Mitchell's land resolution, in a nine-hour closed session, took place in an atmosphere of organised hostility to the liberals that they were responsible for the defeat in 1958. They were attacked in speeches and howled down when they attempted to speak. De Beer was shaken by the hostility, as he explained to Lawrence who was on vacation in Europe, "The venom of speeches was quite unbelievable."[2]

Graaff afterwards conceded to Lawrence that "Mitchell himself was perhaps over robust" in his speech.[3] Despite Graaff's best efforts in opposing the resolution (according to Mitchell it was a bluff as he knew that the liberals would misrepresent his resolution as a break with the Hertzog pledge, and he wanted to avoid the risk of any misunderstandings and possible repercussions)[4] it was accepted with an overwhelming majority.

De Beer and Eglin realised that they had crossed their personal

---

1 *Rand Daily Mail*, 12 August 1959.
2 Barnard, Marais, *Die Verenigde Party*, pp. 116, 118.
3 Unisa, UPA, Graaff papers, File 99.1, Graaff – H. Lawrence, 9 September 1959.
4 Wilks, *Douglas Mitchell*, p. 120.

Rubicon. Turning Graaff and the UP into a more liberal direction would never happen. Seeing their position as untenable they decided to leave the party.

De Beer was requested to inform Graaff of their intentions. He caught him getting into a lift ready to leave the hotel. He conveyed the message, but Graaff said he could not stay and left for the airport. On reflection De Beer felt guilty that he should have expressed his message with more conviction and force as Graaff seemingly did not realise that the liberals were going to leave the party if he did not do something about it.[5] Steytler and Waterson then rushed to the airport to warn Graaff of a possible break. The UP leader still insisted on leaving for Cape Town. He was in hurry to return home as he was in severe pain. He was recovering from a dislocated broken collar-bone after a horse-riding accident a day or two before the conference. During the conference the supporting strapping to stabilise his shoulder had slipped, causing him some discomfort. He urged Steytler and Waterson not to make any decision and to see him in Cape Town.[6]

Eglin and De Beer, after cancelling their return flight to Cape Town, met with some of the liberals in Steytler's room, number 309, in the Maitland Hotel to discuss what to do. De Beer wrote a statement explaining their intention to break with the UP:

> The United Party Congress today took a decision to oppose further purchase of land for settlement by the present government. This is a clear breach of the promise given by the United Party Government in 1936, and as such a backward step from the 1954 statement of United Party policy. None of us can accept this decision. It is indicative of the general unwillingness of the Congress to face up to what we believe to be the increasingly urgent problems of our multi-racial country. For this reason we doubt we can any longer serve any honest and useful purpose as members of the party and we have therefore to consider our position and to discuss it with Sir De Villiers Graaff. We

---

5 Wits, Hackland papers. Hackland's interview with De Beer, 14 July 1980.
6 Graaf, *Div looks back*, p.161.

have had no opportunity of consulting with other Party members who may share our views.⁷

The statement was signed by De Beer, Suzman, Steytler, Van Ryneveld, Waterson, Eglin, Williams and Swart, all parliamentarians and Jacqueline Beck, Cape provincial councillor for Vasco, Leo Boyd, leader of the UP in the Natal provincial council, and Willie Steytler, Jan's brother. Despite the caution of some that they first had to discuss the situation with Graaff, De Beer with the support of Suzman and Eglin insisted on the statement's immediate release to the press and it appeared the next day. (The note meant so much for De Beer that he had it enlarged, framed and mounted in his home.)⁸

Cope, Ronald Butcher, and Wilson who had left Bloemfontein earlier, as well as Fourie who had missed the conference due to illness, promptly endorsed the statement and gave their full support to the breakaway. To secure support De Beer flew to Johannesburg on Friday to meet Oppenheimer and leading figures in the business and newspaper world. Eglin, who had travelled by car, joined him later that day. On meeting Oppenheimer his response, to whether he would support the breakaway was, "Zach, what has my whole life been about if I don't support you."⁹

Wilson felt that instead of rushing to Johannesburg they should have returned immediately to their constituencies to explain their actions as they created time for Graaff to grab the initiative and to isolate them with a campaign of vilification. The UP leader played with great effect the role of a disenchanted victim of political intriguing, that the liberal breakaway was not based on political principle but on intrigue and disloyalty. In a letter to Lawrence, he was desperate to keep him in the UP, he refused to see the acceptance of the Mitchell motion as a matter of principle and accused the liberals of using it as an occasion, rather than a cause, to break

---

7   Strangwayes-Booth, *A cricket in the thorn tree*, pp.158.
8   Correspondence with Wendy de Beer Furniss, 1 December 2020.
9   Barnard & Marais, *Die Verenigde Party*, pp. 68–74.

away.[10] As a result, party members who had no time for Mitchell turned their backs on the breakaways. Major Piet van der Byl, MP for Green Point, former minister in the Smuts government and a popular figure in the UP, viewed Mitchell's actions as stupid, but felt that the dissidents were looking for an excuse to break with the party. This was shown by their release of the statement to the press before discussing it with Graaff, and De Beer's rush to see Oppenheimer.[11] Cathy Taylor, the liberal-minded and energetic provincial councillor for Wynberg, who had vehemently opposed Mitchell's land resolution, concurred with Van der Byl and felt that personal clashes and not principles lay behind the breakaway.[12]

Mitchell, who joined Graaff on his farm outside Cape Town the day after the conference, also used his considerable influence in the party to vehemently reject the notion that the intention of his resolution was to purge the liberals. According to him it was the liberals who were intriguing to break with the party and who were looking for a convenient excuse to do so.[13] He based his accusation on the fact that Eglin and De Beer had met Steytler on his farm, and then travelled with him to Bloemfontein. Ultimately, it would have made no difference whether De Beer and Eglin had rushed back to their constituencies.

Graaff had built up a base of unquestioning loyalty at grass-roots level in the Cape Peninsula. His popularity bordered on worshipping. When Graaff met the breakaway MPs on 17 and 18 August, he was in a position of power and managed to get Waterson and Van Ryneveld to recant and to publicly apologise for their actions. (On 20 August, Van Ryneveld withdrew his apology and resigned from the UP.) De Beer resigned from the UP on the 17th, before he went to see Graaff. This made it possible for Graaff to prohibit

---

10   Unisa, UPA, Graaff collection, File 99.1, Graaff – H. Lawrence, 9 September 1959.
11   Unisa, De Villiers Graaff papers, File 295, P. van der Byl, "Notes on the future – 11.9.1959".
12   C. Taylor, *If courage goes: My twenty years in South African politics* (Johannesburg, 1976), pp. 85–86.
13   Wilks, *Douglas Mitchell*, p. 121.

him from addressing the UP's Cape Peninsula General Council, of which Eglin was the chairman and De Beer the vice-chairman. On 20 August the Council unanimously accepted a motion to approve the conference decisions and the actions of Graaff.[14]

The breakaways received a big boost when, on 30 August, Lawrence telephoned Oppenheimer from Italy to reassure De Beer, who was lunching with Oppenheimer, that he would join them.[15] The next day he wrote to De Beer to assure him of his support, and to let him know that "You have done well for South Africa".[16] Lawrence's support could not counter Graaff's success in keeping the breakaways on the back foot by accusing them of breaking their position of trust with their constituents and by not resigning their parliamentary seats. De Beer had a stormy reception at a public meeting in Maitland when he attempted to explain his resignation. He was verbally abused and instructed that since he had been elected under the UP's colours, he had to resign immediately. His response was that he first wanted to explain his stance to the voters of Maitland.[17] The Progressives – as the liberals were dubbed in the press – had the additional challenge that the provincial election was to take place in September. Steytler, Eglin and De Beer felt that without a formalised party they should not contest the elections. Two of the breakaway provincial councillors, Leo Boyd and Lester Hall, stood as independents in Natal and were defeated.

On 13 and 14 November 1959, at the founding congress of the Progressive Party (PP) in the Cranbrooke Hotel in Johannesburg, De Beer as the chairman played a leading role in the proceedings. Steytler opened the congress with a ringing declaration on the mission of the Progressives:

> In future colour and colour alone should not be the yardstick by

---

14 *Cape Times*, 21 August 1959.
15 Lawrence, *Harry Lawrence*, p. 244.
16 The Brenthurst Library, H.F. Oppenheimer papers, OPP/HFO/J1 (51:8) Lawrence – De Beer, 31 August 1959.
17 *Die Burger*, 28 October 1959.

which people are judged. We consider that all South Africans should be given the opportunity to render a contribution to the political and economic life of our country ... we want to face the future not with fear but with confidence that we can live together in harmony in a multi-racial country.[18]

He was then elected as party leader. Steytler was an Afrikaner, his father was a South African War hero and a founder of the NP who had served in the South African military during World War II. In the North Africa campaign, he was twice mentioned in despatches. Although a medical doctor, Steytler farmed in the Queenstown district and represented this rural constituency in parliament. He was a warm and charming person and would become a much-loved party leader. He was not especially good in parliamentary debates or public speaking, nor was he an administrator or details man, but as De Beer reflected in his obituary of Steytler, he had a bulldog determination to stick to his liberal principles:

> There have been cleverer politicians than Jan Steytler, smoother, more polished ones, certainly more subtle ones. I have not known one braver, or more strongly principled. Jannie was a man no one could ignore. He had a powerful presence, an indomitable will. In a certain sense of the word, he was simple. He did not like being bothered with detail. Nuances and shades of emphasis were never his game. Where he saw injustice, he roared defiance at it. Once he determined his standpoint, he fought for it like a lion, and the greater the odds against him, the greater was his strength of conviction.[19]

Steytler left the day-to-day running of the party to others. This weakness combined with the remoteness of his farm would eventually create difficulties in the party.[20]

---

18 Strangwayes-Booth, *A cricket in the thorn tree*, p.171.
19 Z126, Obituary of Jan Steytler, 31 October 1990. (In the possession of Wendy de Beer Furniss.)
20 Swart, *Progressive Odyssey*, p. 21, 135.

For the Progressives, the main task of the party was to persuade the white minority to save itself from a potential bloody race revolution. The conference accepted a programme of political reform and constitutional reforms, namely the abolition of pass laws and of influx control, the restoration of trade unions and the right of black workers to form unions. On the republican issue the party resolved to oppose such a move as it could endanger internal and external security and peace. For Fourie, a republican, this stance was unacceptable, and he resigned from the PP to sit as an independent in parliament.[21] On the issue of political rights for the black majority, De Beer as the head of the party's committee on the constitution and franchise, requested the conference to appoint Donald Molteno. He was to lead a commission to formulate a policy in accordance with the values and concepts of Western civilization. De Beer joined the Molteno Commission consisting of individuals such as ex-Chief Justice A. van de Sandt Centlivres, ex-Justice L. Blackwell, Leonard Thomson, historian at UCT, J.S. Marais, historian at Wits, Dr Edgar Brooks, a former liberal senator and lecturer in Political Science at the University of Natal, as well as advocate Arthur Suzman and Harry Oppenheimer.

The main task of the Molteno Commission was to decide on the non-racial qualifications to ensure a civilised electorate. The commission's report, which would eventually be accepted as party policy in November 1960, approved a franchise based on literacy and wage qualifications, as well as the ownership of immovable property. On the recommendation of De Beer and Oppenheimer, the conference also accepted the establishment of a "B" electoral roll for those who did not qualify for the ordinary roll but could pass a literacy test in one of the official languages. These voters – through special delimitated constituencies – would not elect more than 10 per cent of the MPs. Ultimately the Progressives accepted that whatever the qualifications to be a voter, the day had to come when black voters would be in the majority; but the process would be gradual. The Molteno Commission furthermore proposed a Bill

---

21   Strangwayes-Booth, *A cricket in the thorn tree*, p.173.

of Rights to entrench the rights of the individuals and to invalidate the Group Areas Act, the Urban Areas Act, the Pass Laws and the Immigration Act. The final report also envisaged a geographic federation consisting of several states or provinces. The rights and powers of the provinces would be widened and entrenched to safeguard their own affairs from central interference. The appointment of judges would be taken out of political hands and entrusted to special panels consisting of judges and lawyers of distinction. This would ensure that the courts were free of political interference. To bring about these far-reaching constitutional changes, a Progressive government would convene a national convention of all races, representing all political parties and organisations, to enact a new constitution.

The Molteno Report provided the PP with an alternative to apartheid, but it would be a daunting task to sell it to a sceptical and conservative white electorate. According to *Die Transvaler*, mouthpiece of the NP in the Transvaal, the Molteno Report was "so revolutionary that one wonders how the Progressive Party can hope to get popular support from the whites in South Africa". De Beer was proud of his contribution to the Molteno Report as he felt that it addressed the main challenge facing South Africa. The Progressives brought out a booklet, *Safeguard your future*, to set out PP policy for the public. For many years, the booklet would be repeatedly reprinted.[22] Thirty-six years later the recommendations of the Molteno Report would be the essential features of the South African Constitution adapted in 1996.

With messianic zeal De Beer set out at public meetings to convince the electorate of the merits of the Progressive platform. In a meeting at the Woodstock City Hall on 3 December 1959, he was adamant that the value of a person could not be assessed by the colour of his skin. The only solution was to live as one nation in accordance with the concepts of Western civilization, and that political rights had to be based on education, income, or property. The Progressives

---

22　D. Scher, *Donald Molteno. Dilizintaba – he-who-removes-mountains* (Johannesburg, 1979), pp. 81–87, 92, 96–98, 100.

would provide a constitution which would protect the rights of the individual. When asked whether he was prepared to accept that the time would come when blacks would have a political as well as a numerical majority, his answer was blunt, "Yes, I am" as it was obvious that political security was not based on "baasskap".[23]

He was especially effective in addressing university students. At the University of Stellenbosch, he stated that he was not interested in white leadership but "only in leadership by civilized people", as civilisation was more important than the colour of a person's skin.[24] Robin Carlisle, a student in Johannesburg, attended a meeting addressed by De Beer in a crammed lecture hall a few weeks after the founding of the PP. He left the meeting impressed with his charm, eloquence, and his ability to connect with his younger audience.[25] De Beer was the star performer and the face of the Progressives. To dedicate himself full time to the party, he sold his medical practice.

---

23 *The Cape Argus*, 4 December 1959.
24 *Cape Times*, 2 June 1960.
25 Interview with R. Carlisle, 14 April 2020.

CHAPTER 7
The winds of change
January–March 1960

The PP approached the 1960 parliamentary session in a buoyant mood. The party was well received by the media, and a growing number of people were joining the Progressives. Parliament provided an opportunity to build on this political momentum. A dull session was expected as there was no proposed contentious legislation. The focus of the government was on the celebrations for the unification of South Africa fifty years earlier. The Governor-General in his opening speech on 15 January 1960, a speech written by the government, listed the proposed legislation bills to reconstruct the Senate, to deal with the wattle bark industry, and to amend the Factories and Machinery Act. These were perfect conditions for the PP to show its wares and to make the public aware that it, and not the UP, was the real parliamentary opposition to the NP.

With the opening of the session, the Progressives were met by a wall of hostility.

The NP viewed liberalism as a legacy of British imperialism, an alien ideology fuelled by hatred of the Afrikaner. Even Schalk Pienaar who had serious concerns and doubts about the oppressive way apartheid was being implemented, condemned liberalism in *Die Burger* as just another weapon of English-speaking jingoists and "Boerehaters" (haters of Afrikaners) to get at the Afrikaner. Because of the party's close ties with Oppenheimer, the PP was seen as an instrument of big capital, the traditional enemy of Afrikaner nationalism.

In reality the PP would be perennially poor as big businesses refused to be associated with liberalism, and the party had to rely on Oppenheimer's personal donations.[1] But the main reason why NP MPs hated and reviled the PP was its exposure of the brutality and hardships of the apartheid system. They did not want to hear about the dark side of apartheid as they had convinced themselves that it was a just and Christian policy.[2] For them, any black discontentment with apartheid was the result of communist agitation with liberals acting as their useful idiots. On the other hand, the UP MPs had worked themselves into a state of rage that the Progressives had not resigned their seats to fight the by-elections under the new colours. They would continuously, to the merriment of the NP, interrupt their speeches.

The progressives were shocked that even Margaret Ballinger, the highly respected native representative and former leader of the Liberal Party, was hostile to them. She was much admired by them as an unbending opponent of apartheid. She was the one person in parliament who could match Verwoerd in debates and cut him down to size. Many felt that the Promotion of Bantu Self-Government Act was motivated by his desire to get rid of her. When the Progressive MPs were still in the UP, she was friendly, helpful and encouraging. There were high hopes that she would join the PP. However, Ballinger was unhappy with the founding of the party as she felt that they should have joined the Liberal Party. She was particularly hurt that in December 1959, Walter Stanford, a fellow native representative and someone she viewed as a protégé, had resigned from the Liberal Party to join the Progressives. (Stanford's membership of the PP parliamentary caucus would be short as his term as a native representative would come to an end in June 1960.) She blamed De Beer for pressing him to do so, and as a result refused to share her front bench in the House of Assembly with him.[3] Her haughtiness and arrogance were also a factor as she

---

1 E.R. McKensie, "Its master's voice? The South African "Progressive" parties and business, 1959–1983", *Journal for Contemporary History*, Vol. 1, No. 3 Dec 1996.
2 *Die Burger*, 24 March 1960.
3 Interview with Zach de Beer, 22 September 1986; University of Cape Town, V.M.L. Ballinger collection, A2.13, Diary, 6, 10, 12 and 13 December 1959.

expected to be treated with respect and was extremely sensitive to her status as South Africa's foremost liberal. She took it badly that the PP was formed without involving her opinion. A contributing reason for this hostile attitude was that Ballinger was a close friend – there was widespread gossip in parliament that they were lovers – of P.A. Moore, the UP MP for Kensington, a member of the party's right-wing and someone who was antagonistic to the Progressives.[4] Her antipathy towards the Progressives was such that she believed that they were under a moral obligation to resign the seats they had won as UP candidates.

Fortunately, the Progressive caucus was filled with a harmony of purpose, excitement, and mutual respect that they had not found in the UP. Suzman would describe the 1960 and 1961 parliamentary sessions as the tensest and most bitter ones she had ever experienced, but they were also the happiest years of her parliamentary career as the Progressives formed a happy and effective unit.[5]

The ritual no-confidence debate opened on 19 January with the public galleries packed to hear Steytler's speech. Normally Verwoerd would immediately respond to Graaff, but on this occasion he remained seated. It was obvious that he wanted to hear what the Progressive leader had to say. When Steytler did rise it was late afternoon, but it was only to request an adjournment. This would ensure that he was the first speaker the next day, and in doing so would not have to share the front page of the newspapers with Graaff.

That evening De Beer addressed the Progressive's first ever public meeting in an NP-held constituency, namely Bellville. About 100 people were present, and apart from an interruption when thunder-crackers exploded at the entrance of the hall, he could complete his speech. He made it clear that if a man could prove his civilisation, he was entitled to political rights regardless of his race. He emphasised that in the economic sphere each man should have the right to do the best work his hands were capable of. As regards

---

4 Interview with H. Suzman, 2 August 1986.
5 Strangwayes-Booth, *A cricket in the thorn tree*, p. 189

the social sphere, he stated that the PP did not believe that people should be forced to live together while they wish to live apart, but the Progressives would not tolerate the open injustice of the Group Areas Act, nor the miserable indignity of the Immorality Act. He ended his speech on a stark warning note:

> We as the White people of South Africa, must choose. We may choose to maintain our domination now, and go under in the long run: or we may choose now to cooperate with the dark-skinned peoples, and save ourselves and them, for a future of progress and peace.[6]

The next morning Steytler delivered his much-anticipated speech in the House. He rejected the Bantustan policy as a fantasy that could never work. Whatever the government did, or future governments may do, black people would one day be the ruling majority in South Africa. The only way to ensure that the country would be in the hands of civilised men when this day arrived was to place all people who met certain civilised standards on the common voters' roll.

Verwoerd's response was that the Progressive policy would lead to black domination, and that a Bill of Rights could not protect the white minority. He argued that once in power, the black majority would wipe out minority groups, the whites, Indians and coloureds. He did concede that he knew what the PP's policy entailed and that the Progressives could force the UP to make clear what it stands for. Verwoerd then stunned the House with an announcement that there would be a referendum to decide whether South Africa should become a republic. He gave the assurance that there would be no drastic constitutional change as a ceremonial State President would replace the Governor-General. The President would be above politics as a symbol of national unity and would be elected by parliament. Only whites could participate in the referendum.[7]

---

6 *Cape Times*, 21 January 1960.
7 *Cape Times*, 21 January 1960.

With the announcement of the referendum, Steytler's speech was only mentioned in passing by the press. From the press gallery Pienaar assured those who did take note of Steytler's speech that it was mere fear mongering, and that nothing would come of the PP.[8] That the Progressive warning about the dangers of a race revolution had to be taken seriously was emphasised on Sunday, 24 January when the country was shaken by the news that nine police officers in Cato Manor, Durban, were hacked and stoned to death during a raid for illicit liquor.

On 3 February the visiting British Prime Minister Harold Macmillan delivered his "Winds of change" speech to both houses of parliament. He warned about a changing Africa:

> The wind of change is blowing through the continent. Whether we like it or not, this growth of national consciousness is a political fact. We must all accept it as a fact. Our national policies must take account of it.[9]

He made it clear that apartheid South Africa could no longer rely on Britain's support. Macmillan had echoed the Progressive's warnings about apartheid. For De Beer the speech was an exciting and wonderful event.[10] But the "Winds of change" speech, instead of benefiting the PP, enhanced Verwoerd's reputation. Caught by surprise, as he had no inkling to what Macmillan would say, his impromptu, measured, and forceful response that his policy of separate development was not at variance with events in Africa even impressed Verwoerd's enemies.[11] It certainly persuaded some conservative English speakers to support the republican ideal.[12]

---

8 *Die Burger*, 21 January 1960.
9 H. Kenney, *Power, pride & prejudice. The years of Afrikaner nationalist rule in South Africa* (Johannesburg, 1991), p.132.
10 Recording of Wendy's conversation with Maureen de Beer, 1 May 2020.
11 H. Giliomee, *The last Afrikaner leaders. A supreme test of power* (Cape Town, 2002), p. 74.
12 S. Dubow, "Macmillan, Verwoerd, and the 1960 'Wind of change' speech", *The Historical Journal*, Dec 2011, Vol. 54, No. 4, p. 1102.

The day after the excitement of Macmillan's speech, the House returned to the petty racism of apartheid with the Reservation of Separate Amenities Amendment Bill. The Bill empowered local authorities to make beach apartheid practicable by providing separate amenities for different races in the sea beyond the high-water mark. De Beer rejected the Bill for enshrining in the law the principle of unfairness and injustice and argued that the House was legislating for the comfort of one racial group, the whites, without any regard to the needs and requirements of other groups.[13] Parliament, with the support of the UP, approved the Bill with 115 votes to 15.

On 5 February, to counter these types of law, Steytler introduced a motion for a reformed constitution which would give each racial community a due share in the government and would guarantee the fundamental rights and liberties of individuals. He condemned the policies of Verwoerd as impractical and a dangerous deception of the position of whites in the country and debated that political rights should not be based on the basis of colour and oppression, but on merit, the granting of rights to civilized men, whether black or white, on a common voters' roll. De Beer, "quick and fluent, as he always is" in the words of the *Cape Times* (6 February 1960), seconded the motion. He argued that consent of the governed was a basic principle:

> ... the present situation in South Africa is inherently a dangerous one because of all the people on whose respect for the law and maintenance of law and order depends, of all those people only a small proportion are consulted in the making of the laws of the country.[14]

The solution to this worrying situation was a non-racial franchise based on a civilisation test. He also argued that in 1960 black people needed protection against the white minority, but that the day would come when whites would badly want such protection

---

13 House of Assembly debates, 4 February 1960, Col. 936–938.
14 House of Assembly debates, 5 February 1960, Col. 1010.

against a black majority. This could be achieved with a Bill of Rights safeguarding all communities.[15]

It was a powerful speech, but it was overshadowed by the announcement that all hope of saving 437 trapped miners at the Coalbrook colliery south of Johannesburg – the pit had collapsed on 21 January – had been abandoned.

Undaunted, De Beer would use every opportunity to push the Progressive stance of extending political rights to the black majority. With the Senate Bill that reduced the membership of the upper house from 90 to 54 members, he argued that the reconstituted Senate did not represent the population of South Africa and provided no protection for the rights of individuals or groups.[16]

On 4 March, the Progressives supported a motion by Ballinger that the pass laws and influx control for black people had to be abolished. The UP opposed the motion, appealing instead for leniency and the application of these laws with greater fairness.[17] The motion was rejected by the House, while outside parliament black anger was building up against pass laws. The newly created Pan Africanist Congress (PAC) in an attempt to pre-empt the ANC called for a nationwide campaign against the pass laws. Combined with a call for a stayaway from work, black people were urged to march to police stations without their passbooks and to insist on being arrested, and then to refuse any bail. The hope was that the apartheid state's penal system would be overwhelmed.

On 21 March, in an atmosphere of simmering anger with the apartheid laws, thousands of black people marched on police stations. The police at Sharpeville outside Vereeniging panicked and fired more than 1000 rounds on between 15 000 to 20 000 protesters at the police station. Sixty-nine people were killed and 180 wounded. At Langa, near Cape Town, a similar incident took place but on a smaller scale.

News of the killings at Sharpeville reached Verwoerd while he

---

15 House of Assembly debates, 5 February 1960, Col. 1014–1019.
16 House of Assembly debates, 2 March 1960, Col. 2559.
17 Barnard & Kriek, *Sir De Villiers Graaff*, p. 101.

was in the House of Assembly. The House was acrimoniously debating the proposed republican referendum. Mitchell was at his apoplectic best on the dangers of a republic. On receiving the message, Verwoerd said to his bench mate, Ben Schoeman, "Nou gaan ons groot moeilikhede hê" (Now we are going to have big problems).[18] However, in his statement to the House, he projected confidence that the situation was under control and he blamed the opposition's anti-apartheid propaganda for inciting black people to defy the state. The republican referendum debate then continued.

Tony Delius, the political correspondent of the *Cape Times*, was horrified. He was a liberal who loathed apartheid, and mercilessly mocked NP MPs and ministers in his column "Notes in the House". Delius published his column under the pseudonym of Adderley, the name of the man who had led the protest against Britain's attempts to settle convicts in the Cape in the 19th century. He told Joel Mervis, editor of the *Sunday Times*, that Adderley had tried to prevent South Africa from becoming a convict station, while he was trying to prevent it from becoming a police state.[19] Under the heading "Death and chaos outside – unreality inside" he pointed out that while Sten-gun fire could be heard on the edges of Cape Town, the echoes of modern South Africa were lost in the House amidst wild cries about a future republic. In addition, P.J. Luttig, the NP MP for Mayfair, asked Steytler whether he would allow his daughter to marry a black man.[20]

---

18 Schoeman, *My lewe in die politiek*, p. 260.
19 J. Mervis, *The fourth estate. A newspaper story* (Johannesburg, 1989), p. 409.
20 House of Assembly debates, 21 March 1960, Col. 3799.

CHAPTER 8
Opposing the banning of the African National Congress and a republic
March–December 1960

In the wake of the massacre, the ANC called for a day of mourning and a general strike. South Africa was in the grip of a growing violence and seemed to be on the brink of an uprising. The situation seemed so desperate that on 26 March the pass laws were suspended. In parliament Mitchell launched a savage attack upon Verwoerd for showing weakness. The NP MPs needed no encouragement to be unbending. Their faith in apartheid was unshaken, and they were firmly of the opinion that the unrest was the result of white liberals spreading lies and poison about apartheid. They went on the offensive when the PP demanded that the government negotiate with black leaders to determine the root causes for the violence. Scorn and anger were poured upon the Progressives, that they, together with the ANC, were responsible for the violence.[1]

The Minister of Justice, Frans Erasmus, tabled the Unlawful Organisations Bill that outlawed the ANC and the PAC on 28 March. The Verwoerd government believed that without the agitation of the two movements, the black majority would be happy and content with apartheid. Initially, the UP viewed it as a vicious piece of legislation, and Graaff was determined to oppose it.[2] Verwoerd met him privately, informing him that the country was in turmoil, that the situation was far worse than the press had reported, and that national interests demanded that the Bill be passed. Graaff, feeling that it was the duty of any responsible opposition to assist

---
1 *Cape Times*, 24 March 1960.
2 House of Assembly debates, 28 March 1960, Col. 4200.

in the maintenance of law and order, decided to support the Bill. Without any debate, or protest, the UP MPs obeyed him.[3] Mitchell accused the Progressives of "trying to make political capital out of bloodshed" when they made it clear they were determined to oppose the Bill.[4]

On 30 March, while parliament debated the Unlawful Organisations Bill, a local PAC leader, Philip Kgosane, a 23-year-old UCT student, led a mass protest march of 30 000 people from Langa to Caledon Square police station. It was to protest a brutal police raid earlier in the day on the township. It was an unplanned protest, and the police – caught by surprise – was unable to stop the march before it entered the city. When Colonel I.P.S. Terblanche, Deputy Commissioner of Police in the Western Cape, saw the size of the crowd, he was shocked and fell to his knees in the police station to pray for strength to deal with the situation. Ignoring Erasmus's order to use force on an illegal march, he ordered the police, all armed with a Sten submachine gun, into the police station while he accompanied two fellow senior officers unarmed to negotiate with Kgosane. The march dispersed peacefully when he gave Kgosane his personal assurance that he would meet the Minister of Justice later that afternoon.[5] While the march was in progress, armoured cars and heavily armed police and soldiers protected parliament. Wilson stood with some NP MPs outside parliament in the company of soldiers to watch the march, and he witnessed how pale and strained the faces of these MPs were. They were speechless.[6] All Suzman could see peering out of the basement office of the PP was the trembling boots of a terrified young police constable.[7]

In the House of Assembly press gallery, Delius observed that events outside the chamber did not even lead to a ripple of concern

---

3   Graaff, *Div looks back*, pp. 166–167.
4   *Cape Times*, 29 March 1960.
5   T. Heard, *The Cape of Storms: A personal history of the crisis in South Africa*, (Johannesburg, 1991), pp. 90–100.
6   Wilson, *A time of innocence*, p. 379.
7   Strangwayes-Booth, *A cricket in the thorn tree*, p. 180.

amongst NP MPs. It was as if they were listening to the troubles of Tibet. Verwoerd assured the House that any violence would be suppressed without any hesitation. Daan De Wet Nel, Minister for Bantu Administration, proclaimed that race relations had never been better and that only a small minority was responsible for the unrest. Erasmus then announced a state of emergency. Strict censorship was enforced, meetings were banned, and the police started arresting opponents of apartheid. An estimated 23 000 people would be incarcerated.

When Kgosane returned to Caledon Square police station for his promised meeting with Erasmus, he was arrested. According to Graaff, Colonel Terblanche never forgave Erasmus for this and bore the scars of that betrayal to his dying day.[8] The government took a dim view of Terblanche for not using the force at his disposal to break up an illegal march and refused to promote him to Brigadier, a promotion he was due for. (In July 1987, the Minister of Law and Order, Adriaan Vlok, rectified this wrong by promoting him to the honorary rank of Brigadier as a symbolic recompense for the treatment he had received.)[9]

Amid the crisis, the second reading debate on Unlawful Organizations Bill continued and would last more than 19 hours. The Progressive MP's fought through the night to oppose the Bill. The *Cape Times* (1 April) observed that at 02:30 in the morning all twelve PP MPs were in the chamber, compared to the seven of the 42 UP, and the 23 NP MPs out of a 102. Mitchell gave the UP's full support to the Bill, and then sat back watching the NP MPs fiercely attacking the Progressives. In the early morning hours of 31 March, De Beer got to address the House. He condemned the NP's attitude that as the Progressives had warned of the dangers facing the country, they had to be the cause of the disturbances. The reason for the unrest was the abject failure of apartheid. Whites would not submit to the laws that apply to blacks only, for example the pass laws, or to be banned from trade union activities. He emphasised

---

8   Graaff, *Div looks back*, p. 166.
9   G. Shaw, *The Cape Times. An informal history* (Cape Town, 1999), p. 164.

that real peace could only come about by consulting with black leaders and by meeting their grievances and that the future would be bleak if these grievances were not addressed.[10]

The NP attacks on the Progressives became fiercer during the third reading of the Bill. Blaar Coetzee, NP MP for Vereeniging, was adamant that the government would never negotiate with agitators and arsonists. De Beer made it clear that the Progressives opposed the banning of the ANC and PAC, because it was healthy for the body politics that these organisations should be allowed to operate. The outlawing of the movements would not prevent any future uprisings. It would not silence the views to which the government takes exception to, nor would it put a stop to the activities to which the government objected. He furthermore pointed out that the duty of parliament was to avoid placing excessive power in the hands of the executive and allowing it to act without the supervision of the House.

While the debate was taking place, the police was resorting to brute force to intimidate black people in Cape Town. De Beer used the debate to produce reports that he had received that the police were assaulting black people at random, and indiscriminately, with whips and truncheons and demanded a statement from the Minister of Justice.[11] Erasmus replied that the police were at last free to deal with agitators and to restore law and order. Steytler responded with anger, "You speak of maintaining law and order. But what sort of law, and what sort of order?".[12]

With the country in a crisis, the House debated the dignity of parliament. This was after Hamilton Russell, UP MP for Wynberg, in a public speech had condemned the enlarged Senate as a "house of ill-fame peopled by gentlemen of easy virtue". The *Cape Times* reported this statement and a select committee of parliament found the editor, Victor Norton, guilty of contempt of parliament. Norton was summoned to the Senate where its president rebuked

---

10 House of Assembly debates, 30–31 March 1960, Col. 4579–4590.
11 House of Assembly debates, 4 April 1960, Col. 4762–4766.
12 *Cape Times*, 5 April 1960.

him. Russell's fate was to be decided by the House of Assembly. He defended himself with vigour and refused to apologise. De Beer came to his defence by proclaiming that he did not criticise the Senate but an act by political leaders to create the enlarged Senate.[13] This was to no avail as the NP was determined to punish Russell. The House voted to expel him from parliament for two weeks.[14]

The ANC and PAC were outlawed on 8 April. The next day, Verwoerd, while opening the Witwatersrand Agricultural Show, was seriously wounded in an assassination attempt by David Pratt, a deranged white man. With Verwoerd hospitalised, Paul Sauer, the Minister of Lands, troubled by the events at Sharpeville and Langa, felt that the harshness of apartheid had to be addressed. At a public meeting, he urged that the pass system had to be softened and the wages and living conditions of people be improved. Despite these sentiments, the security forces continued to use considerable violence in urban areas to crush black resistance. The pass laws were reinstated on 10 April. In some rural areas, resistance continued for a while, but by the end of August the state of emergency was ended.

On 26 April parliament returned to the Republic Referendum Bill. The PP opposed the Bill as it would only accept a republic if the rights of every individual were guaranteed and if the Union's continued membership of the Commonwealth was safeguarded. The referendum could not be a proper test of the country's feelings for or against a republic as not a single coloured or black person, no matter what his qualifications, could express his opinion. The Progressives supported the UP's appeal that qualified coloured people on the separate voters' roll should be given a voice in this decision, but went further in demanding that this right should also be extended to all qualified black people.[15]

De Beer, in what Delius in the *Cape Times* (27 April) described in

---

13　House of Assembly debates, 5 April 1960, Col. 4876.
14　*Cape Times*, 6 April 1960.
15　*Cape Times*, 26 April 1960.

"one of those rapidly-reasoned and able speeches that the House came to expect of him", rejected the government's stance that the referendum was a matter between whites only:

> We say there is only one criterion which can be defended in a connection like this, and that is that the qualified citizens of the country who are to become subjects of the republic should have the right to participate in a decision of this sort.[16]

In his response Abraham, who seemingly had developed a dislike to De Beer, expressed his appreciation that he would disappear from the House with the coming general election. To all observers it was obvious that PP MPs at most had a remote chance to retain their seats in the next general election. Fortunately for the party, the election was still three years away, ample time to strengthen its organisation and to convince voters of the need to vote Progressive. In the report stage of the Bill, De Beer demanded that there could not be a referendum without considerable constitutional reform. During the third reading, he once more demanded that all qualified South Africans, irrespective of race, who were to become citizens of the republic should take part in the referendum. That Western civilised standards, he reminded the NP, were not only good enough to be preached but had to be practised.[17]

On 11 May, De Beer, as the Progressives star debater, had the difficult task of explaining why the PP had to vote with the NP during the Bantu Administration vote for money to buy additional land for black people. This was after Graaff had moved an amendment deleting £500 000 from the amount as long as such land was to become part of independent Bantustans. De Beer argued that in 1936 a promise had been made to provide this land and this promise had to be carried out. He continued by saying that this was the reason why the Progressives had split from the UP in Bloemfontein. It was also essential to add more land to the

---

16 House of Assembly debates, 26 April 1960, Col. 6442.
17 *Cape Times*, 3 May 1960.

reserves, not as a political solution as they were still part of a unified country, but for the adequate development and rehabilitation of existing eroded and overcrowded areas and to improve living conditions.[18] However noble the Progressives' intentions, their support for the Bantu Administration vote created the perception that while the country was burning, they were playing petty party politics by settling a score dating back to Bloemfontein with Graaff and Mitchell. In his "Notes in the House" Delius did not hide his disappointment.

Despite the traumas of the year, Verwoerd was determined that the republican referendum should proceed on 5 October. The republican campaign was bolstered by Verwoerd's increased stature after the failed assassination attempt. He addressed large and enthusiastic meetings. But what really boosted the republican campaign were the bloody events in the newly independent Congo, and the desperate fleeing of white settlers after the withdrawal of the Belgian colonial authorities. To secure the votes of conservative English speakers, the NP's slogan was "To unite and keep South Africa white, a republic now".[19] In the words of the *Rand Daily Mail*, the republican referendum had been reduced to "the simple question whether you want your daughter to marry an African, or more to the point, to be ravished by a Congolese soldier".[20]

The Progressives under the slogan of "Reject this republic", campaigned hard against a republic as it would perpetuate "baasskap" domination and racial hatred, and would be interpreted throughout the world as confirmation of the NP's racial policies. Steytler urged all freedom-loving South Africans that if they wanted progress and believed that the government should be the servant and not the master of the people, they had to reject a republic.[21] However, the UP dominated the anti-republican campaign and Graaff

---

18 House of Assembly debates, 11 May 1960, Col. 7290–7291.
19 S. Dubow, *Apartheid 1948–1994* (Oxford, 2014), p. 85.
20 Kenney, *Power pride and prejudice*, p. 157.
21 *Cape Times*, 27 September and 4 October 1960.

attracted vast crowds to his public meetings, much bigger than those of the Progressives. The referendum had halted the PP's momentum. The UP's campaign created the perception that it, and not the Progressives, was the true opposition to the NP. In a tight result the pro-republican vote would win with a majority of 73 380 votes. Maitland voted with 7029 votes to 3866 against a republic, but it did not signify support for the Progressives.

And yet, De Beer remained optimistic about the PPs future as was evident in a speech he gave to the Commonwealth Correspondents Association in London on 25 October. He argued that in the past ten years a growing number of whites realised that their domination could not be maintained, and that political rights and opportunities had to be extended to blacks. For this reason, many supported the Bantustan policy. On the other hand, there were many good and moderate people who felt that maybe the Progressives were too hasty with their policies. However, the realisation by so many whites that white supremacy could not be maintained through oppression created an opportunity for the Progressives to spread its message, and to gain support.[22]

De Beer was too optimistic, as the events of 1960 had bolstered Verwoerd's reputation as a man of granite that would secure their survival in Africa. Amongst whites it led to a false sense of security and complacency that the Bantustan policy was the solution to South Africa's racial challenge. This exorcised any doubts about the future, making it near impossible for the PP to make any political headway.

---

22 *Die Burger*, 26 October 1960.

CHAPTER 9
A session of petrified minds
January–June 1961

Boris Wilson was so depressed by the 1960 parliamentary session that he decided to resign his seat. He felt that parliament was an exercise in futility, that proceedings had an air of complete unreality, and that by remaining in parliament he was providing a veneer of legitimacy to the apartheid state. Another motivating factor was his unhappiness with the management of the party. When parliament was not in session, Steytler spent most of his time on his farm, leaving De Beer and Eglin in de facto control of the party. According to Wilson, this led to tension in the party as De Beer, who was frustrated and had high leadership ambitions, developed an antipathy towards Steytler, and he felt that De Beer's political selfishness was damaging the growing PP. De Beer never made a secret of his political ambitions, but there is no evidence that he undermined Steytler. The reality was more complex as Wilson's memoirs reflects a prickly person that felt unappreciated and victimised by those who did not value his talents and achievements, and revealed that he was envious of De Beer.[1] Wilson left parliament on 30 January 1961. His departure was a blow for the Progressives because he was an outstanding parliamentarian and it left the fledgling party to deal with a difficult by-election.

It was a deflated PP that returned to parliament on 20 January 1961. The only hope to regain momentum was to win the upcoming by-elections in Hospital and Green Point, and to oppose the NP in such a way that it was seen as the main opposition party. This was a considerable challenge, since after the departure of Stanford and Wilson, the Progressive caucus was reduced to ten members.

---

1   Wilson, *A time of innocence*, pp. 351, 365, 388–390.

To be active in the House and to spread the party's message outside parliament placed immense pressures on them. Especially as the electorate was in no mood to listen to any liberal message. Wilson, while sharing a flight to Cape Town with Albert Hertzog, the ultraconservative Minister of Posts and Telegraphs, asked an obviously relaxed Hertzog how he could stand all the tension in the country since the previous year. He was astonished by his response: "Tension?", he asked. "What tension?" He put his hands out wide, and smiled. "There is no tension in the country – everything is beautiful."[2]

His attitude reflected that of the government and NP. In the House of Assembly there was a complete absence of urgency to deal with the revolutionary potential in the country. All Verwoerd and the NP could focus on was an early general election to weaken the UP, and to eliminate the PP.[3] It was as if Sharpeville, Langa and the protest march in Cape Town had never taken place.

As usual, parliament opened with Graaff's no-confidence motion. After the referendum victory, the NP, high on self-confidence and arrogance, treated the motion as a joke. NP MPs bashed the UP for its lack of South Africanism, patriotism and an unwillingness, with an emotional Mitchell in the lead, to accept the referendum result. In this atmosphere De Beer condemned the lack of urgency to deal with the challenges facing the country. "To debate our problems as if we had decades to solve them in is almost as tragic as not debating them all." He also condemned as silly statements by De Wet Nel that race relations in South Africa have never been so good, and that there was no country in the world in which the masses had greater rights than in South Africa; despite Verwoerd's lofty rhetoric of separate development, crude "baasskap" was being implemented in the country. He urged the government to remember that in history there are examples of discrimination on the grounds of language and religion, and that such systems never succeeded. The only solution was to remove racist restrictions

---

2 Wilson, *A time of innocence*, p. 405.
3 House of Assembly debates, 25 January 1961, Col. 100.

and to extend political rights with a qualified franchise based on Western civilisation.[4] It was a powerful speech, but it left NP MPs unmoved.

In the press gallery it had an impact on Pienaar who had started to fear for Afrikaner survival. After Sharpeville he and Piet Cillié, editor of *Die Burger* and his close friend since their primary school days, initiated a campaign to address what they saw as the damaging influences and negative aspects of apartheid. *Die Burger* in carefully worded editorials and in Cillié and Pienaar's column "Uit my politieke pen" (From my political pen), under the pseudonym of "Dawie", started a campaign against petty regulations to control every aspect of black lives. For them racially separate post office counters or bathrooms was senseless and undermined what they saw as the separate freedoms of grand apartheid, the Bantustan policy. *Die Burger* also initiated a debate on the future of the coloureds as the homelands policy could not be applied to them. The paper reflected the attitude of many Western Cape Afrikaners that coloureds – and not white representatives – should represent themselves in parliament.[5] For this reason the newspaper supported the Cottesloe declaration.

From 7 to 14 December 1960, eight Afrikaans- and English-speaking churches met in Johannesburg to discuss the political situation in South Africa. It led to the Cottesloe declaration, supported by the DRC delegation, in which the churches agreed that no one should be excluded from any church on the grounds of race; that there were no scriptural grounds for the prohibition of mixed marriages. It also criticised migrant labour and low black wages. Moreover, the declaration made it clear that there could be no objection in principle to the direct representation of coloureds in parliament. Cottesloe was seen as a challenge to the moral legitimacy of apartheid and Verwoerd was offended, vowing that he would never allow direct coloured representation in parliament. He had made it clear that he saw no reason to depart from

---

4 House of Assembly debates, 27 January 1961, Col. 268–281.
5 L. Louw (ed.), *Dawie 1946–1964* (Cape Town, 1965), pp. 182–183.

established apartheid policies. His survival from the assassin's bullet convinced him that he was protected by Providence and had strengthened his belief that apartheid was the only policy for a prosperous South Africa. For him the Cottesloe declaration would be the thin end of the wedge that could lead only to black domination. In support of Verwoerd, Dr A. P. Treurnicht, the ultra-conservative editor of *Die Kerkbode* – influential mouthpiece of the DRC – initiated a campaign of vilification to undermine the DRC's delegation.[6]

Verwoerd squashed the internal NP debate in January 1961 when a declaration of the Federal Council of the NP stated that the party, meaning Verwoerd, was the sole arbiter of policy. For Verwoerd it was either integration that would mean the downfall of the whites, or stricter segregation to ensure their survival. He had no doubt that the only solution was more and stricter apartheid and he went to absurd lengths to ensure racial separation at all levels. Pienaar was convinced that Verwoerd was a danger to Afrikanerdom as his stifling of any debate contributed to a dangerous complacency and intellectual laziness amongst Afrikaners. He feared that the prime minister created a false sense of security that exorcised any doubts about the future.[7] Amongst friends he was outspoken that Verwoerd was leading South Africa into an abyss.

Pienaar concurred with a lot of what that De Beer had said in the no-confidence debate, but felt that he was wasting his talents with the Progressives. In his influential and widely read parliamentary column "In die Volksraad" (In the House of Assembly) of 28 January, he condemned Graaff for not being able to keep De Beer in the UP as he would wither away with the Progressives in the political desert. He conceded that he could be unfair to Graaff, as he wondered whether the member for Maitland did not end up in this desperate position because his words were more effective than his political ideas. That he was too loquacious for his own good. De

---

[6] H. Kenney, *Architect of apartheid: HF Verwoerd, An appraisal* (Johannesburg, 1980), pp. 216–217, 263.

[7] S. Pienaar, *Getuie van Groot Tye* (Cape Town, 1979), p. 63.

Beer took Pienaar's criticism in his stride as he had a high opinion of him, and they would become friends later on.[8]

After the no-confidence debate, De Beer played a leading role in opposing the Defence Amendment Bill, which provided powers in a time of internal discontent for the military to commandeer goods. For him this would reduce South Africa to a permanent state of emergency.[9] In between parliamentary debates, he had to campaign in a provincial by-election set for 22 February in Green Point, Cape Town. It was such a safe predominately English-speaking opposition seat that since its delimitation in 1943 the NP had never contested the constituency. For the Progressives to make progress, they had to win Green Point, and they threw everything into the contest. The UP responded with black-peril tactics. Marais Steyn, UP MP for Yeoville and Graaff's adviser and speechwriter, and a captivating speaker with a strong platform presence, claimed at a public meeting that the Progressive policy was a threat to white survival as black people in South Africa were too primitive for a qualified vote.[10] Ironically, he owed his political career to Leo Kowarsky, a prominent Progressive. After Steyn had lost in Vereeniging in the 1958 general election, Kowarsky resigned as the representative for Yeoville to make it possible for him to return to parliament. Steyn would use his new lease on a political life to hound the Progressives. (He would eventually join the NP in the early 1970s.) On election day, UP supporters welcomed voters with calls that a vote for the PP was a vote for Albert Luthuli, leader of the ANC, and that support for the UP was a vote against black nationalism. The wife of a UP MP called out "Vote Thompson [the UP candidate], vote white!" to arriving voters. In the end, the PP could only secure 23 per cent of the vote.[11]

The Progressives, desperate to avoid another Green Point, threw everything into a Johannesburg City council by-election in Ward 24

---

8 Correspondence with Wendy de Beer Furniss, 3 December 2020.
9 *Cape Times*, 21 February 1961.
10 *Cape Times*, 1 February 1961.
11 *Cape Times*, 1, 23 and 24 February 1961.

on 1 March. The ward was in the Hillbrow constituency, regarded as one of the country's most cosmopolitan and liberal parliamentary seats. The Progressives nominated a strong candidate – Kowarsky, a World War II veteran, who had been wounded in the battle of Sidi Rezegh. The UP nominated Alf Widman, also a combat veteran of World War II, who had served as a company commander in Italy, and the provincial councillor for Orange Grove.

The UP once more resorted to black-peril tactics. Exploiting the publicity surrounding racial clashes in the Notting Hill area of London in Britain, the party distributed a pamphlet "If you want Notting Hill Politics here – vote Progressive", warning that the PP's franchise policy meant that whites would be outvoted by blacks within 20 years. The fear of racially mixed municipal swimming pools was also exploited, especially as the Progressives had voted against separate beaches for blacks and whites. On 1 March, the *Rand Daily Mail* supported the Progressives on the basis that they were at a particularly vulnerable stage after the trouncing in Green Point. The newspaper wanted to prevent another setback for the fledgling party which could lead to its obliteration on the general election that was rumoured to take place in September or October. With the voters of Ward 24 being more concerned about the possibility of racial mixing in a municipal swimming pool, Kowarsky narrowly lost with 1146 votes to the 1411 of Widman.[12]

In March Verwoerd left for London to attend a Commonwealth meeting and to apply for membership as a republic. But on 15 March after an emotional condemnation of apartheid by countries such as India, Ghana, and Canada, he withdrew the application. Against this background, De Beer dealt with the policies of the UP and the NP in a wide-ranging speech during the budget debate on 27 March. As far as the UP's new policy of a race federation based on ethnic groups and not on geographical regions was concerned, he accepted that the ideal of a federation to bring about freedom and liberty to the individual was a possible solution. But a federation implied a central parliament in which all races should have

---

12 *Rand Daily Mail*, 1 and 2 March 1961.

and enjoy the same rights.[13] Dealing with government policies, he pointed out that South Africa's departure from the Commonwealth was not the consequence of becoming a republic but a result of the NP's racial policies. The question was how South Africa could win back the respect of the Commonwealth and of the world. To do so, he said, the government had to accept that the country was a multiracial one, and to apply the basic concepts on which Western standards were based — the belief that the individual had the right to be judged according to his own merits, and to be allowed to achieve for himself what he could in his own right. To think in racial groups and to classify people as such could only lead to injustice and unpleasantness. He reiterated that although Verwoerd spoke of apartheid as a policy of non-subjugation, it was nothing but domination by one race over another; a policy that has been rejected by civilised nations all over the world. He ended his speech with an emotional warning:

> That apartheid threatens us firstly and most dangerously with internal strife, and secondly with economic impoverishment and thirdly with external hostility, and finally it is threatening us in our own conscience as we sit here, because we cannot face what we are doing. If this is to continue, I can only say as Jefferson said long ago: "I tremble for my country when I reflect that God is just."[14]

In the press gallery Pienaar listened intently. In his column of 28 March 1961, he inserted De Beer's use of Jefferson's statement without any comment, but he obviously wanted to alert his readers to the injustices of apartheid that had to be addressed. De Beer's warning had a lasting influence on him. Years later in a column he wrote for *Rapport* (22 September 1974), he urged his fellow Afri-

---

13 *Cape Times*, 28 March 1961.
14 House of Assembly debates, 27 March 1961, Col. 3698. De Beer was using Thomas Jefferson's statement on the system of slavery in the United States of America. "I tremble for my country when I reflect that God is just: that his justice cannot sleep for ever."

kaners to reconsider their treatment of black people, and then to "ask yourself if the vengeance of the eternal God can be kept at bay".

On 7 April, the South Africa Constitution Bill came before the House. It was proposed that the constitution remain unchanged except that a President without executive powers replace the Governor-General. With the decision to leave the Commonwealth, all emotion and passion surrounding republicanism had evaporated. For observers it was striking how flat the atmosphere in the House was. Not even the NP MPs seemed enthusiastic, while the UP maintained a sort of dispirited boycott of the debate.

The Progressives opposed the Bill clause by clause on the grounds that it did not include a Bill of Rights guaranteeing fundamental rights and liberties, the political participation of all qualified citizens irrespective of race, adequate safeguards to prevent domination by one racial group over others, and the decentralisation of executive power on federal lines.[15]

It left Delius unimpressed:

> Probably the most unreal feature of the whole debate was the Progressive attempt to stage something like a ditch-by-ditch resistance to its passage. One wondered why on earth they were wasting all that breath on a constitutional dodo. One had the weird impression that the Progressives were a kind of cricket on the hearth of a deserted house. All that was needed to be said was said in the first half-hour or so of the debate.[16]

The most significant part of the debate was when Jan de Klerk, Minister of the Interior, explained that the republican ideal was a great tree of freedom with deep roots which would spread its branches over both white groups as well as black people. He was astonished that there could be any opposition to this irresistible, unstoppable political force, urge and ideal. De Beer responded that

---

15 *Cape Times*, 1 February 1961.
16 *Cape Times*, 7 April 1961.

the global movement against colour discrimination was also such a force, and the NP was moving against the political ideals of the whole civilised world.[17]

A few days later De Beer directly confronted Verwoerd during the Prime Minister's vote by condemning the Bantustan policy as arrant nonsense and the rejection of Western civilized principles: "What is Western civilization if it is not the doctrine that the individual human being is supreme?" F.S. Steyn, NP MP for Kempton Park, was outraged and condemned him as "deliberately malicious".[18] This did not deter De Beer from confronting Erasmus to explain the banning of people in terms of the Suppression of Communism Act. Patrick Duncan, a prominent member of the Liberal Party and whom he knew personally, had just been banned although he was most violently anti-communist. He wanted to know what the limits were to the Act's powers and whom it could penalise. As the PP stood for the end of white domination, could its supporters be next in line to be banned?[19]

In this period the Progressives had the uphill task of fighting the Hospital by-election. Once more they were condemned as a threat to white survival. Although the NP did not contest the seat, P.W. Botha, MP for George and the Deputy Minister of the Interior, warned that if the PP had its way South Africa would "be engulfed by Black hordes of uneducated, uncivilised barbarians".[20] Against this background, Steytler's call on voters to support the granting of political rights to all civilised people on a basis of merit made no impact.[21] On election day a UP party organiser stood outside the polling station to welcome voters with calls that they had to vote against the PP to prevent another Congo. Eventually emotions boiled over, and the police had to intervene when a fistfight erupted between supporters of the two parties. After exerting them-

---

17 House of Assembly debates, 6 April 1961, Col. 4005.
18 House of Assembly debates, 12 April 1961, Col. 4401.
19 House of Assembly debates, 19 April, Col. 4886 and 20 April 1961, Col. 4985.
20 *Rand Daily Mail*, 1 May 1961.
21 *Rand Daily Mail*, 1, 2 and 4 May 1961.

selves to the utmost, the Progressives could only secure 36 per cent of the vote. [22]

While most white voters rejected Progressive policies as too radical, black people viewed the principle of a qualified non-racial franchise as racist. On 1 May, De Beer experienced this sentiment at a multi-racial meeting at the Gandhi Hall in Durban when he was harangued for two hours by a group of around 500 black people. His response that the country can best be governed by people who are able to understand the law and its value, and that in power the Progressives would provide educational facilities for every citizen to enable him or her to qualify for the vote, did not convince his critics and led to a mass walkout.[23]

After the Hospital defeat, the Progressive MP's had to return to a hostile parliament and its sense of unreality. This was typified by the government's refusal to take any note of the reasons for the violence the previous year. Verwoerd's focus was on the maintenance of law and order with the General Law Amendment Bill which, without declaring a state of emergency, allowed the detention of a person for 12 days without granting bail. For the Progressives the Bill signified slipping down the totalitarian path towards a state of permanent undeclared emergency. De Beer, in opposing the Bill, had to cope with a barrage of interjections. For him to be heard, the Speaker had to intervene more than once to silence the House. He was adamant that the Bill could not counter unrest and resistance to apartheid as it would only raise the levels of frustration and discontent. It was a move towards a catastrophe as it could not alleviate the troubles facing the country.[24] However, Delius was disappointed with the Progressives as they seemed to have little sense of outrage at this new inroad into civil liberties. He felt that their parliamentary performance was not up to standard as they were too distracted by a succession of by-elections.[25]

---

22 *Die Burger*, 4 May 1961.
23 *Rand Daily Mail*, 2 May 1961.
24 House of Assembly debates, 8 May 1961, Col. 6121–6128.
25 *Cape Times*, 9 May and 27 June 1961.

Delius had a point, because while the debate on the Bill was taking place, the Progressives were contesting the Constantia provincial council by-election in an affluent part of Cape Town. It ended in another heavy defeat as the PP could only attract a paltry 28 per cent of the vote.[26] The PP MPs were indeed exhausted, not just by the succession of demoralising by-election defeats but also by the daily struggle to be heard above the uproar of a hostile House.

However, De Beer rose to the occasion when Jim Fouché, Minister of Defence, with the Defence Further Amendment Bill for the first time introduced conscription in South Africa. The intention was to create a standing army of at least 10 200 citizen force troops to be conscripted annually for nine months to deal with external and internal threats. De Beer cast doubt on the government's belief that a larger and stronger army could be used to deal with internal disturbances:

> An army consists of people trained to kill the maximum of people in the shortest possible time. But troops on internal security are trained to control crowds with the minimum loss of life. How are the two aspects of training to be combined for our troops?[27]

He had reason to be concerned as the military was extensively used in the protection of the republican festivities. The republic was proclaimed on 31 May 1961 with C.R. Swart as the first President. The day passed without any incidents as the government had banned all political meetings while mobilising Citizen Force units. Henry Brown and Neville Rubin, two young article clerks at a Cape Town legal firm, were determined to challenge the ban in court and they approached Eglin for support. When Eglin showed no interest, they went to De Beer, who was enthusiastic and urged them to discuss it with Molteno. If he supported their argument, he would consider pursuing it further. When Molteno gave his approval, De Beer instructed them, with a promise to cover the

---

26 *Cape Times*, 11 May 1961.
27 *Cape Times*, 23 May 1961.

legal costs – he had convinced Oppenheimer to provide the funds – to lodge an application at the Supreme Court in Cape Town to challenge the banning as "grossly unreasonable. That it was oppressive and incapable of being observed by any person pursuing the activities of normal daily life" and demanded the government to prove in court that the ban on political meetings was not "invalid, bad in effect". As the 31st passed without any incidents, Erasmus did not oppose the legal challenge and lifted the ban on meetings. The government had to pay De Beer's legal costs.[28]

On 20 June, during the Appropriation debate – against the background of rumours of an early general election – a note of desperation crept into De Beer's pleading to the House to accept constitutional reforms. He once more rejected the NP's claims that it was defending Western civilisation in South Africa, and that apartheid brought economic prosperity to all. He stated that apartheid as a policy based purely on prejudice would bring nothing but poverty and should be replaced with one that would secure prosperity in a multiracial society. His heartfelt plea fell on deaf ears. J.E. Potgieter, NP MP for Brits, condemned it as "multiracial nonsense!"[29]

The only reform that came out of the trauma of 1960 was the Liquor Laws Amendment Bill that allowed black people to buy hard liquor on the same basis as whites. Enforcing the existing prohibition was one of the reasons for the poor relations between the police and black people. For Delius it was a curious experience to see the House debating whether the black man should be allowed a drink while so many urgent problems were simply ignored.[30] Ironically, the Bill divided the Progressives and they were given a free vote. Eglin and Townley Williams opposed the Bill as they felt that drastic reform in the social and economic circumstances of

---

28 *Cape Times*, 27 May and 7 June 1961; H. Brown, *A lawyer's odyssey. Apartheid, Mandela and beyond* (Pietermaritzburg, 2021), pp. 33–35; While presenting a paper at Unisa on 11 May 2022, Brown confirmed that the funding was provided by Oppenheimer.
29 House of Assembly debates, 20 June 1961, Col. 8502–8503.
30 *Cape Times*, 23 June 1961.

black people were necessary to remove the root causes of the abuse of liquor. De Beer, who passionately stated in his speech that "I hate all race discrimination", supported the Bill as he had no doubt that it was a measure to ameliorate racial discrimination.[31]

One positive development in a period of utter gloom for the Progressives was that with the republic, Fourie rejoined the PP on 20 June. It was a boost for the hard-pressed Progressives as he was an outstanding parliamentarian. Delius pointed out it was the best bit of news the Progressives had had for a long time. On 27 June, a cold Cape winter's day, the parliamentary session came to an end. For Fourie it was a session of petrified minds. Delius called it "this monumentally uninspired session". For De Beer it was a sad day for South Africa as the session had ignored the challenges facing the country:

> We now have proof that neither internal order, international status nor our stability can be maintained on the basis of apartheid. People must realize that they have to choose between prosperity and racialism.[32]

There was no announcement on a general election with the closing of the session, but it was accepted that it would take place in October. The Progressives left parliament with the realisation that they would not return. Delius was saddened that all the dull repetitive UP and NP propagandists of the House were in safe seats, while the Progressives, "[a]ll the people with some adventure and even gaiety about their thought were in considerable danger of disappearing."[33]

---

31 House of Assembly debates, 19 June 1961, Col. 8447.
32 *Cape Times*, 28 June 1961.
33 *Cape Times*, 24 June 1961.

CHAPTER 10
A young man with a great future behind him
August–December 1961

On 1 August, Verwoerd announced that as he wanted the republican era to start with a newly elected parliament there would be an election 18 October. The PP, organisationally still finding its feet, fought the election with the slogan: "Look ahead – think ahead". Steytler led the campaign with the message that South Africa was a multiracial country, and that exploitation and suppression could not secure white survival in Africa. Whites had to "adapt or perish". To adapt, political rights had to be extended to the black majority with a qualified vote, while the pass laws, influx control and job reservation had to be removed. No person deserved special protection just because he was white.[1] It was a message De Beer propagated with messianic zeal.

The UP, realising that it would not be able to capture NP seats, focused its campaign on the PP. Graaff was determined to destroy the Progressives before they could become a real threat. He was in a strong position to do so as he had considerable personal standing in the English-speaking community, and its newspapers. Apart from the *Rand Daily Mail* and the *Natal Witness*, they were supportive of the UP as it was seen as the real opposition to the NP. From the first day of the campaign, the UP had the PP on the back foot with the accusation that the Progressives would divide the opposition vote, delivering opposition seats to the NP.

The PP decided not to contest those seats in which its candidates could benefit the NP. Steytler left his Queenstown constituency to stand in Port Elizabeth South. Swart withdrew from Zululand,

---

1   Mervis, *The fourth estate*, pp. 343–344.

and Fourie abandoned his Germiston District constituency to contest Sea Point in Cape Town. These selfless actions which the Progressives portrayed as placing country before party did not secure any gratitude from the UP, which exploited it as proof that it was the main opposition party.[2]

In Maitland, De Beer expected a three-corner contest with the UP and the NP but was determined to contest it as it was a safe opposition seat. An uphill struggle awaited him as Maitland was in the proverbial backyard of Graaff. His UP opponent was Tony Hickman, a salaried party official as the Cape Provincial secretary, and a member of the Bellville Town Council. His candidature was unpopular amongst local UP members as it was felt that he was forced on them. They would have preferred J.G. Killian, Maitland's provincial councillor.[3] The Maitland contest became complicated when Frank Waring, a former UP MP for Orange Grove between 1943 and 1958, announced his candidature as an independent candidate. He was a mediocre MP, but his likeability and status as former Springbok rugby player ensured him a high public profile. His wife, Joyce, the daughter of Arthur Barlow – a legendary former parliamentarian and journalist – was the real force in his political career. She had her own political ambitions. In 1953 she had lost the UP-nomination contest against Suzman for Houghton and was encouraged by her father to join the NP as the political future was with the Nationalists.[4] Joyce pushed Waring to be part of the revolt against Strauss. This led to his expulsion from the UP and the end of his parliamentary career by 1958. To ease his way into the NP, he portrayed himself as the victim of a liberal purge. Aware of Verwoerd's desire to secure the support of conservative English speakers, he approached the prime minister in 1960 with the suggestion that he was willing to serve in his government.[5] With

---

2 Swart, *Progressive Odyssey*, pp. 93–96.
3 *Die Burger*, 15 September 1961.
4 Unisa, Joyce and Frank Waring papers, File 20.1.1, Barlow – Joyce Waring, 7 November 1951, and 23 June 1953.
5 B.M. Schoeman, *Van Malan tot Verwoerd* (Cape Town, 1973), p. 214.

the opposition vote in Maitland divided, he saw an opportunity to get back into parliament.

Initially De Beer did not take Waring's candidature seriously. Maureen said that in all the time she knew Waring, she never heard him utter a word as Joyce always spoke on his behalf. She viewed him with some amusement as a henpecked former rugby player with little between the ears.[6] However, Waring was a dangerous opponent as he had won the support of Verwoerd with his sycophantic flattery and with his vocal support of republicanism and apartheid. He portrayed his candidature as a rallying cry for English speakers to support the government. Although Verwoerd would have preferred to have him stand as an NP candidate,[7] he ordered the Maitland branch of the party not to put up a candidate.

Waring kicked off his campaign with a public meeting in which he praised Verwoerd as the greatest leader South Africa has ever had, and apartheid as the solution to South Africa's racial situation. He further portrayed himself as a bridge builder between conservative English speakers and Afrikaners to help the NP to keep the country for white people.[8] On a visit to Cape Town, Verwoerd urged all Afrikaner nationalists to support Waring as he was a good friend of the NP. *Die Burger* (4 October 1961) placed this instruction on its front page.

In contrast to Waring's apartheid stance, De Beer's 68-page pamphlet *Multi-racial South Africa*, published by the British Institute of Race Relations, appeared during the campaign. He was adamant that white supremacy could only be maintained for a short time, and then at the expense of severe restrictions on civil liberties and of grave unrest. The only solution was a non-racial qualified franchise:

> The least that the White man must do is to adopt a policy which will give the Black man a majority in Parliament if and when he

---

6   Recording of Wendy's conversation with Maureen de Beer, 7 July 2020.
7   J. Waring, *Sticks and stones* (Johannesburg, 1969), pp. 78–83.
8   *Die Burger*, 22 September 1961; *The Cape Argus*, 30 September 1961.

deserves it. This means a qualified franchise ... a multiple vote or some franchise system which is not racially discriminatory ... The African must accept something less than his universal adult suffrage; the White man must accept a future Black majority ...[9]

In a letter to the voters of Maitland, he explained Progressive policy in the following terms:

> [Apartheid] ... is unjust and it leads to hostility, bitterness and internal disturbances. The right kind of protection is through a constitution which makes it impossible for even parliament to destroy the rights of any section of the population. This sort of protective constitution is used today in the Americas and indeed in most Western Countries. I stand for it here. We also reject injustice. I am, for example, a doctor by profession: I cannot refuse to another doctor the rights I give myself. This would be unjust. Therefore I stand for what is called a 'qualified franchise' – votes on merit and not on colour. ... roughly, I believe in extending full voting rights to anyone who has passed Standard Six and has at some time earned R600 per year, or who has certain equivalent qualifications.
>
> I believe that South Africa can only become richer if every South African is given the opportunity to do the best work he can – to produce more, to earn more and to spend more. Socially, I believe every South African should be allowed to choose his own company. Nobody should be forced to mix with people of other races if he does not wish to: equally, no one should be forbidden to meet people of other races if he chooses to do so. This is my policy in brief: on this basis I have the honour to seek your support.[10]

This was a message the majority of white South Africans did not want to hear, and they were susceptible to the black-peril tactics. Mitchell was crude in his approach. "Let the Progressives go and

---

9   *Cape Times*, 13 September 1961.
10 University of South Africa, Progressive Party papers, File 5.4.1, De Beer's letter to the voters of Maitland.

frolic in the surf with the coolies and non-Europeans."[11] In a UP pamphlet titled "The Progressives and their policies are a danger to you and your country" the PP was condemned as working for a "multi-racial parliament with a black majority". John Vorster, who had been appointed the Minister of Justice in August, urged that the Progressive threat to white South Africa had to be eliminated.[12]

Against the background of black resistance to apartheid and the bloodshed in the Congo, De Beer's admission at a public meeting in Cape Town that to prevent a race revolution the PP's qualified non-racial franchise plan could lead to a black majority government, did not endear him to his constituents.[13] In Maitland at a public meeting on 12 September, a questioner – to loud supportive cheering – proclaimed that "[t]he natives are barbarians and will be barbarians for the rest of their lives". De Beer responded that South Africa was a multiracial country and that each racial group was entitled to ask for protection against domination by any other.[14]

Addressing a public meeting in George – an NP fortress and the seat of P.W. Botha – in support of Ogies van Heerden, the Progressive candidate, he declared that if a black man was elected as an MP in a democratic manner and was elected as prime minister, the Progressives would accept him. He warned the 500 people present "that unless a move is made soon to give peaceful expression to the political aspirations of our non-White people there is likely to be a dreadful clash which may well result in Black domination of the worst possible type." He was given an attentive hearing, but a motion put to the meeting by NP supporters that it had confidence in Verwoerd and the NP was carried with a large majority.[15] (On election day Van Heerden could only attract 506 votes compared to the 7624 of Botha.)

De Beer's attentive reception in George was the exception. At

---

11 *Cape Times*, 31 September 1961.
12 *Die Burger*, 6 September 1961.
13 *The Cape Argus*, 8 September 1961.
14 *Cape Times*, 13 September 1961.
15 *Cape Times*, 5 October 1961.

all his Cape Town meetings he had to deal with continuous and concentrated heckling. And yet, with his charm and friendly demeanour, he usually succeeded in turning rumbustious meetings into good-humoured ones. This was evident in Observatory on 11 October, his birthday. Despite the Progressives being vastly outnumbered and his speech being interrupted with shrill blasts on a tin whistle, stamping and jeering, a good spirit existed between De Beer and the audience. The meeting closed with them singing happy birthday to him.[16] His campaign ended on 16 October with 600 enthusiastic supporters cheering him on at the Gordon Institute Hall in Mowbray.[17] Despite the rousing end to his campaign, De Beer knew that he faced defeat.[18]

Election day was marked by grey skies, rain showers and gusty winds. At the Maitland Town Hall, a group of female Waring supporters welcomed arriving voters with the call: "Vote for Waring and for a white South Africa." From early on it seemed that voters took the slogan seriously as it was obvious that the contest was between Hickman and Waring.[19] When the result was announced in the early hours of the next morning, Hickman secured 4610 votes to the 3703 of Waring and the 1688 of De Beer.

The UP captured all but one of the Progressive seats. In the Western Cape the Progressives suffered heavy defeats. In Durban, Pietermaritzburg and Johannesburg they did better, but only managed to retain Helen Suzman's Houghton constituency with the enthusiastic support of the *Rand Daily Mail*.[20] She hung on to her seat with a majority of 564 votes. The election was a triumph for Verwoerd. Compared to the 1958 election, the NP had increased its votes in every constituency apart from one it had contested, while it captured two seats from the UP.

As a parliamentarian, Hickman was not in De Beer's class. When

---

16 *The Cape Argus*, 12 October 1961.
17 *Cape Times*, 17 October 1961.
18 Interview with D. Cox, 13 April 2020.
19 *The Cape Argus*, 18 October 1961.
20 Mervis, *The fourth estate*, pp. 342–344.

Gideon Jacobs was elected to parliament as the UP MP for Hillbrow in 1966, he was told what a loss De Beer was to the party.[21] Hickman would become a leading right-winger in the UP caucus, and would in the 1980s end his political career as an NP appointee to the President's Council. The real victor in Maitland was Waring. His good performance was made possible by a significant number of former UP supporters voting for him as they were concerned about growing black anti-apartheid resistance, the collapse of colonial control in Africa, while being impressed with Verwoerd's confidence that apartheid was the only viable policy for South Africa. Verwoerd, eager to secure English-speaking support for the NP, used Waring's good performance in Maitland to give him a parliamentary seat and to elevate him to the cabinet as Minister of Information.

De Beer was shaken by the scale of his drubbing at the hands of lightweight opponents. Compared to his fellow Progressive candidates in the Cape Peninsula, he had, with his 16,8 per cent of the vote attracted the least support. In Salt River, Lawrence secured 31,7 per cent, Eglin in Pinelands 30,7 per cent, Jacqui Beck in Simon's Town 20,4 per cent, and Fourie with 35,4 percent of the vote in Sea Point. *The Cape Argus* (19 October 1961) pointed out in a leading article that De Beer's position at the bottom of the poll at Maitland must have been a hard blow to his prestige. It was indeed the case as De Beer experienced that rejection by his constituents as a deflating experience that dented his confidence. (Lawrence descended into a deep depression after his beloved Salt River had rejected him.) In 1994, De Beer would describe his 1961 defeat as the lowest point of his political career.[22] According to Maureen, he was so gutted and shattered that she had to remind him he was still the same man as the one that had woken that morning.[23] For

---

21 G. Jacobs, *Beckoning Horizons* (Johannesburg, 1985), p. 247.
22 The O'Malley Archives, Nelson Mandela Centre of Memory, O'Malley's interview with Zach de Beer, 8 November 1994, https://omalley.nelsonmandela.org/omalley/index (accessed 28 August 2019).
23 Recording of Wendy's interview with her mother, Maureen de Beer, 1 May 2020.

his daughter Wendy, although only seven years of age, it was clear that her father's defeat was a cataclysmic event.[24]

Publicly De Beer did his utmost to appear positive. A few days after the election at a function to thank 200 Progressive supporters for their efforts during the campaign, he told them that the party had "gloriously won its battle for survival", and that in Natal and the Rand it was nearly as strong as the UP. That the PP was on the road which may be hard and long, but a straight road, that would lead to inevitable success.[25] Personally his political prospects were bleak. At a post-election function, the chairman – with a sense of humour – articulated the state of De Beer and Eglin's political careers by referring to them as "these brilliant young men who have great futures … behind them".[26]

De Beer's political wounds were soothed with the prospect of a two-and-a-half-month tour of the United States of America (USA) on a leadership grant award by the American government. He left for the USA on 22 October. While travelling the country, De Beer was struck by the pessimism amongst Americans about South Africa. That "many Americans simply expected a great, big bloody revolution". What Americans wanted from South Africa was a change of direction. "They want us to accept the principle of government with the consent of the governed. They want us to end race discrimination."[27]

---

24 Interview with Wendy de Beer Furniss, 15 April 2020.
25 *Cape Times*, 23 October 1961.
26 Eglin, *Crossing the borders of power*, p. 96.
27 *Cape Times*, 15 December 1961.

CHAPTER 11
To be shaped by defeat
1962–1966

On his return to South Africa, De Beer was determined to be part of the process to bring about reform to prevent "a great, big bloody revolution". As chairman of the PP's National Executive, he was in charge of the party's overall organisation. The responsibilities and time-consuming nature of a general medical practitioner meant that he decided not to revive his practice. To have the time to remain active in politics and to secure an income to provide for his family, he entered the business world.[1] After joking that "As jy die Progge kan verkoop, kan jy enige iets verkoop" (If you can sell the Progs, you can sell anything), his friend Paul Rands, the director of P.N. Barrett, a leading advertising and marketing agency, offered him a partnership.[2] In January 1962, he moved to Johannesburg to head the agency's marketing and research department. Maureen and the children stayed behind in Cape Town. The *Sunday Times* (14 January 1962) viewed his move as an attempt to secure a more contestable seat for the next general election. The PP had narrowly failed to win the Johannesburg constituencies of Parktown, Johannesburg North and Orange Grove. This could have been a contributing factor, but the real objective was to build a business career. Despite his lack of experience, he excelled in his new job, but then according to Suzman, he was a person that would do well in anything he chose as a career.[3] He raised his profile in the world of economics by writing leading articles for P.N. Barrett's *South African Business Bulletin*.

---

1   Interview with Debbie de Beer, 23 April 2020.
2   *Finansies & Tegniek*, March 1985.
3   Suzman, *In no uncertain terms*, p. 193.

As the chairman of the PP's National Executive, De Beer travelled the country to spread the Progressives' message to increase grassroots support, to raise the morale of members, and to build up party structures. It was a challenging task as after the heavy expenditure in the general election, the party was in a financial crisis. Despite energetic efforts the party was unable to attract any financial support. Had Oppenheimer not poured sums of money out of his private funds into the party, it would not have been able to continue.[4] But even with his generous support, the PP was so poor that it was unable to appoint salaried staff and the party had to rely on voluntary workers. Most of them had to earn their living and were consequently busy, with little time for politics, leaving the party's administration and organisation in a poor state. This led to tension between De Beer and Steytler, who did not concern himself with the daily running of the party. De Beer admired Steytler as a brave and good man, but felt that he was a poor administrator, and due to his isolation on the farm an absent leader. With Eglin and Suzman he felt that this was a problem that had to be addressed. For them the task of a party leader was not just to be the political head, but also the administrative one. De Beer's objective was to create a strong head office which could provide daily initiative and required the regular attendance of the leader at this office. Steytler, who had made enormous sacrifices for the party, was hurt by this, seeing it as a vote of no-confidence in him.[5]

The Progressives started 1962 with high hopes as they were confident of victory in the Johannesburg North and Parktown Transvaal provincial council by-elections of 14 February. In October 1961, the Progressives narrowly lost these seats; in Parktown with a mere 85 votes. The PP expected to win Parktown and had high hopes for Johannesburg North. The party had well-organised

---

4   B. Hackland, "The Progressive Party of South Africa, 1959–1981: Political responses to structural change and class struggle", (PHD, Oxford University, 1984), pp. 222–229.
5   Wits, PFP/DP papers, Ab2.2.1, Minutes of the National Executive, 11 June 1966.

party structures in these two seats and the vocal support of the *Rand Daily Mail*. Progressive expectations were raised by the UP's apathetic campaign. The Progressives in contrast had a succession of well-attended and enthusiastic meetings. On 22 January, De Beer had addressed a crowd of more than 600 people, mainly young people. He described the PP as a movement of conservation and reform, but never of revolution.[6] On the eve of the election, the Progressives were confident that Parktown was in the bag. Even the UP expected to lose the seat and feared that Johannesburg North could go the same way, a view shared by the press.

The Progressives, and political observers, were stunned when the UP hung on to both seats, increasing its majority to 465 votes in Parktown. In a leading article "Why the Progs lost" on 18 February, Joel Mervis as editor of the *Sunday Times*, explained that the voters of the northern suburbs of Johannesburg were not prepared to stand and watch an effective opposition be divided and dismembered. That it was clear to them that the PP, however unintentionally, was a disruptive force playing straight into the hands of the NP. For him the Parktown result signified that the Progressives had little hope of becoming a political force. The sensible thing for them to do was to rejoin the UP and to try and bring about reform from within the party. The fear of divided opposition was certainly a factor benefitting the UP, but what Mervis ignored, and what *Die Burger* (16 February) gleefully pointed out, was the UP's effective use of crude black-peril tactics, portraying the Progressives as selling out the whites with its policies.

A week later the Progressives suffered another provincial by-election defeat in Greenpoint, exactly one year after the one of 1961 that did so much to derail the party's momentum. The Progressives once more threw everything into the contest. To generate enthusiasm, they arranged a mass meeting on the eve of the poll, bussing in support from as far as George and Worcester. The meeting of more than 1000 people roared its approval when Steytler stated that the differences between the UP and NP were micro-

---

6 *Rand Daily Mail*, 23 January 1962.

scopic.⁷ By using black-peril propaganda, the UP held the seat with ease. The Progressives secured 1634 votes compared to the 1708 of February 1961.⁸ With its messianic approach to politics, the party accepted the defeat stoically. The PP's pugnacious propagating of liberal views was worrying the government and this was evident in John Vorster's address in the opening ceremony of the University of Stellenbosch's academic year on 21 February. A big part of his speech was dedicated to the threat of liberalism to the apartheid state:

> Liberal thinking does not remain confined to political philosophy. It ultimately taints the entire being. It gives the impression of stimulating and leading to reform, but actually there is no reform, because the reformer is conservative. The liberalist in whatever sphere was a nihilist, who destroyed and did not reform, and if you transform, then you disfigure.⁹

Unbowed by the Greenpoint defeat, the PP set out to contest three by-elections on 11 April 1962 in traditional opposition seats in predominately English-speaking areas, namely the parliamentary seats of East London City and Durban Musgrave, and the Natal provincial council seat of Umbilo. East London City and Umbilo were such safe UP seats that the PP avoided them in 1961. Contesting these seats was an opportunity to spread the Progressives' liberal message. Musgrave was a different matter as Townley Williams had lost the seat with 959 votes the previous year. The PP had a strong candidate in Ray Swart and with an element of desperation threw everything they had into the contest. De Beer did his part. On 20 March at a public meeting, he warned Musgrave's voters that the NP's talk of fighting in the last ditch to maintain white supremacy was a threat to their survival. "The Government's policies are despised and detested by the whole world. If we become involved

---

7   *The Cape Times*, 20 February 1962.
8   *Die Burger*, 20 and 22 February 1962.
9   *The Cape Times*, 22 February 1962.

in a shooting war, we could not possibly win. It is the task of the Government to avoid such war, not invite it." The worst part was that the UP encouraged the government to "rattle their puny little sabres and shake their puny little fists in the face of civilization". It was the task of the opposition to tell the government that it was talking nonsense. Whites should not allow themselves to be stampeded like cattle into a position from which they were forced to defy providence.[10] It was not a message the average white voter wanted to hear.

In East London City the PP candidate fared dismally, while in Umbilo the party did better but still suffered a heavy defeat. But it was the Musgrave result that was a shattering blow. The UP, using black-peril propaganda, increased its majority to 1448 votes. In his memoirs, Swart vividly describes the hatred the Progressives had to endure during the campaign:

> A woman standing just below me was beside herself with disapproval of me as she screamed hysterically: "You bloody kafferboetie! Go back to your kaffers! We hate you! We hate you!" and then to give final vent to her venom she spat at and on me. It was an awful experience and a disgraceful example of how naked racism can degenerate human behaviour. It was not easy being a Progressive in those days.[11]

Musgrave was a decisive defeat for the Progressives. For R.W. Johnson, a young liberal student who was actively involved in the campaign, the defeat after the huge effort by the Progressives was a bitter pill to swallow. He had naively assumed that the liberal cause would make steady progress and he had never imagined it going backwards.[12] After 11 April 1962, the party ceased to be seen as a serious political force. The popular perception was that the PP

---

10 *The Cape Argus*, 21 March 1962.
11 Swart, *Progressive odyssey*, pp. 104–105.
12 R.W. Johnson, *Foreign native, An African journey* (Johannesburg, 2020), p. 40; R.W. Johnson, "The DA on the brink", *politicsweb*, 12 October 2011.

was an eccentric and ineffectual splinter party and to support the PP was to waste your vote.

Although these by-election defeats were painful for De Beer, he had the tenacity to deal with them. He was fond of quoting a phrase attributed to William the Silent: "It is not necessary to succeed in order to undertake, and it is not necessary to hope in order to persevere."[13] It was these types of defeat that led to the statement in the 1990s by Ken Owen, editor of the *Sunday Times*, that "[t]o be a liberal South African was to be shaped by defeat."[14] How difficult it was to be a liberal in this period was reflected in De Beer publishing a newspaper article, "Liberal view is still democracy's cornerstone", under a nom de plume of Ian McCrae. Ian was his mother's name for him and McCrae her maiden surname. It can only be concluded that he felt that under his own name many would not read the article as it would be seen as Progressive propaganda. The article was a response to Vorster's condemnation of liberalism, especially his statement that "liberalism is a danger almost as great as communism and even more insidious". In his response he set out the philosophy of liberalism:

> ... a liberal is someone for whom the individual is of supreme importance. He believes that every human being must be given the greatest possible freedom to develop his personality, his character, his talents. The liberal, if put to the test, will always be guided by the interest of the individual rather than those of the party, the group, the community or the state. ... a liberal is a man who believes in individual freedom and the integrity of the human personality. This belief is the cornerstone of Western democracy, and in attacking it Mr. Vorster and his colleagues are attacking democracy too.[15]

---

13 Interview with T. Leon, 3 April 2020.
14 K. Owen, *These times. A decade of South African politics* (Johannesburg, 1992), p. 292.
15 Undated and unidentified newspaper clipping in the possession of Wendy de Beer Furniss.

In May 1963, the article would be republished under De Beer's name in *Progress*, the newssheet of the PP in the Transvaal. In this article he also praised the liberalism of F.S. Malan.

The Progressives' concern about the state of the country, and the desire to prevent a race revolution was fuelled by the ANC resorting to armed resistance. A military wing, Umkhonto we Sizwe (Spear of the Nation), was founded, and as from December 1961, this group was responsible for a series of sabotage attacks on power stations, railway lines, telecommunication installations and symbols of apartheid. Umkhonto was smashed when in July 1963 the police arrested the ringleaders near Rivonia, Johannesburg. During the subsequent Rivonia Trail, five of the ten accused, including prominent ANC leaders such as Nelson Mandela and Walter Sisulu, were sentenced to life imprisonment.

To crush any black resistance, the apartheid state undermined the rule of law. The UP supported the 1963 General Laws Amendment Bill that introduced the system of ninety-day detention without recourse to the courts. The procedure could be repeated indefinitely on the expiration of the ninety days. In addition, the Bill made it possible to continue the detention of those who were convicted of political offences after the completion of their sentences. Robert Sobukwe, leader of the PAC, would be detained on Robben Island for six years after he had served his three-year prison sentence. Graaff refused to oppose the draconian security legislation as white voters accepted them as a necessity for the maintenance of law and order.[16] Suzman, the only MP to oppose the Bill, was disgusted, pointing out that the UP "meekly acquiesced in South Africa's abdication from the ranks of democratic countries".[17]

And yet, the UP's support for draconian security legislation did the party no harm at the polling booth. In May 1963, Hamilton Russell resigned his Wynberg seat in protest of his party's support of the General Laws Amendment Bill. In the subsequent by-election, Donald Molteno, as a high-profile PP candidate, campaigned on a

---

16 Graaff, *Div looks back*, p. 195.
17 House of Assembly debates, 29 April 1963, Col. 4923.

platform as a protector of the rule of law, and accused the UP that they had betrayed the principles of the rule of law. Cathy Taylor, the UP candidate, beat off his challenge with ease by portraying support for security legislation as a necessity for law and order. In a three-candidate contest, Molteno could only attract 21,1 per cent of the vote, coming third behind an independent candidate supporting Verwoerd's Bantustan policy.[18] After the Wynberg result, *Die Burger* (2 August 1963) confidently predicted that the PP had reached the end of the political road. The Progressive leadership pronounced itself happy with its performance in Wynberg as the PP had few members and no party structure in the constituency. The votes Molteno had attracted reflected the slow but steady progress of the Progressives.[19]

De Beer was under no illusions that it would be a long haul for the Progressives. However, it became increasingly difficult for him to be involved in the PP. By September 1963, his business responsibilities and a crisis in his personal life led to him standing down as chairman of the National Executive. After the unexpected death of Rands, he had to return to Cape Town in August 1963 to manage the local P.N. Barrett office. In this period, he and Maureen separated, and they would divorce in 1964. (Maureen and the children moved to Johannesburg to be with her parents in Houghton. After a short stay in Britain, they eventually settled in Pretoria.)

Wendy, the oldest daughter, speculates that De Beer's early political success could have been challenging for the marriage.[20] Maureen was a strong and forceful personality who had to sacrifice her ambitions for a legal career (she was admitted to the Cape Bar as an advocate in April 1953)[21] to be a mother and the wife of a parliamentarian. And she had to make considerable sacrifices as her husband was continuously on the road to address public meetings, leaving her alone with three young children, at the same

---

18   Taylor, *If courage goes*, pp. 103–104.
19   Scher, *Donald Molteno*, pp. 103–105.
20   Interview with Wendy de Beer Furniss, 17 November 2021.
21   *Cape Times*, 7 April 1953.

time sharing some of his political responsibilities. For example, when De Beer left for the USA in October 1961, it was left to her to clear out the PP's election office in Maitland.[22]

In September 1965, De Beer married Mona Glasser, a divorcee with two children. Mona, according to Tony Leon, was a sharp and intelligent person, and the De Beer marriage was a tempestuous one with arguments and quarrelling, even in public.[23] De Beer once confided in Douglas Gibson that he was a person who after his divorce had married the same type of woman for a second time.[24]

Despite numerous setbacks, De Beer had succeeded as the chairman in creating the basic party structures on which the Progressives would build over the years.[25] He was replaced by Prof. P.V. Pistorius, a professor in Greek at the University of Pretoria. Pistorius also found it difficult to give his undivided attention to the post due to work pressure and the hostility of students and the university management who accused him of neglecting his teaching duties due to his political commitment.

De Beer remained active in the PP and he became chairman of the PP's National Public Relations committee.[26] In this capacity he became increasingly concerned that Steytler's leadership was harming the party as he was not living up to his obligations. On 15 July 1964, he wrote in desperation to Oppenheimer: "I think the party has a slim chance – very slim – of survival under a different leader, provided the change is smoothly and efficiently handled."[27] He was prepared to take the initiative to bring about this change. In the end nothing came of this plan as Steytler was too popular with the rank-and-file of the party. His unhappiness with Steytler's

---

22 Recording of Wendy's interview with her mother, Maureen de Beer, 1 May 2020.
23 Interview with Tony Leon, 3 April 2020.
24 Interview with Douglas Gibson, 1 April 2020.
25 *Impact*, May 1980.
26 Wits, Progressive Federal Party and Democratic Party papers (hereafter PFP/DP papers), Af1, De Beer – John Cope, 23 September 1963.
27 The Brenthurst Library, H.F. Oppenheimer papers, OPP/HFO/J1 (109:37), De Beer – Oppenheimer, 15 July 1964.

leadership increased after the PP's disastrous performance in the provincial elections of March 1965. The party had failed to win a single seat. Even in Houghton it did not come close to victory. By the end of August, a frustrated De Beer requested to be relieved from his chairmanship of Public Relations. As no replacement could be found, he was asked to continue.[28] A month later, he once more submitted his resignation, also as a member of the National Executive. However, his resignation from the National Executive was not accepted.[29]

By March 1966, the PP was in no state to contest the general election, and neither was De Beer. Apart from his business responsibilities, he could not financially afford to be a candidate. With the PP lacking funds, candidates had to carry some of the costs, and he was unable to do so. Apart from alimony to Maureen and supporting his three children, he had to run a second household in Cape Town with Mona and her children, Adam and Sue. He was financially strapped and Oppenheimer had to provide him with a loan.[30] However, he did campaign for Progressive candidates. In Stellenbosch rowdy university students refused him the right to speak when he addressed a public meeting in support of Mrs H.E. Spottiswoode.[31] This hostile political climate was encouraged by the NP with its message that liberals were the useful idiots of the communist onslaught against South Africa. In Welkom in the Free State, Steytler was abused as a "Boereverraaier" (Boer traitor) and was pelted with eggs, tomatoes and doused with water. The next day he received the same abusive treatment at the hands of aggressive university students in Pretoria. Their behaviour was so thuggish that the police had to intervene to protect the Progressives in the hall.[32] In Natal the PP's rejection of Ian Smith's uni-

---

28 Wits, PFP/DP papers, Ab4.1, P.V. Pistorius – R.F. Hurley, 30 August 1965.
29 Wits, PFP/DP papers, Ab4.1, Minutes of Action Committee, 25 and 26 September 1965.
30 The Brenthurst Library, HF Oppenheimer papers, OPP/HFO/J1 (109:37), De Beer – Oppenheimer, 15 July 1964.
31 *Die Burger*, 23 March 1966.
32 *Cape Times*, 24 and 25 March 1966.

lateral declaration of independence cost it the support of English speakers who had voted Progressive in 1961 but who had returned to the UP with its emotional support for the white minority in Rhodesia.

On election day the NP won by a landslide victory. The growing faith in apartheid as a political solution, combined with the fact that South Africa's status as a republic in 1961 had removed some of the rivalry between the two white groups, meant that a significant number of English speakers flocked to the NP. The party captured several UP seats, including Maitland. The UP's tally of parliamentary seats dropped from 49 to 39. Even though there were two more candidates standing than the 24 in 1961, the Progressives could only attract 43 869 votes compared to the 68 045 five years earlier. Most PP candidates suffered heavy defeats and 12 lost their election deposits. In Stellenbosch, perceived as the most politically enlightened Afrikaans university, Spottiswoode only secured 416 votes to the 7133 of the NP and the 2842 of the UP. In East London North, Steytler lost his deposit after attracting a dismal 13,5 per cent of the vote. In Sea Point, Eglin suffered a defeat with 29,5 per cent of the vote. The Progressive vote dropped significantly in Johannesburg North, Parktown, Orange Grove and Musgrave, constituencies where the PP did well in 1961. Suzman was once more the only successful Progressive candidate with a majority of 711 votes. Her victory was made possible by a leading article of Mervis in the *Sunday Times* (27 March) in which he made it clear that although the newspaper supported the UP, Suzman was a special case and that the voters of Houghton had to support her. The PP seemed to be doomed to extinction. In the words of the magazine *News/Check* (27 January 1967), the party was one MP away from oblivion. Spirits in the party were at an all-time low. For De Beer, the 1966 election was the darkest hour in the history of the PP.[33]

---

33 *Progress*, February 1979.

CHAPTER 12
The Progressive Party as a propagator of modernity
1967–1970

In the wake of the election Eglin asked De Beer to analyse the position of the party and to provide advice on the best way forward. The result was a document titled "The Progressive Party, 1966–1971". He did his utmost to be positive by claiming that the image of failure was not unrelieved as the Progressives looked active, courageous and modern, and that many who rejected the party believed that it will sometime in the future have a role to play. To do so, the party had to portray it as the propagator of modernity:

> The Progressive Party must base itself upon the most modern sophisticated elements in South Africa: the employers, the intellectuals, the top-level technologists and executives who provide the leadership in any modern industrial state. It will be argued that these people are few. The reply is that they are trendsetters, and that their number and the number of those who follow them must and will grow. We must do all we can to associate ourselves with jets and nuclear power and computers and space travel and everything modern. We must do all we can to identify ourselves with the Kennedy spirit. ... Kennedy said: "Let us get America moving again." This must be the kind of approach we adopt. We must deal with issues rather than theories. We must associate with success rather than failure. We must constantly look for practical, positive suggestions to make. We must involve ourselves with what is modern, Western, progressive, sophisticated. We must avoid everything that is pious, pompous and ponderous.

He also recommended that the party improve its administrative system, and that in the next election the party had to prevent the wasteful expenditure of money, talent and time. The party had to focus on six or seven conceivably winnable seats.[1]

As De Beer was unable to be present at the National Executive Meeting of 17 April, Eglin tabled the memorandum. However, proceedings were dominated by Steytler submitting his resignation as leader because he felt that his image was harming the party. This led to two motions being tabled. One being that before his resignation could be accepted, there had to be a full discussion on the administration and organisation of the party as well as the party's performance during the election. The second one was that it was vital in the interest of the party that there had to be continuity in the leadership and that he should withdraw his resignation. This motion was accepted, and Steytler temporarily withdrew his resignation. Only after a lengthy analysis of the party's poor performance did De Beer's memorandum come up for discussion. Steytler was unimpressed as he felt that it was too American, and that what works in the United States would not necessarily do so in South Africa. Pistorius was equally unconvinced as he felt that the acceptance of the memo would reduce the PP to a pressure group instead of a political party. It was then decided that the memorandum would be discussed in detail at the next Action Committee meeting. Eglin, newly elected as the chairman of the National Executive, was determined to have it accepted.[2]

As mentioned, Steytler's resignation was at the National Executive meeting of 11 June. He explained that he felt obliged to resign as the top rung of the party lacked confidence in him. De Beer responded that there were two issues at stake: whether the party leader resigned or not, and the necessity to overhaul the party. On the first issue, he said, Steytler had to make his own decision, and

---

1 Wits, PFP/DP papers, D2, Z. de Beer, "The Progressive Party, 1966–1971", 11 April 1966.
2 Wits, Ab2.2.1, PFP/DP, Minutes of the National Executive Committee, 17 April 1966.

that the period after an election was not a bad time for a leader of political party to resign. He made it clear that there had never been any doubt that Steytler's political judgement was particularly good and that his personal prestige character and determination was valuable, but that he had had differences with him over a period of years on how the party should be run. This view was endorsed by Suzman as she also felt that there were grave shortcomings in the party's administration. There had to be a strong executive administration. She also urged that a speechwriter be appointed to help Steytler to prepare his speeches and to overcome the downward trend of the party, he had to come out with some really first-class speeches. For Steytler it must have been a harrowing experience to listen to the criticism. In his response he made it clear that he was fully aware of his shortcomings, conceding that his isolation on the farm made his task difficult. He acknowledged that he was bad at speech writing, but declared that he would continue as party leader if it was the wish of the committee. He did not want to do anything that could harm the party. In the end he withdrew his resignation on the urging of the majority of the committee members who felt that it would be fatal for the image of the party.[3]

Steytler's decision to remain the leader came at a financial and a personal cost. Political duties meant the neglect of his farm that needed his undivided attention to stay afloat financially. On the other hand, his relationship with Eglin as chairman of the National Executive Committee was fraught with tension and rivalry, and caused him unhappiness. Eglin was of the opinion that Steytler was too lethargic, that he had lost heart, and that he was not fulfilling the role of a leader, leaving the running of the party to him.[4] Steytler, on the other hand, felt that Eglin was too pushy and was plotting to replace him.[5] In reality, Eglin did nothing to

---

3   Wits, PFP/DP papers, Ab 2.2.1, Minutes of the National Executive Committee, 11 June 1966.
4   Swart, *Progressive odyssey*, pp. 111–113.
5   Wits, Hackland papers, Brian Hackland's interview with Jan Steytler, 25 August 1980.

undermine him as he felt that Steytler was trapped in a leadership he did not want. However, it was obvious to all that he, De Beer, and Suzman felt that it would have been better if he was replaced by a younger and more energetic leader.

The decisions of the 11 June 1966 National Executive meeting would come to haunt Eglin and De Beer in the 1970s and 1990s. This meeting set out to determine the role of the party leader. Was he responsible for the administration of the party? If so, would it not be a burden on his shoulders as political leadership was already enough responsibility? For some of the Council members the leader's focus had to be on policy guidance. For De Beer and Eglin it was the task of the party leader to create an efficient administrative and organisational structure, as well as to provide political leadership. In getting this approach accepted, they created a burden for themselves when they became party leaders. In addition, they established a precedent for National Executive meetings to ruthlessly evaluate the shortcomings of the leader. Years later they would be at the receiving end of this gruelling process.

Despite Steytler's reservations De Beer's memorandum on the future of the party was accepted by the National Executive on 6 October. De Beer was also elected by the Committee as the chairman of the Public Relations committee. In combination with Eglin, pugnacious and confident with an attitude that the PP had to dust itself off and continue with the struggle to save South Africa, they set out to revive the party. It was an increasingly challenging task as the Progressives remained financially poor. One of the objectives of his memorandum was the hope of getting financial support from industrialists and financiers by focusing on free enterprise. Nothing came of this hope as big business was too timid, petrified of alienating white customers and the government that viewed liberalism as a subversive ideology.

The loathing of liberals was reflected on 6 September 1966 when Verwoerd was stabbed to death in the House of Assembly by Demetrio Tsafendas, a parliamentary messenger. As Verwoerd was being carried out of the House, P.W. Botha, the Minister of Defence, raged at Suzman: "It's you who did this. It's all you liberals. You incite people. Now we will get you. We will get the lot of you."[6] Botha grudgingly apologised when the Speaker obliged him to do so, but he reflected the opinion of most whites, and certainly of Verwoerd's successor, John Vorster, that the PP was a subversive party. And that the black majority would be happy with the apartheid system if dangerous and devious liberals did not whip up resentment amongst them. The Progressives' uncompromising opposition to security legislation bolstered this perception. In 1967 the UP supported the Terrorism Act, which allowed indefinite detention in solitary confinement without trial. The prestige attached to Graaff's name meant that the UP's support for security legislation made it easier for the apartheid state to brand the Progressives' defence of the rule of law as "soft on security", "unpatriotic" and as "enemies of the state".

The perception of the Progressives as a threat to white survival led to legislation specifically aimed at the party – the Prohibition of Political Interference Act of 1968 which banned multi-racial political parties. This Act was a direct result of the PP winning both coloured seats in the Cape provincial council election of 1965. The Progressives immediately set their sights on the four coloured parliamentary representatives to be elected in the 1966 general election. Steytler was to contest one of the seats which would secure his return to parliament. Desperate to keep the Progressives out of parliament, Verwoerd brought in legislation to extend the terms of the coloured representatives. In 1968, the system of white coloured representatives was abolished and replaced with a Coloured Persons Representative Council. The Prohibition of Political Interference Act left the Liberal Party no choice but to disband, but the PP, with a number of coloured and black members, decided under protest to compromise by becoming an all-white party to continue its opposition to apartheid.[7]

By then De Beer had moved to Johannesburg as he had joined

---

6   Suzman, *In no uncertain terms*, p. 69.
7   Strangwayes-Booth, *A cricket in the thorn tree*, pp. 221–222.

AAC's public relations department in January 1968 as a marketing adviser in the industrial division.[8] A year later he became secretary to the Executive Committee of the corporation. Oppenheimer wanted clever and talented men to work for him and long before 1967 had urged him to join AAC. Being an employee of Oppenheimer did not affect their friendship. They socialised a fair bit, the De Beers would stay with them at their holiday home on the Natal South Coast. There was a mutual respect and trust between them to such an extent that Oppenheimer even discussed private family matters with him. Once, sitting next to each other on a flight from Johannesburg to London, they talked throughout the night, enjoying each other's company.[9]

In April 1968, after a period as a lecturer at Unisa in Pretoria, Maureen immigrated with the children to Britain. (She never lost her interest in politics and would be active in local elections, serving in Harrow as a Liberal Party town councillor.) De Beer remained close with his children and he would visit them regularly. His position at AAC meant that he had to visit Britain regularly, making it possible for him to see his children often.[10] (He continued to write his letters in Afrikaans to Wendy so that she did not forget her Afrikaner heritage.) After some initial strain, this led to a warm relationship with his former in-laws, as they appreciated his role of postman for their gifts, letters and photographs to Maureen and the children.[11]

In this period, while rejecting with contempt the Progressives' calls for political reform, the government gradually started to adapt Verwoerdian apartheid. Vorster, despite his well-deserved reputation as an authoritarian, was – compared to Verwoerd – much more pragmatic. He accepted that the apartheid state could only keep its enemies at bay by adapting to a changing world and attempted to smooth the rough edges of apartheid with tightly controlled

---

8   The Brenthurst Library, H.F. Oppenheimer papers, OPP/HFO/G6.4 (88:41), De Beer – Oppenheimer, 25 September 1967.
9   Interview with Wendy de Beer Furniss, 27 August 2021.
10 Interview with Wendy de Beer Furniss, 2 November 2022.
11 Correspondence with Wendy de Beer Furniss, 28 April 2020.

domestic reforms. The result was changes to selected apartheid measures, for example, to open some parks and hotels to all races, and to allow the visiting New Zealand rugby team to include Maori players. Vorster's pragmatism aggravated the growing internal struggle in the NP between the ultraconservatives, the "verkramptes" (narrow-minded ones), and those who favoured a more tolerant outward-looking Afrikanerdom, the "verligtes" (enlightened ones).

Many ultraconservatives, especially Albert Hertzog, who was a member of Vorster's government, soon lost faith in the prime minister as he proved too pragmatic in his attempts to counter the growing isolation of South Africa. Vorster's statement in February 1967 that Maori players in a visiting New Zealand rugby team would not be a threat to white domination was unacceptable for Hertzog and his followers, and the divisions in the NP widened dramatically. The internal differences in the party had reached a climax at the Transvaal NP congress of 9–11 September 1969. Delegates had to vote on resolutions expressing full confidence in the government's policies. Hertzog and some followers refused to support the idea of Maori rugby players visiting South Africa. They were expelled from the party.[12] Hertzog formed the Herstigte (Reconstituted) Nasionale Party (HNP) on 24–25 October 1969.

To crush the HNP at birth, Vorster announced a parliamentary election for 22 April 1970. The PP, once more advocating the defence of the rule of law and the urgency to bring about constitutional reform, lacked the money to fight an election. The party's financial situation was so dire that during the election campaign it ran out of money and had to curtail its expenditure.[13] De Beer, newly established at AAC, did not put himself forward as a candidate, but he did campaign for Eglin in Sea Point. The sitting UP MP, the ultraconservative Jack Basson, stood with the slogan of

---

12 *Hoofstad*, 15 June 1971.
13 B. Hackland, "The economic and political context of the growth of the Progressive Federal Party in South Africa, 1959–1978", *Journal of Southern African Studies*, Vol. 7, No. 1, 1980, p. 7.

"Keep Sea Point white". With the endorsement of the *Cape Times*, which was disgusted with Basson's racism, Eglin lost with 231 votes. Despite the good showing in Sea Point, it was another disastrous election for the Progressives. The UP and its supporting press portrayed the PP as a tiny and marginal party that only divided the opposition vote. This led to some voters who were supportive of the PP and its ideals voting for the UP as they did not want to waste their vote. According to Leif Egeland, a friend of Graaff, thousands of UP supporters like him were Progressives at heart but were not prepared to waste themselves with the PP as an ineffectual splinter party.[14] Suzman was once more the only elected Progressive candidate. Vote-wise the PP did slightly better than in 1966, but the total vote of 51 760 was still below the tally of 1961 and compared badly with the 553 290 of the UP. The UP had regained eight of the seats it had lost to the NP in 1966. The reason for these gains was that the NP focused its campaign on the HNP, which was electorally crushed, attracting only 3,5 per cent of the vote. However, the thuggish methods used by the NP to disrupt the HNP's election campaign led to some former NP voters voting for the UP.

In the wake of the election, there was a strong feeling in the party that Steytler, who had suffered another heavy defeat in Durban Musgrave, had to be replaced by a more energetic leader. De Beer's unhappiness with his leadership was reflected in his resignation as the chairman of Parktown's Progressive branch, and from its national executive three days after the election. Giving work pressure as reason for this step, he at the same time made it clear that he would be available to speak for the PP from time to time as his job did not prohibit him from expressing his political affiliations.[15] On 28 October, the Progressives performed even worse in the provincial council elections. In all three top seats the Progressives had targeted as possible victories, they suffered defeat.

---

14 Unisa, UPA, Graaff collection, File 1.12.8, L. Egeland – Graaff, 12 March 1973.
15 *Sunday Express*, 3 May 1970.

In Houghton where Suzman had won in March with a majority of 2049 votes, the UP retained the seat with 1341 votes. In Sea Point the UP won with 974 votes, and in Parktown the UP raised its 1116 majority of 1965 to 2566 votes. The photograph on the front page of the *Cape Times* (29 October) of a weeping Progressive supporter in Sea Point symbolised the state of the PP.

After the election there was talk that Eglin would oppose Steytler in the next party conference. At the end of November 1970, Steytler announced his decision to retire from politics. His political career had come at a considerable cost as it placed his farming under financial pressure. By the end of 1970, a severe drought forced him as a once wealthy farmer to become a general medical practitioner in the isolated Namaqualand mining village of Okiep.[16] His integrity, honesty, moral courage and unbending liberalism left a broad and solid foundation for the PP on which his successors could build. De Beer, despite his spiky relationship with Steytler, never forgot his sacrifices and would go out of his way to help him with his financial problems.[17]

Eglin thought that De Beer would be most suitable for the leadership position. After a meeting in Oppenheimer's study in his Brenthurst home, a frank assessment was made of the merits and availability of him and De Beer. It was eventually decided that Eglin should make him available as leader while De Beer would assist him on the managerial side of the party.[18] This was a role reversal. For many years, De Beer was politically the more senior figure with a star quality, and was seen as the next Progressive leader.

---

16 *The Argus*, 16 December 1972.
17 The Brenthurst Library, H.F. Oppenheimer papers, OPP/HFO/J1 (101), De Beer – Oppenheimer, 27 September (no year).
18 Eglin, *Crossing the borders of power*, p. 119.

CHAPTER 13
The comeback
1971–1977

In February 1971, Eglin was duly elected as Progressive leader. In his acceptance speech he stated that he believed that the old political order was dying, and that the PP should provide a political vehicle for all "verligtes". This entailed enlightened English-speaking voters who remained loyal to the UP, and Afrikaners, especially the "modern city Afrikaner", who rejected the values of the "verkramptes" in the NP.[1] Eglin had reason to be optimistic that he could attract Afrikaner support as the NP seemed unable to cope with the challenges facing the country. Vorster was obsessed that the HNP should not increase its support and this dampened any initiative for change. The prime minister, despite his public image as a "kragdadige" (forceful) leader, was insecure and ultrasensitive to criticism.[2] Vorster increasingly lost all drive and ideas and was content to tread water and drift with the political tide of relative calm between 1970 and 1974.

Unknown to most whites, black resistance was stirring amongst the black youth with the forming of the South African Students' Organisation (SASO) and the rise of black consciousness. This led to the founding of the Black People's Convention in 1972. Black consciousness promoted self-confidence and raised expectations, whilst black workers became increasingly restless about exploitative working conditions. In "verligte" circles there were fears about the NP's blindness to the flaws of apartheid and these "verligtes" demanded reforms. This made some of them increasingly receptive to the PP's message. De Beer's Political Planning Com-

---

1   *Sunday Times*, 21 February 1971.
2   Schoeman, *My Lewe in die Politiek*, pp. 334–335.

mittee with the support of Piet Vermeulen, leader of the Progressives in Pretoria, arranged a symposium with Afrikaner academics to convince them of the need to embrace liberal reforms. One of these academics was Van Zyl Slabbert, a future leader of the Progressives.[3]

To assist him, Eglin formed five advisory committees, with De Beer as the chairman of the Political Planning Committee.[4] In this capacity he did his utmost to support Eglin with memorandums on requested issues such as the Bantustans and urbanised black people. He found it a challenging task as most of the committee members, apart from Peter Soal, did not make any significant contributions.[5] De Beer also supported Eglin in the municipal elections of March 1972 when he actively campaigned in Johannesburg for the PP's 14 candidates. The party secured its first election victory, apart from Suzman's, when Dr Selma Browde was elected to the City Council.[6] By then De Beer did not just focus on reform through the ballot box, but did his utmost to convince fellow businessmen that they had a duty to take the lead to bring about change in the country, and to remove all those measures that inhibited opportunity and denied rights to the black majority.[7] He set an example by using his position at AAC to improve the living and working conditions of black miners.[8]

Under De Beer's guidance the Political Planning Committee developed in some detail the Progressives' federal policy to meet the challenges and diversity of the South African racial, political and economic scene. At the party's national conference on 19 August 1972 in Silverton, Pretoria, he explained that to establish a proper federation the provincial borders had to be substantially redrawn

---

3   Wits, Max Borkum papers, De Beer – Borkum, 30 August 1972; Swart, *Progressive odyssey*, pp. 119, 121.
4   *Progress*, May 1971.
5   Wits, Max Borkum papers, Z. de Beer, Progressive Party: Political Planning Committee, 5 May 1972; De Beer – Borkum 30 August 1972.
6   *The Star*, 29 February and 2 March 1972.
7   *Rand Daily Mail*, 11 May 1972.
8   A. Boraine, *A life in transition* (Cape Town, 2008), p. 71.

to take demographic factors into account, as well as other sensible factors such as distance, climate, communities and economic resources to create an unspecified number of provinces based on a liberal democratic constitution.[9] Eglin, who was not easily pleased, praised the plan and commented: "It will provide a valuable blueprint for the evolution of constitutional government. It shows that the party has become concerned with realities and not dreams."[10] The conference reflected a new vitality. The party had shaken off its gloominess after a succession of defeats and was facing the future with confidence and vigour. In contrast, the UP was riveted with political divisions.

After 1970, a reformist movement, impatient and dissatisfied with Graaff and eager to revitalise the UP – supported by Mervis in the *Sunday Times* – came to the fore in Johannesburg. The press dubbed them the Young Turks after the army officers who attempted to modernise the moribund Ottoman Empire at the beginning of the twentieth century. Harry Schwarz, dynamic leader of the UP in the Transvaal provincial council, a Jewish refugee from Nazi Germany and a former Air Force navigator with combat experience in North Africa and Italy, became their leader. As a victim of anti-Semitism, he loathed racism, and was a vehement opponent of the NP. He was hard-working, ambitious and able. In September 1972, he secured a surprise victory over the conservative Marais Steyn for the Transvaal leadership. He brought energy and enthusiasm into a stale UP as he was determined to fight for equality of opportunity, civil liberties and human dignity, and the removal of discrimination.[11]

The UP conservatives, dubbed the Old Guard by the press, felt that the Young Turks were too far ahead of the conservative white electorate and would alienate them. By the time an early

---

9 Wits, PFP/DP papers, Jc 8.1, Z. de Beer, The federal policy of the Progressive Party.
10 *Rand Daily Mail*, 21 August 1972.
11 Unisa, UPA, Graaff collection, File 281, Schwarz – Graaff, 19 December 1974.

election was announced for April 1974, the divisions in the UP had paralysed the party. The Young Turks in the Transvaal used their position of authority to veto Old Guard candidates, while in the Cape Province the Old Guard kept reformist candidates out. The internal strife meant that the party had little time and energy to fight the NP and PP.

By then De Beer was residing in Zambia. In July 1972, he was appointed as chairman of Anglo-American Central Africa, and also as the managing director of Nchanga Consolidated Copper Mines, and in October went to live in Zambia. However, he did return to South Africa to support Progressive candidates. On witnessing De Beer addressing a small public meeting in Green Point, Johan Vosloo of the NP-supporting *Rapport* was impressed by his control of the meeting and the quality of his speech. After reminding his readers that De Beer had once been the golden boy of South African politics, he predicted that he would soon return to politics.[12] By then the political tide was turning for the Progressives. The hounding of the Young Turks had convinced many enlightened-UP supporters that the PP would provide more effective opposition to the NP. The Progressives made a breakthrough with victories in five UP-held constituencies, namely Sea Point, Rondebosch, Johannesburg North, Parktown and Orange Grove.

A few months later the PP faced the UP in a by-election in Pinelands, Eglin's former constituency. There was a widely held belief amongst Progressives that this was the opportunity for De Beer to join his old friend on the green benches of the House of Assembly. The *Rand Daily Mail* (2 May 1974) reported it as a certainty that he would be the PP candidate, but his AAC responsibilities made him unavailable and he was replaced by Alex Boraine, who won the seat.[13] While in Zambia, De Beer helped to raise the profile of the PP and that of Eglin when he arranged a meeting for him and Slabbert, the newly elected MP for Rondebosch, to meet President Kenneth Kaunda. It was a coup for the Progressives that brought

---

12 *Rapport*, 14 April 1974.
13 Boraine, *A life in transition*, p. 81.

them significant publicity as a serious player in South African politics.[14]

After a 14-month-period of negotiations with the Zambian government to terminate the AAC's contract to manage four mines in the country, De Beer returned to South Africa at the end of 1974.[15] He left with some regret. In an interview with the *Financial Mail* (25 April 1980) he described his period in Zambia as the most enjoyable years of his working career; that it bolstered his faith in free enterprise as the only way to bring about prosperity and to eradicate poverty. To *Rapport* (18 February 1990) he pointed out that the nationalisation of the copper mines brought the Zambian government great financial losses. By 1977 the income from the mines had dropped to a paltry 12 million rand from 280 million rand, when it still could tax the private copper mines as well as the salaries of workers, and the various companies that delivered goods to the mines.

Back in Johannesburg he became an executive director of AAC with special responsibility for manpower and administration, and was made chairman of LTA Ltd, a large construction company. Eglin, who was determined that the PP's policies had to adapt to a changing South Africa, appointed De Beer to a Constitution Committee led by Slabbert, to examine the party's policies, especially the non-racial qualified franchise.

Politically South Africa was in a state of flux as the government was paralysed by internal feuding. Amongst "verligtes" the collapse of the Portuguese Empire in 1974 and the fear that time was running out for reforms added an edge to their demand for more reforms. On 2 June 1974, under the heading, "Moet hulle hul hiervoor laat skiet?" (Must they be shot for this?), Schalk Pienaar in his influential column in the *Rapport* asked whether it could be asked of young white conscripts to take up arms in order to protect discrimination that could not be justified:

---

14 *The Star*, 11 November 1974.
15 Profile of Zach de Beer in *Optima*, undated clipping in the possession of Wendy de Beer Furniss.

> Our sons go in increasing numbers to the borders where they must shoot and be shot at. The numbers and the shooting can increase dramatically. These sons, can they really believe that everything they see about them is worth their lives? And we, dare we send them to their death in defence of so many practices that in our souls we know are not defensible.

He demanded that the government had to focus on the conditions which created a revolutionary climate.

On the other hand, the "verkramptes" under the leadership of Dr A.P. Treurnicht, former editor of *Die Kerkbode* and MP for Waterberg, opposed even trifling changes to apartheid rules and dogma. He was adamant that no distinction could be made between petty apartheid (separate post office counters, beaches etc.) and grand apartheid, the Bantustan policy:

> If petty apartheid lapses completely, then grand apartheid is senseless, superfluous and unnecessary, because if white and non-white are acceptable to one another at all levels of everyday life and they mix everywhere without reservations, then it is senseless to force them to live in separate or residential areas.[16]

This led to the English-medium press dubbing him "Dr No". The result was a paralysed NP unable to deal with the challenges facing the country. While a dispute raged in the NP on whether a racially mixed South African invitational rugby team would be allowed to play against visiting international sides,[17] the growing resentment amongst blacks about their oppression and exploitation was ignored. This led to some Afrikaners, although not in large numbers, turning to the Progressives.

The internecine struggle in the UP came to a head on 10 February 1975 when Schwarz left the UP with three fellow MPs, one senator and ten Transvaal provincial councillors, 14 Johannesburg

---

16 D. Welsh, *The rise and fall of apartheid* (Johannesburg, 2009), 85.
17 A.P. Treurnicht, *Noodlottige Hervorming* (Pretoria, nd), 1–12.

city councillors, and four Randburg town councillors to form the Reform Party under his leadership.[18] Eglin immediately started talks with Schwarz on a possible merger with the Reformists. Amongst Johannesburg Progressives, this led to some unhappiness with Eglin as Schwarz in the 1960s and early 1970s was uncompromising in his condemnation of Progressives. Many Progressives with long memories found it difficult to forget and forgive his past behaviour.[19] In a letter, Ruth, a long-time member of the party, raised these concerns with Eglin, especially his fear that the honour and integrity of the party would be tainted by the Reformists, who had neither.[20]

In a memorandum to Max Borkum, chairman of the Southern Transvaal Regional Council of the party, De Beer came to Eglin's support. He made it clear that he "strongly believe that the advantages to the Progressive Party of merger far outweigh the admitted risks that will have to be run"; that a new party would have a significant number of safe seats, and that the English-language press would be solidly behind the merged party, and that it would also remove the Reformists as competitors for fundraising. He admitted that there were risks that Schwarz might prove to be a powerful divisive influence because of his difficult personality, but continued that he hoped that the superior principles and policy of the PP would cause him to be a positive and not a negative force. In addition, if he would be difficult, he believed the leaders of the party would be quite strong enough to control him. He also condemned the attitude of some Progressives who stated their less than full confidence in Eglin to maintain the attitude of the party as they would wish it to be:

> This, to me, is an unwarrantable and ungrateful imputation against a man who has firstly played a great role in the party throughout its existence and, secondly, been an enormously successful leader.

---

18   *The Star*, 12 February 1975.
19   *Rand Daily Mail*, 24 and 26 July 1975.
20   Wits, Max Borkum papers, Ruth – C. Eglin, 12 May 1975.

> I have no doubt that Colin Eglin, Helen Suzman, you yourself and others would continue to determine the attitude of a merged party. ... If we do drop it [the merger] then in effect the school of thought to which I belong, which says that the Progressive Party must work to build up political power in order to try to reform South Africa, will have given way to another school which avers that the maintenance of purity of attitude is to be preferred to the extension of political power. Under these circumstances – if merger is rejected in principle – I shall certainly maintain my loyalty to the Progressive Party, but shall always believe that it has lost a great opportunity.[21]

The combination of Schwarz's peppery and volatile personality and Eglin's brusque and domineering attitude led to some strain in the negotiations. As Michael Green pointed out in *The Daily News* (9 May 1975), "together they don't exactly form a mutual admiration society". Schwarz's announcement that he had no interest in the leadership, and the acceptance of the principles of the Progressives, led to a merger of the two parties on 26 July 1975 to form the Progressive Reform Party (PRP). The new party with Eglin as the leader was launched amid scenes of 1200 cheering supporters in Johannesburg. And yet, many Progressives continued to view the Reformists with suspicion. Max Borkum, the veteran of many bruising battles with the UP as Suzman's election campaign manager, secured De Beer's election as his vice-chairman to keep any of the Reformists out of leadership positions.[22] He was also elected to the party's Federal Executive Council and remained a member of the reconstituted Slabbert Commission to examine the Progressive's qualified franchise proposals.[23] The Progressives would find Schwarz a difficult colleague, his relationship with Suzman was a stormy one, but he would be a valued member of the parliamentary caucus as an expert on financial affairs. De Beer came to respect his work ethic and abilities.

---

21 Wits, Max Borkum papers, Note for M.M. Borkum, ESQ. J.P., 5 May 1975.
22 Wits, Max Borkum papers, De Beer – Borkum, 8 July 1975.
23 *Sunday Times*, 27 July 1975.

Support for the PRP was reflected in by-election victories in the Bryanston Transvaal provincial council seat in November 1975, and in the Durban North parliamentary seat in May 1976. In Bryanston, which the UP had won with ease in 1974, the Progressives won with 435 votes. Durban North was once such an impregnable UP citadel. When the Progressives contested it in the 1966 general election, they only managed to attract a dismal 879 votes. In a three-cornered contest between the PRP, UP and NP, the Progressives won a narrow victory of 324 votes. The defeat was a kiss of death for the UP. If it could not hold on to Durban North, none of its seats were safe.

Eglin confidently proclaimed that Durban North had established the Progressives as the real parliamentary opposition. However, the merger and electoral success did not make the challenge of fund-raising any easier. The PRP struggled with the lack of funds and growing bank overdrafts. De Beer did his utmost to provide advice on how to cut back on costs, and to organise employment at AAC for party officials. He even attempted to secure business contracts for Ray Dunlee, the owner of a printing business and the Randburg member of the Transvaal provincial council who was experiencing financial problems and possibly had to resign as a councillor. This would create a difficult by-election for the PRP.[24]

On 16 June 1976, Soweto erupted. The immediate cause of the uprising was the compulsory use of Afrikaans as a language of instruction in schools, but it was just the spark that unleashed pent-up forces of frustration and anger with the lack of political power and the poor socio-economic conditions in the township. As the Bantustans were incapable of sustaining their growing populations, black people, despite influx measures, streamed to urban areas to live in poor and degrading circumstances. The uprising quickly spread countrywide, as well as to coloured areas. The apartheid state responded with force. The Internal Security Amendment Act of 1976 gave the police extensive powers to deal with the uprising.

---

24 Wits, Max Borkum papers, De Beer – Borkum, 9 January and 21 June 1976.

Repression measures brought back some stability, but it came at a cost as black youths fled the country, joining the ANC or PAC in exile. This led to the revival of both movements. More crucially, blacks were no longer cowed by the threat of state violence, and unrest would always be under the surface.

De Beer's desire to improve the living conditions of urban black people to prevent a possible revolution led to his involvement in the Urban Foundation, an organisation consisting of black and white businessmen that was founded in the aftermath of the Soweto uprising. It was the brainchild of Clive Menell, a prominent figure in the mining industry, and his wife Irene, a leading Progressive, based on the "New Detroit" programme of the late 1960s in the USA to improve the quality of life in deprived black urban areas. They sold the idea to Oppenheimer through De Beer, whom they viewed as part of the "do-gooder wing" of AAC. The Urban Foundation was founded by Oppenheimer and Anton Rupert, a leading Afrikaner businessman, at an urban housing conference in Johannesburg on 29 and 30 November 1976, with Oppenheimer as its head. De Beer served as one of the Foundation's directors.[25]

The Soweto uprising drastically altered parliamentary politics. For Graaff the Soweto uprising required a national government, a united front of the NP and UP, to make the necessary reforms to save the situation. During a long interview with Vorster on 16 August 1976, the prime minister made it clear that he did not need the support of the UP. The next day at the UP's Cape conference in East London, Graaff initiated the "Save South Africa campaign" to create a new unified opposition party to attract disenchanted NP supporters. In doing so, he was prepared to disband the UP and to stand back for a new leader of the parliamentary opposition.[26] A committee was appointed under retired judge Kowie Marais to examine and report on the feasibility of a new party. The subse-

---

25 E. Dommisse and W. Esterhuyse, *Anton Rupert. 'n Lewensverhaal* (Cape Town, 2005), pp. 316–319: A. Butler, *Cyril Ramaphosa. The road to presidential power* (Johannesburg, 2019), pp. 112–113.

26 Graaff, *Div looks back*, pp. 244, 248.

quent negotiations with the PRP led to an outcry in the UP. Some Old Guard MPs refused to have any dealings with the Progressives. In January 1977, they were expelled from the UP and would form the short-lived South African Party (SAP) before joining the NP.

In the end nothing came of the negotiations between the UP and PRP as the differences between them were too great. The Progressives believed in equal political rights on a common voters' roll, while the UP insisted on separation of power on a race basis at all levels of government. The PRP refused to budge and eventually Graaff withdrew from negotiations but continued meetings with the Democratic Party, an insignificant splinter party without any public representation, to form a new party. On 28 June 1977 on the ice-skating rink at the Carlton Hotel in Johannesburg, the UP disbanded. The next day the New Republic Party (NRP), based on UP policies, was formed with Graaff as the interim leader. Early in October, Radclyffe Cadman, a former protégé of Mitchell, became leader of the party.

The PRP had to face the immediate challenge of a by-election in Hillbrow. De Beer was confident the Progressives would win the seat and provide an opportunity to eliminate the NRP before the next general election. He wanted a strong candidate in the form of the highly respected former judge Kowie Marais, who after the failure of negotiations with the UP identified with the principles of the Progressives. He even provided the reasons the judge should use to justify his involvement in active politics.[27] In the end there was no by-election due to a general election in November in which Marais as a Progressive candidate won the Johannesburg North seat.

---

27 Wits, Max Borkum papers, De Beer – Borkum, 5 August 1977.

CHAPTER 14
Member for Parktown
1977

After the disbanding of the UP, the Progressives were in negotiations with five former UP MPs under the leadership of Japie Basson, an outstanding parliamentarian with a reputation as a political maverick who refused to be part of the NRP. On 5 September 1977 at the Carlton Hotel in Johannesburg, they joined the Progressives to form a new party. The name for the new party led to a heated debate as the former Reformist led by Schwarz fought hard to retain their name. After numerous votes the name Progressive Federal Party (PFP) was accepted. This wrangle somewhat dampened the enthusiasm of the delegates.[1] The new party had 18 members in the House of Assembly. The core principles of the PFP were full citizenship for all South Africans, and a constitution negotiated and agreed upon by representatives of all South Africans. Slabbert's Constitution Committee was once more reconstituted with De Beer remaining a member. In addressing the conference, De Beer, who was elected to the new party's Federal Executive, proclaimed that the PFP spoke for 90 per cent of all South Africans. *Die Burger* (7 September 1977) in a leading article took exception and accused him of living in a dream world. The newspaper was adamant that there were no alternatives to the NP's policies.

The PFP had no time to find its feet as Vorster on 20 September announced a snap general election to be held on 30 November 1977 to test the opinion of the electorate on the new constitutional proposals of three parliaments. After 16 June he realised that Verwoerdian apartheid was unworkable. He was fully aware that repression was not the solution but was at a loss on how to deal with

---

1 *The Star*, 6 September 1977.

black demands for a fully democratic society. The result was that he tinkered with some aspects of apartheid: to accept that black schools can decide on their language of instruction; to accept the permanency of urban black people in the townships; to give black urban areas a measure of self-government with community councils, and to pump more money into the Bantustans.

Vorster was especially concerned about the rising militancy in the coloured community. In August 1976, he appointed a cabinet committee under the chairmanship of P.W. Botha, the powerful leader of the Cape NP, to investigate possible constitutional adjustments to politically accommodate the coloured and Indian community. By then Vorster realised that the political position of these groups was untenable, while he desired to co-opt them to bolster white domination. In 1977, the Botha committee recommended three parliaments, one for each race group in which they could decide their own affairs, while provision was made for consultation and co-responsibility with regard to common affairs in a council of cabinets controlled by an executive president with autocratic powers. In reality, he was anxious to paper over the deepening divisions in his own party, and to exploit the state of flux in opposition politics.

Five days after Vorster had announced the election, De Beer and Suzman attended the funeral of Steve Biko, a prominent anti-apartheid activist, in King William's Town. While in detention without trial in Port Elizabeth, he had suffered a head injury at the hands of the security police and was taken unconscious and naked in a police vehicle to Pretoria where he died. The size of the funeral and the anger of those present were reminders of the necessity to bring about political reform to prevent a revolution.[2]

In the wake of the Soweto uprising, De Beer felt that he had to do something to be of value to a country in crisis but was unsure about what to do.

As he explained to Wendy:

---

2 Suzman, *In no uncertain terms*, pp. 226–227.

Maar die probleme van Suid-Afrika – of liewer Suider-Afrika, wat as 'n eenheid gesien moet word – doem bergagtig in die voorland op. Hoe om op te tree, hoe om 'n mens se eie, noodwendig beskeie bydrae te probeer maak, dit is die vraag.[3] (But the problems of South Africa, or rather southern Africa, which must be seen as a unity, appear insurmountable in front of us. How to act, how to make your own modest contribution, that is the question.)

He decided to return to electoral politics. His son, Zach jr, was under the impression that Oppenheimer had encouraged him to return to parliament to be an agent for change, and felt that his father still had the desire to lead the Progressives. He was fully aware that his father, although a humble person, was also an ambitious one.[4] This is also the view of Peter Soal, a long-term friend, who observed that De Beer had never given up on this dream to lead the Progressives.[5] If he wanted to succeed Eglin, he had to prove himself in the House of Assembly. More importantly, he was inspired to enter parliament again by the example F.S. Malan had set as an Afrikaner liberal with his efforts to reconcile the aspirations of Afrikaner nationalism and black nationalism.[6]

De Beer, by then chairperson of the PFP's national fundraising committee, was nominated to contest the constituency of Parktown, a seat covering the older, mostly affluent northern Johannesburg suburbs. René de Villiers, a former editor of *The Star*, had narrowly won the seat for the PP in 1974. After three years in the House of Assembly, he had enough of politics and decided to retire. The NRP and NP also contested Parktown. Brigadier Rocco de Villiers, a retired police officer, was the NRP candidate, and Stephan du Toit, an attorney, stood for the NP.[7] Although the PP had only won Parktown with a majority of 391 votes in 1974, it had become

---

3 De Beer – Wendy, Easter Monday 1977. (In the possession of Wendy de Beer Furniss.)
4 Interview with Zach de Beer junior, 22 April 2020.
5 Interview with P. Soal, 11 April 2020.
6 *Financial Mail*, 25 April 1980.
7 *The Star*, 12 November 1977.

a safe Progressive seat. As De Beer confidently informed *The Star* (5 November 1977), "[i]f the PFP is in danger in Parktown, God help us elsewhere." For him the NRP only had nuisance value. It was a straight fight with the NP, a party that paid lip service to moving away from discrimination while its approach was based upon the worst form of discrimination, the denial of rights to black people on the grounds of their skin colour.[8] He set out the following goals for the PFP:

> We are asking people to vote for the concept of a single multiracial South African nation. A common society. I am trying to establish the concept that we are all citizens of one nation having a common patriotism. The common society, sharing swimming baths and so on, will follow, but that is not my main concern now. We (black and white) are irrevocably intertwined economically and in other ways. We must make up our minds to take this into account in our political structure also.[9]

In an election without any real excitement – as it was clear from the first day that the NP would win with a massive majority – De Beer's candidature caused a stir. *Beeld* (20 October 1977) speculated that his nomination was part of a move by the liberal establishment to replace Eglin, as his Afrikaner identity would be an electoral benefit for the Progressives. The *Beeld* pointed out an open secret that many Progressives were unhappy with Eglin's leadership, they felt that in an era of television-dominated politics he lacked charm and glamour. His abrasiveness to friend and foe alike alienated many Progressives.[10] In 1975, Soal, a friend and admirer of Eglin, told Tony Leon that Eglin had the "bedside manner of an angry crocodile".[11]

---

8   *Rand Daily Mail*, 1 November 1977.
9   *The Star*, 5 November 1977.
10 Suzman, *In no uncertain terms*, p.173; Correspondence with Peter Soal, 6 November 2014.
11 Tribute to Colin Eglin MP by Tony Leon at a gala banquet held in Cape Town, 14 June 1997. Supportservices.ufs.ac.za/userfiles/documents/00004/3614 – eng.pdf. Accessed on 2 December 2013.

However, the main concern was that on television a bald and chubby Eglin came over as uninspiring, dull, and plodding. Many Progressives started to look at the trim, handsome, loquacious and charming De Beer as his replacement. To squash any rumours that he had his sights on the party leadership, he informed Helen Zille of the *Rand Daily Mail* (1 November 1977) that his main weakness was "a lack of driving ambition". This statement would come to haunt him as it raised concerns that he was not serious about his political career.

After his selection as a candidate, De Beer was quickly reminded that parliamentary politics can be a gladiatorial contest. On 4 October, P.W. Botha, while addressing a meeting in Vorster's Nigel constituency, launched a direct attack on him for discouraging international businesses to invest in South Africa. He quoted from the *Business Week*, an American journal, a statement De Beer had made about investments in South Africa in November 1976: "If I were a foreigner looking clinically at South Africa I would refrain from investing here until South Africa looked safe for private investment." He then vowed to hound De Beer from meeting to meeting until he stated where he stood. The background to this statement was that in a paper he presented to a *Financial Mail* investment conference in Johannesburg on 10 November 1976, a concerned De Beer had urged the government to bring about reforms as it was the only way to ensure international investment in the South African economy:

> If I were a foreign investor, looking clinically at South Africa as one might look at Venezuela or Mexico or Thailand, I think I would be aware of South Africa's great long-term potential, but would refrain from investment here until such time as South Africa looked safe for private enterprise – which means until the obviously essential liberal political reforms had been carried out.[12]

---

12 Z426, The political factor in investment. (In the possession of Wendy de Beer Furniss.)

An unrepentant De Beer responded that he had attempted to warn the government that its policies were likely to lead to problems on the capital account of the balance of payments, which was precisely what had happened.[13] Botha's attack was an early indication that the NP would target the PFP as an unpatriotic party.

Of all the opposition parties, the PFP was organisationally in the best state to fight an election. The Progressives also had the bonus that the English-medium newspapers, freed of their traditional loyalty to the UP, supported them. Eglin campaigned with the message that the country was heading for siege and conflict if it did not eliminate discrimination based on colour and that apartheid had to be replaced by an open society, free from either compulsory integration or separation, and this could only be achieved by negotiating with the black majority.[14] De Beer, certain of a victory in Parktown, campaigned for other Progressive candidates and made it clear in a public meeting in his old constituency of Maitland that he was willing to accept a black prime minister and a black majority government.[15]

The NP in its campaign simply ignored the fact that apartheid was failing, while its constitutional proposals of three parliaments were played down as it was feared that it could deepen the division between "verligtes" and "verkramptes". Instead, Vorster attacked President Jimmy Carter of the USA for criticising apartheid. He claimed that an election victory for the NP would make it more difficult for the USA to put pressure on South Africa. De Beer rejected this as a spurious argument as a larger NP majority could not counter growing international pressure on the country. He emphasised that South Africa's deteriorating international position was the result of government policies.[16] Vorster's enmity to Carter was accompanied with emotional rhetoric of fighting to the last man, or last drop of blood, to defend South Africa. He accused the PFP

---

13 *The Citizen*, 2 November 1977: *The Star*, 5 October 1977.
14 *Sunday Times*, 13 November 1977.
15 *Beeld*, 15 November 1977.
16 *Rand Daily Mail*, 1 November 1977.

of a lack of patriotism, declaring that the party was disgraceful and un-South African and that it had no right to exist.[17]

The NP campaign was supported by the South African Broadcasting Corporation's (SABC) new television service which bent over backwards to convey the government's agenda. The NP received 80 per cent of the political coverage during the election campaign. The perception was created that it was unpatriotic not to vote for the NP.[18] Vorster's tactic of exploiting the fear of white people paid off as the NP secured its biggest ever parliamentary victory with a majority of 135 seats. Up to 1974, mainly elderly conservative English speakers only voted UP simply out of a traditional loyalty to the old party of Smuts. After June 1977, they transferred their support to the NP with its promise that it would maintain law and order in the wake of the Soweto uprising, and that it would fight to the last ditch to maintain white supremacy. Former opposition constituencies with lower-middle-class voters such as Maitland became NP strongholds. As in 1961, De Beer's stance that he would accept a black prime minister did not go down well with the Maitland voters.

The PFP managed to win 17 seats. All these constituencies were concentrated in the affluent and predominately English-speaking suburbs of Cape Town and Johannesburg. As the NRP had been reduced to ten seats, the PFP became the official parliamentary opposition. In Parktown De Beer had won with a solid majority of 4160 votes after securing 7089 votes to that of the 2929 of Du Toit, and the 1183 of De Villiers. Immediately after his victory, rumours started that he would replace Eglin as party leader. De Beer rubbished this as nonsense. He responded: "I hope my colleagues at Anglo American can find it possible to still make use of my services."[19] It was an odd response that fuelled the perception amongst

---

17 *Cape Times*, 28 October, and 17 November 1977.
18 E.R. McKenzie, "The relationship between the Progressive Federal Party, the English-language press and business with special reference to the 1983 referendum", (MA Unisa, 1992), p. 71.
19 *The Star*, 1 December 1977.

some Afrikaans newspapers that he was representing the interests of the corporation and Oppenheimer in the PFP, and that he was a part-time politician.[20]

---

20   *Hoofstad*, 6 April 1979.

CHAPTER 15
Impatience with parliament
1978–1979

To prepare for his return to the House of Assembly, De Beer read all his old parliamentary speeches. It must have been a demoralising experience as all his warnings had been realised, while no effort had been made to address them. In January 1978, he entered a parliament he hardly recognised. Only a handful of his former contemporaries were still in the House of Assembly. Of the original eleven Progressives of 1959, only himself, Eglin, Swart (also elected in 1977), and Suzman were still in parliament. In his memoirs Swart describes that it was striking how over a period of 16 years the power had shifted from the House to the executive. The prime minister and his cabinet treated parliament with aloofness and arrogance, as if it was a waste of time to deal with even their own MPs. He also found the NP in a state of trauma. Many of its MPs had lost the conviction that apartheid was a moral, just and workable policy, and only paid lip service to Verwoerd's Bantustan dream.[1] An exhausted Vorster was unable to rise to the occasion and provide an alternative policy.

For Eli Louw, elected as an NP MP in 1977, the most striking aspect of parliament was the enormous power Vorster had, but that he did not do anything with this power. For most NP MPs it was obvious that in the government things had become stuck. The party was drained and paralysed by the divide between the "verligte" and "verkrampte" wings. Vorster was so concerned about a split in the party that he allowed the proposal of three parliaments to fade away. He clung to the Bantustan policy, hoping that by turning them into independent states it would resolve all the problems of

---

1 Swart, *Progressive odyssey*, p. 147.

the apartheid state. By then many in the NP knew that this was nonsense.[2] This uncertainty in the party and a lack of direction left the NP MPs in a volatile mixture of arrogance, insecurity and they were hypersensitive to criticism. As a fellow Afrikaner, De Beer understood their state of mind, realising that many of them, especially the "verligtes", shared N.P. van Wyk Louw's stance that Afrikaners would only survive in Africa if the apartheid state was based on justice.[3] For this reason he would never take a sneering or mocking attitude in debates towards NP MPs, but delivered his speeches in a tone of sorrow and desperation, hammering on the inbuilt injustices and destructiveness of apartheid and that apartheid could only end in bloodshed and the destruction of the Afrikaner.

On 30 January 1978, in a motion of censure, Eglin condemned the government for aggravating racial tensions, escalating violence, and for increasing authoritarian and repressive measures, all of which threatened the security and stability of South Africa. He especially castigated the government for the murder of Biko.[4] His attack set the tone for the rest of the parliamentary session. The Progressives hammered on the point that all South Africans should enjoy full political rights, or the growing black resentment would erupt in a revolution. The only way forward was a national convention to bring all South Africans together so that a new constitution could be drawn up to secure freedom and justice for all.[5]

The NP resented the Progressives' criticism, especially their morally superior attitude grated on the party. It was seen as sanctimonious and hypocritical as they could escape the consequences of their integrationist policies. For them the Progressives were mainly affluent, living in secluded upmarket suburbs, buying their own apartheid, or they could leave the country at any time.

The PFP was sneeringly referred to as the acronym for "Packing

---

2 Giliomee, *The last Afrikaner leaders*, pp. 109, 138.
3 Louw, *Liberale Nasionalisme*, p. 63.
4 House of Assembly debates, 30 January 1978, Col. 19–41.
5 Boraine, *A life in transition*, pp. 96, 105, 111–114.

for Perth".⁶ From the first day of the session, the 135 NP MPs, supported by the SAP and occasionally by the NRP, launched a massive attack of abuse on the Progressives.

The volatile atmosphere in the House of Assembly was aggravated by the so-called Information Scandal. In 1978, allegations became public about the Department of Information's extravagance and misappropriation of public funds, and that the government was funding *The Citizen*, an NP supporting English-medium tabloid, with taxpayer money. Eglin doggedly led the attacks on the government. Desperate to regain the initiative, the NP launched vicious personal attacks on the Progressives, accusing them of encouraging black resistance to apartheid. Eglin's speeches in the House of Assembly were delivered in a hostile atmosphere with a wall of noise. His task as leader of the opposition was made more challenging by the fact that he was no great orator or parliamentary debater.⁷ Vorster, although past his prime-ministerial prime, was still an outstanding parliamentary performer, and a bully who ruthlessly exploited Eglin's flaws. Some PFP MPs felt that Vorster ran circles around Eglin.

De Beer, as the Progressives' spokesperson on commerce and industry, found it challenging to find his feet as an MP. It was a drastic jump from genteel boardroom meetings to the rowdy House of Assembly. After years of being an influential AAC director, it was difficult to be a humble backbencher in a small party. (The Progressive parliamentary caucus had fewer members than the cabinet.) The Progressive MPs had a heavy workload and had to endure long hours in the chamber. De Beer had to deal with all legislation relating to industry, commerce, and tax. But more challenging was the hostility and merciless heckling they had to endure from the NP, NRP and SAP MPs. Personally, he became a target from the first day when Vorster responded to the motion

---

6   T. Leon, *On the contrary. Leading the opposition in a democratic South Africa* (Johannesburg, 2008), pp. 66, 100.

7   J. Basson, *Steeds op die parlementêre kolfblad. Met insigte oor die Afrikaner en Afrikaans* (Cape Town, 2008), p. 106.

of censure with the personal attack on him accusing De Beer of encouraging foreigners not to invest in South Africa and that he was drafted into parliament to replace a plodding Eglin.[8]

De Beer responded alternately in Afrikaans and English that the statement on investment had been used out of context. He reacted that for him as a director of a South African company and with all his savings invested in the country to encourage disinvestment made as much sense as a maize farmer praying for a drought in the growth season. He again emphasised that to encourage investments in the country, the political temperature had to be lowered. To do this, black people had to own property in urban areas and secure trade union rights, while the education model of people of colour had to be improved. It was a forceful speech that impressed the House. Paul Greyling, the parliamentary representative of *Beeld*, observed that when De Beer started talking, there were mocking calls of "new leader" from the NP benches, but that there was a feeling that he was indeed the new leader after the speech, as he was so much more impressive than Eglin.[9] *Beeld* in a leading article, "Zach mielies" (Zach maize), speculated that he would soon be the PFP leader. Determined to cut De Beer down to size, the government refused to accept his explanation. Senator Owen Horwood, Minister of Finance, dedicated the biggest part of his speech to condemn him for smearing South Africa in the eyes of foreign investors.[10]

De Beer in his report-back meeting to his constituency admitted that the Progressives were shaken by this onslaught: "We weathered that storm of abuse and vituperation – I will not say completely unscathed – and settled down to the hard work of fighting the Government day by day in the house. ... Gradually our confidence grew and our performance improved."[11] His opening

---

8 *Beeld*, 31 January 1978.
9 *Beeld*, 2 February 1978.
10 House of Assembly debates, 2 February 1978, Col. 288–292.
11 Z390, Extracts from a speech to be made by Z.J. de Beer, Parkview Senior school, 18 July 1978. (In the possession of Wendy de Beer Furniss.)

speech set the pace for the rest of the parliamentary session. In a volatile atmosphere in which personal insults and abuse was the norm, he refused to descent to this level and his contributions were lucid, analytical and balanced. During the Part Appropriation debate he warned that South Africa's economic difficulties could be attributed to the lack of confidence engendered by the policy of the government; that "we must choose between prosperity and apartheid, because we cannot have both at the same time".[12] A message he repeated in the Budget debate – that the luxury of apartheid meant the drying up of foreign investments and that foreign confidence could only be restored if all South Africans shared the same opportunities.[13]

De Beer also played a leading role in exposing the corruption in the Department of Information as a member of the parliamentary select committee on Public Accounts. In the House, after giving examples of how officials did everything in their power to circumvent treasury regulations, he demanded a public investigation into the Department.[14] During debate on the budget of the Department of Information he condemned the government for its lack of control of public funds and the refusal to accept responsibility for the misuse of funds.[15] When the report of the Select Committee on Public Accounts on the Department of Information was debated in the House, he demanded that the relevant minister, Connie Mulder, had to resign. He admitted that Mulder was a man of great personal attributes and warmth, and that there was no doubt that he could do many things in the world, but added that administrating a government department was clearly not one of them.[16]

Even in the heat of the Information Scandal, De Beer never let the destructive effects of apartheid out of his sight. In the last

---

12 House of Assembly debates, 20 February 1978, Col. 1496.
13 *Beeld*, 7 April 1978.
14 House of Assembly debates, 21 April 1978, Col. 5300–5311.
15 *Beeld*, 10 May 1978.
16 House of Assembly debates, 16 June 1978, Col. 9714.

reading of the budget debate, he pointed out that the biggest challenge facing black people was an economic one, and that they viewed political rights as crucial to rectify this situation. In *Beeld* (10 June 1978) an impressed Greyling described it as a solid speech. It was, however, his financial expertise that made the House listen to him. His criticism of the legislation for the implementation of sales tax, namely that it would punish the poor and would cause confusion, received extensive coverage by *Beeld* (15 June 1978). This was a compliment as *Beeld* was a newspaper that went out of its way to deny any positive publicity to the opposition parties. However, this did not exempt him from all the personal attacks. When he condemned the way money was budgeted for secret intelligence work without parliamentary control, it unleashed emotional accusations that he and fellow Progressives were a threat to state security.[17]

The 1978 parliamentary session was an exhausting and dispiriting one for the Progressives, but De Beer had made a good impression. His fluent oratory and bilingualism, a quality much admired by fellow MPs, made him a highly respected figure in the House. This raised the expectation in parliamentary circles that he would replace a struggling Eglin as the leader of the opposition. However, De Beer had serious doubts about his parliamentary career. The triviality of much of parliamentary business and "its marginal relevance to the main issues facing South Africa", compared to commercial initiatives that were setting the pace for social change, meant that he felt that he could wield more influence outside parliament.[18] In a March 1985 interview with the Afrikaans financial magazine *Finansies & Tegniek* he explained his discontentment with parliament:

> Die sakewêreld het my ongeduldig gemaak en ek kon dit nie met die betreklike rustigheid van die politiek versoen nie. Dinge word in die sakewêreld gedoen, besluite word geneem en daardie besluite word

---

17 *Beeld*, 17 March 1978.
18 Undated *Optima* in the possession of Wendy de Beer Furniss.

uitgevoer. So werk dit nie in die politiek nie. (The business world made me impatient and I could not reconcile it with the relative ease of politics. Things happen in the business world. Decisions are made, and those decisions are implemented. This does not happen in politics.)

His growing doubts about remaining in parliament did not dilute his dedication to the PFP and the cause of liberalism. He did his utmost to address the chronic poverty of the party. The Progressives lacked the resources to open party offices and to appoint full-time organisers, or to have its own publications.[19] At a fundraising dinner he described the desperate financial state of the party:

> To do our proper duty, we need, excluding general elections, something in the order of a million rand a year. We receive something like half a million. That is the size of it. I am sick of firing party staff. I want to start hiring people. What you do here tonight can make a difference. ... I hope you will give this party a great deal of money.[20]

He also played a leading role in Van Zyl Slabbert's Constitutional Committee. At the PFP's conference on 17 and 18 November 1978 in Durban, the Committee's recommendation to adopt the principle of universal suffrage based on proportional representation in a federal form of government was accepted by delegates. (De Beer had found it difficult to depart from the qualified franchise but accepted that it was no longer tenable.)[21] This political system would be based on a Bill of Rights and an independent judiciary. Minority rights would be protected through a form of consensus democracy. This meant power sharing by reconciling the need for majority rule with minority protection and the sharing of executive power between the majority and minority parties, while minorities

---

19 *Beeld*, 12 June 1978.
20 Z395 Speech to be made at a dinner at Mount Nelson Hotel, Cape Town on Monday 25th September 1978. (In the possession of Wendy de Beer Furniss.)
21 Wits, Hackland papers. Hackland's interview with de Beer, 14 July 1980.

would have a veto on crucial issues. The delegates also accepted the Committee's proposal of a national convention at which representatives of all South Africans would draw up a constitution.[22] De Beer praised the PFP's policies as "politics of negotiation", opposed to the government's "politics of confrontation", and that the Progressives were rejecting the "winner-take-all" concept for a "give-and-take" policy.[23]

On 7 December parliament met for a two-day special session to discuss the report of the Erasmus Commission that had been investigating the Department of Information. The commission led by Judge R.P.B. Erasmus had been appointed by P.W. Botha, who had replaced an ill Vorster as prime minister. Vorster was elected as the ceremonial State President. Botha was a formidable political operator with a legendary bad temper and reputation, and whose finger-wagging abusiveness led to him becoming known as the "groot krokodil" (big crocodile).

The Erasmus Commission had exposed massive misappropriation of public funds. The government, for example, had spent 39,1 million rand on the *Citizen* newspaper. Eglin condemned this abuse of the taxpayers' money as the result of the arrogance and dereliction of duty by the government, and demanded that the prime minister had to resign. De Beer joined the attack. He blamed the government for dragging South Africa down to the level of a banana republic and held Horwood responsible for not maintaining any control on how the secret fund of the Department of Information was used. He maintained that the government should have known what had happened to money which had been voted for by parliament.[24]

With the opening of the 1979 parliamentary session, De Beer urged the government to embrace constitutional reform as "doing nothing seems to be the most dangerous of all possible courses of action". Moreover, "baaskap" was still being championed by the

---

22 A. Grundlingh, *Slabbert. Man on a mission* (Jeppestown, 2020), p. 77.
23 *Cape Times*, 18 November 1978.
24 House of Assembly debates, 7 December 1978, Col. 129–137.

NP despite fine-sounding assurances of the prime minister.[25] The NP MPs exploded in anger. During these free-for-all clashes, it was obvious to "Dawie" (*Die Burger*, 14 February 1979) that De Beer was unhappy in parliament, and he wondered if he yearned to be back in the business world. However, despite his discontentment with parliament, De Beer did not let up on his attacks on apartheid. During the debate on the Part Appropriation Bill, he reiterated that South Africa could either have apartheid or prosperity, but not both. During the third reading of the budget debate, he warned that the government would have to learn that the prosperity or poverty of the nations was indivisible and that the gap in the living standards between the poor and the rich was too wide and was a destabilising factor: "If we want to stay rich, we must uplift the poor."[26]

The parliamentary session was once more dominated by the state corruption in the Department of Information. De Beer continued to hound Horwood. This was after the Minister of Finance had conceded that he had taken great care not to see the details of the Department of Information's secret projects on a document he had signed. This led to De Beer taking the unusual step of proposing the elimination of the Minister of Finance's salary from the budget vote as the country needed a Minister "who watches the people's money and checks every cent of it".[27] During the session which De Beer later would describe as "hard, bitter and often unpleasant" in his Parktown report-back meeting,[28] concerns in the Progressive caucus about Eglin's leadership continued to brew as he found it difficult to cope with Botha, who relentlessly bashed and humiliated him.

To support him, De Beer wrote a profile "Eglin – courage and drive has brought success" for the *Progress* of February 1979. He

---

25 House of Assembly debates, 7 February 1979, Col. 252–253, 258.
26 *The Star*, 22 June 1979.
27 *Sunday Times*, 6 May 1979.
28 Z370, Extracts from a speech to be made by Dr Z.J. de Beer at his report-back meeting to be held at Saxonwold School at 8.00 P.M. on Thursday, 19 July 1979. (In the possession of Wendy de Beer Furniss.)

made it clear that intellectual brilliance, charm, wit, good looks and style are gifts that contribute to the success of certain politicians, but that other less spectacular attributes count for much more, namely determination, hard work, strength of mind and body, persistence, courage and judgement, and that Eglin with these attributes had revitalised and rebuilt the PP. Although De Beer conceded that Eglin's speeches sometimes left something to be desired in the manner of their delivery, he praised him as the most successful opposition leader since D.F. Malan, and ended his profile on a ringing note:

> No doubt there will again be opponents who underrate him: assuredly they, too, will learn the hard way that Colin Eglin is a most exceptional and outstanding political leader.

His heartfelt praise for Eglin would be blown away by the so-called McHenry affair.

CHAPTER 16
Farewell to parliament
1979–1980

On 26 February 1979, the United Nations (UN) released a report on a possible settlement on the South African-controlled Namibia. Pik Botha, the Minister of Foreign Affairs, discussed the report with the leaders of the opposition parties and their respective spokesmen on foreign affairs to give the government's side of affairs. Eglin and Japie Basson, the PFP's foreign spokesperson, then met with Western diplomats to discuss the UN report, while Eglin had a telephonic conversation with Don McHenry, an envoy of the United States to the UN. Eglin had informed Pik Botha of these contacts.

On 3 April 1979, Pik Botha in a melodramatic speech during the Appropriation Bill debate, accused Eglin of leaking to McHenry information the government had shared in confidence with him as leader of the opposition. Botha demanded that Eglin, apart from crawling into a hole in the ground and staying there, had to resign as leader of the opposition. This was against the background of outraged NP MPs baying for blood. Eglin, who had already used his speaking opportunity earlier in the Appropriation debate, was allowed a few minutes by the Speaker to respond with a personal explanation. A stunned and wrong-footed Eglin was hesitant and uncertain in his reaction. He conceded in his memoir that his initial response had let the PFP down.[1] De Beer vigorously defended Eglin's right to talk to foreign diplomats and that Pik Botha's dramatic performance was a fine example of a lightning conductor being used to neutralise the Progressive attacks on government corruption. He furthermore mocked his theatrical performance:

---
1 Eglin, *Crossing the borders of power*, p. 184.

> The hon. the Minister of Foreign Affairs is one of the best performers in this house, and he gave a performance this afternoon which was second to none. ... He produced hot air as none of us is able to do, but there was not a single fact in the whole of his attack ... [2]

His support and defence of his friend raised his stature in parliament. Hendrik Schoeman, the eccentric Minister of Agriculture, and the only cabinet minister whom the Progressives found remotely likeable, went as far as to express his fondness for De Beer in a parliamentary speech.[3] However, despite his best efforts to defend Eglin, and his calls for the maximum support for his beleaguered friend, he could not restore the damage done by Botha's attack. He confided in Wendy that the McHenry controversy had severely damaged Eglin's confidence.[4]

Pik Botha never provided any evidence that confidential information was leaked, but it did not prevent a sustained assault on Eglin's alleged lack of patriotism. Amongst Afrikaners it bolstered the perception that the Progressives were unpatriotic. In May 1979 they showed their disapproval when the PFP attracted a paltry 378 votes out of a 9723 cast in a provincial by-election in Swellendam, a predominately Afrikaner rural constituency in the Western Cape. In June 1979, the party could only secure 681 votes of 10 415 cast in a parliamentary by-election in Randfontein, a Transvaal mining town.[5] These results convinced some Progressives that if the party wanted to attract Afrikaner support, De Beer had to be the party leader.[6] To Wendy he confided his reluctance to be the leader, as well as his doubts about his abilities to do so:

> As ek wou aanbly in die politiek, is daar 'n kans dat ek onder druk kom om die leierskap oor te neem. Alleen wil ek dit nie hê nie, maar

---

2 House of Assembly debates, 3 April 1979, Col. 3930.
3 *Hoofstad*, 6 April 1979.
4 De Beer – Wendy, 3 July 1979. (In the possession of Wendy de Beer Furniss.)
5 *Beeld*, 11 May and 7 June 1979.
6 *Rapport*, 29 April 1979.

nog baie erger – ek is hoegenaamd nie seker dat ek dit suksesvol kan doen nie. Tog kan daar 'n kwessie van verpligting wees. (If I were to remain in politics there is the possibility that I would be pressured to take over the leadership. Not only do I not want it, but worse – I am not sure whether I would be able to do it successfully. And yet, there could be the matter of duty.)

By then he had already discussed with Oppenheimer the possibility of returning to AAC, while informally he also had been approached by UCT on whether he would make himself available as a candidate to replace Sir Richard Luyt as the principal.[7]

However, what he did not mention to Wendy was that the once strong feeling in the PFP that he should replace Eglin had dissipated as some Progressives felt disappointed in him.[8] The unrealistically high expectation in 1977 that he would immediately set the political world alight and invigorate the PFP was bound to disappoint. While De Beer's star was fading, the political stocks of Van Zyl Slabbert as the golden boy of the Progressives were on the rise. Gordon Waddell, the former PP MP for Johannesburg North, and an influential figure as chairperson of the party's finance committee, wanted him as party leader.[9] This desire was understandable as Slabbert was an outstanding parliamentarian while his intelligence was complimented by his good looks. He was tall and handsome and had an attractive personality. Boraine described the effect of his charm as falling under his spell,[10] while his self-deprecatory sense of humour made him a highly likeable person.[11] He became popularly known as "Van". His sporting prowess – he represented Western Province in a rugby match and played cricket for South African universities – added to his popularity, which

---

7 De Beer – Wendy, 3 July 1979. (In the possession of Wendy de Beer Furniss.)
8 *Cape Times*, 23 April 1979.
9 Swart, *Progressive odyssey*, p. 155.
10 A. LeMaitre and M. Savage, *The passion for reason. Essays in honour of an Afrikaner African* (Johannesburg, 2010), p. 37.
11 Swart, *Progressive odyssey*, pp. 156–157.

amongst admirers bordered on the adulation. Afrikaners flocked in large numbers to his public meetings.

Slabbert was eager to become the party leader. According to Boraine, his closest political confidant, he was keen to succeed Eglin as he preferred leading from the front.[12] Slabbert was also approached by UCT and expressed his willingness to be considered for the position as principal. This led to prominent Progressives informing him that they wanted him to be party leader and that they would leave the party if he should turn his back on politics. He felt obliged to withdraw his application for the UCT post,[13] and made it clear that he was available if there should be a leadership vacancy. His admirers conducted a whispering campaign to demand a change in leadership. De Beer was aware of the growing momentum for Slabbert and did his utmost to support Eglin. He wrote an article for *Progress* on the necessary qualities for the leader of a political party. After listing all the requirements and challenges, he concluded that "No-one short of a superman could really fill the bill."[14] He concluded the article with a ringing declaration of support for Eglin:

> If it is to some extent true that the leader makes the party, it is at least as true that the party makes the leader. My advice to you is: trust Colin Eglin. Give him the support he needs. Trust one another: work together. Let strength go out from each of us to each. We fight against great odds, but success may well be nearer than it now seems.[15]

Speaking at a report-back meeting in Parktown on 19 July, he reiterated his support: "I remain as convinced as I have been for

---

12 LeMaitre and Savage, *The passion for reason*, p. 39.
13 Slabbert, *The last white parliament*, pp. 53, 63.
14 This statement led to Fred Mouton, the brilliant cartoonist of *Die Burger* depicting Slabbert as leader of the opposition dressed in a superman suit. W.D. Beukes (ed.), *Oor grense heen. Op pad na 'n nasionale pers 1948–1990* (Cape Town, 1992), p. 145.
15 Z375, Article for "Progress" by Dr Z.J. de Beer MP, 21 June 1979. (In the possession of Wendy de Beer Furniss.)

years past that Mr Eglin and no one else was the right man to lead the Opposition."[16]

On 25 July 1979, he wrote to Wendy that Eglin's days as leader were numbered. This filled him with some concern as Slabbert lacked experience, while he had doubts whether he had the unbending willpower required to be a party leader or would have the same dedication to party affairs as Eglin. De Beer's concerns made sense. If Eglin as a battle-hardened veteran who had endured the buffeting of political warfare since 1953 had buckled under the NP's onslaught, what would happen to Slabbert? This led to his decision that if Slabbert should become leader, he would consider remaining in parliament to assist him.[17]

On 27 July, Eglin raised the issue of his leadership at a Federal Executive meeting in Johannesburg. In an informal discussion he urged members to be frank and truthful. De Beer then surprised him by proposing a motion that the meeting express its full confidence in him. The motion was a last-ditch attempt to save Eglin's leadership as De Beer felt the whole issue surrounding the leadership issue was a panicky reaction by some Progressives who lacked experience in dealing with the robust tactics of the NP.[18] A vote of confidence would force those participating in the whispering campaign to come out in the open to vote against the man who had led the Progressives out of the political wilderness. It was a case of put up or shut up. This attempt to force the discontents to support Eglin led to Roger Hulley proposing a motion – "[t]hat a ballot be held to determine whether or not the Federal Executive is of the opinion that Mr. Eglin MP should continue as leader" – which was accepted. Waddell then in a short speech promoted the leadership of Slabbert.

The subsequent discussion was a harrowing experience for

---

16 *The Star*, 20 July 1979.
17 De Beer – Wendy, 25 July 1979. (In the possession of Wendy de Beer Furniss.)
18 De Beer – Wendy, 3 July 1979. (In the possession of Wendy de Beer Furniss.)

Eglin as he had to listen to speakers expressing doubts about his leadership abilities, especially his lack of charisma, to build a new image for the party. Slabbert stated that he would not oppose Eglin but would be available if the party wanted him as leader. At 17:00, after a marathon eight-hour meeting, the Federal Executive voted in a secret ballot by 25 votes to 19, and three spoilt ballots, that it wanted a new leader.[19]

On 6 August in Sea Point at a report-back meeting to his constituents, Eglin announced his retirement as leader, and recommended Slabbert as his successor as they shared the same political principles. At the PFP's conference in Johannesburg on 3 September 1979, he was subsequently elected leader unanimously after De Beer recused himself from the leadership contest. He later admitted to lacking the burning desire to be the leader. To the author of a profile article on him for the *Optima* journal, he admitted that as a parliamentarian he lacked one vital characteristic of the natural political leader – a "sheer drive for power, with its concomitant implacable refusal to brook opposition".[20]

With the opening of the 1980 parliamentary session, De Beer gave his parliamentary bench in the second row to Eglin to prevent his old friend, who had lost his frontbench with his leadership, from being relegated to the backbenches.[21] Slabbert was in the fortunate position that he inherited a well-organised and confident party, while he took to the PFP's leadership like a duck to water. It was obvious to De Beer that he did not need any help or guidance. This eased his decision to return to AAC. On 15 April 1980, during the budget debate, he made his resignation speech to the House of Assembly. But before he did so, he condemned the stranglehold of apartheid on the economy and the lack of freedom in the country as a result of the pass and labour laws, the Group Areas Act,

---

19 *Sunday Times*, 5 August 1979: Wits, PFP/DP papers, Ab 2.2 10, Minutes of the Federal Executive meeting, Johannesburg 27 and 28 July 1979; Eglin, *Crossing the borders of power*, p. 189.

20 Undated clipping in the possession of Wendy de Beer Furniss.

21 Eglin, *Crossing the borders of power*, pp. 192, 194.

the discrimination in education and training that limited black people and handicapped the private sector. He repeated that only by getting rid of apartheid, and by securing a government that had the support of all South Africans could the economy prosper. He made it clear that his resignation was not politically motivated and assured his Progressive colleagues of his continuing affection, loyalty and support.

After making polite comments about De Beer's departure, the NP promptly returned to its favourite activity of bashing the Progressives as unpatriotic and subversive. Louis le Grange, Minister of Police, launched a savage attack on Boraine for daring to support the campaign for the release of Mandela. Portraying the ANC leader as a dangerous radical and part of a campaign to wipe out the white man in South Africa, he insinuated that the PFP supported terrorism and violence. He vowed that the government would not release Mandela.[22]

De Beer viewed Le Grange's behaviour with disdain. In an interview with Tos Wentzel of *The Star* (17 April 1980), he warned that the day was very close, if it had not already arrived, when the white man was going to find it impossible to assert his will over black people. Also that white politics would become reactive and responsive to black aspirations, and that negotiation and agreement with the black majority would become the pattern.

De Beer found his last week in parliament harrowing, with tearful parties as he was bidding farewell to political allies dating back the 1950s. It also meant the end of a political career that had started with such high hopes and ambitions as a 24-year-old. That he had some regrets on how his political career ended is reflected in an interview with the *Financial Mail* (25 April 1980):

> I might have succeeded if I'd had more ambition. My biggest problem has been that I see both sides all too easily. My political epitaph should read that 'he might have succeeded if he had the will'.

---

22   *Beeld*, 16 April 1980.

And yet, he felt that his career did not end in failure: "If I may be so immodest as to say, I've given it all I've got — and seen some results."[23] His return to parliament was a difficult and challenging time, but that he had made his mark was evident in the statement of *Beeld* that his departure would be a great loss for the PFP as he was an outstanding parliamentarian.[24] His standing amongst Progressives was reflected in Eglin's tribute in the party's *Impact* newssheet of May 1980. Under the heading "A remarkably gifted South African" he paid an emotional tribute to him:

> Zac will be missed by his colleagues in Parliament, as he will be by party members around the country. Parliament and politics will be poorer without him. For Zac by any standards is a remarkably gifted South African. He is a man whose strength lies not merely in his razor sharp intellect, his charity of thought and speech, his understanding of people and politics, but also in his firm commitment to the principle of a non-racial South Africa. Thank you Zac. Sterkte ou vriend in die jare wat voorlê. (Good luck, old friend, for the years ahead.)

---

23 *Financial Mail*, 25 April 1980.
24 *Beeld*, 3 and 17 April 1980.

CHAPTER 17
You cannot do good business in a rotten society
1980–1985

On his return to AAC, De Beer replaced Gavin Relly as chairperson of Insurance Holdings. He soon became an executive director responsible for the group's interests in insurance, property and construction as chairperson of SA Eagle, Southern Life, Amaprop and the LTA construction company. He used his position as one of South Africa's leading businessmen to urge the business community to become involved in politics as "you cannot do good business in a rotten society".[1] To secure a prosperous economy, he stated once again, the country had to get rid of apartheid. Charming and loquacious, he was in great demand as guest speaker at university graduation ceremonies, various business functions and conferences which he used to propagate with fervour the message for constitutional reforms to prevent a revolution.

In October 1980, while addressing the annual dinner of MBA students at the UCT Graduate School of Business, he warned that the real danger facing businesspeople was that when black people took over political power – and he reiterated that it was going to happen – they may throw out the baby of free enterprise with the bathwater of apartheid. It was their task as businesspeople to ensure that this did not happen:[2]

> This means that the businessman who wants to serve his system cannot be content just to see to it that his own organisation runs on enlightened lines: he must be seen to demand for blacks their full

---

1   *The Star*, 23 June 1987.
2   *UCT Graduate School of Business*, Number 4, October 1980, p. 5.

share of the fruits of free enterprise. If – and it is a big if – business people will gird up their loins and do all the things I have indicated: if there is a really successful campaign to make the free market system and its benefits fully available to our black citizens now: if their quality of life is demonstrably improved through this process, and if it can be shown that free enterprise, so far from being allied to apartheid is fundamentally inimical to it, then I believe we can succeed. But the approach has to be both urgent and radical: free means free, and free enterprise cannot be reconciled with pass laws, Group Areas Acts, and the like. Change is the theme of our time. If we wish, while changing the bad things in our society, to keep the good economic system, we must act urgently and effectively.[3]

As the LTA chairman, he urged a conference of construction companies in October 1982 that they had to come to grips with the emergence of the new era of political trade unions and that they had to persuade workers that the free enterprise system was "free for them as well as for us".[4] In his address to a graduation ceremony at Wits in December 1984, he called for the scrapping of the Group Areas Act as it was not only "morally repulsive", but also highly inefficient and expensive in practice. It furthermore stifled people's natural aspirations and initiatives.[5] However, his status as an AAC executive meant that those on the left viewed his call for reform as motivated by financial gain. When he advocated in *South Africa: The road ahead*, compiled by G.F. Jacobs, the privatisation of state industries such as Eskom, Anton Harber in his review of the book for the *Weekly Mail* (11 July to 17 July 1985) proclaimed:

As one reads De Beer's essay, one can almost hear Anglo chuckling gleefully at the prospect of getting its hands on some of those industries now controlled by the state.

---

3 *Sunday Express*, 9 November 1980.
4 *The Star*, 26 October 1982.
5 *Business Day*, 17 December 1984.

While at the AAC, De Beer retained close contacts with the PFP. He had regular dinners with Slabbert.[6] In public he praised him to the skies, "… the opposition is being led by a man who is young, handsome, highly intelligent, very well educated and charismatic".[7]

During the general election of 1981, he went to Cape Town to address a public meeting in support of the Maitland candidature of James Selfe. Addressing a group of between 50 and 60 people in the Milnerton City Hall, he made it clear that the PFP stood for full citizenship for all South Africans and that anything less than placing the coloured people on the common voters' roll for one sovereign parliament would be a political fraud.[8] Selfe was grateful for De Beer's support,[9] but the NP won Maitland with a large majority. Nationally, the Progressives did better than in the 1977 election as the NP was in a vulnerable position with the exposure of the misuse of public funds in the Department of Information. The NP also had to defend several seats it had won in the 1977 with the opposition vote divided between the NRP and the Progressives. With the NRP a spent force, the PFP improved its share of the popular vote to 19,09 per cent compared to the 16,71 per cent in 1977 and hence increased its parliamentary representation from 18 to 26 seats.

Disappointingly, the PFP attracted only about five per cent of the Afrikaner vote.[10] The reason for this low level of support was Botha's stance on political reform. He was determined to ensure Afrikaner survival. For him it was a case of "adapt or die", and he was willing to adapt apartheid to changing circumstances. To prevent revolution, he envisaged reform to establish a modernised, improved and more humane apartheid system by abolishing unnecessary and

---

6 Interview with Debbie de Beer, 23 April 2020.
7 *The Star*, 9 March 1982.
8 *The Argus*, 9 April 1981.
9 Unisa, Progressive Federal Party papers, File 32.3. J. Selfe – De Beer, 25 May 1981.
10 H. Giliomee, "Demokratiese Party se werklike rol", *Die Suid-Afrikaan*, June/July 1988, p. 7.

irritating discriminatory measures.[11] His first step was to abolish the Senate in 1980 and replace it with a nominated President's Council consisting of white, coloured and Indian members to investigate and advise the government on constitutional reforms. (The constitution was also adapted to make provision for twelve nominated MPs. The President could nominate four, while the rest were proportionally indirectly elected based on the number of MPs in the various parties. The PFP qualified for one such MP, and Nic Olivier was elected.)

Botha, however, made clear that these reforms would never include the principle of a one-man-one-vote election for a single parliamentary chamber. In his response Slabbert was adamant that the PFP would not be "hijacked for apartheid" and refused to be drawn into a process of constitutional reform that fell short of the political aspirations of the black majority. With the support of the parliamentary caucus, he decided to boycott the President's Council.[12] This led to the Progressives being labelled by the NP, and the Afrikaans-medium press, as a "boycott" party of orderly reform.[13]

It was a perception that convinced most enlightened Afrikaners to retain their faith in the NP, despite all of its shortcomings. Their confidence in Botha was bolstered by his impatience with Treurnicht's tiresome defence of petty apartheid and he simply steamrolled him. Botha was determined to rid the NP from Treurnicht, and the opportunity arose when he opposed a proposed new constitution to share power with the coloureds and Indians in a tricameral parliament with an in-built white majority, and a powerful executive president. In Treurnicht's eyes Botha was committing treason. After a stormy NP parliamentary caucus meeting on 24 February 1982 in which Treurnicht refused to support a vote of confidence in Botha, he and his closest followers were expelled from the NP.

---

11 D. & J. de Villiers, *PW*, (Cape Town, 1984), p. 168.
12 *Sunday Times*, 8 June 1980.
13 Slabbert, *The last white parliament*, p.69.

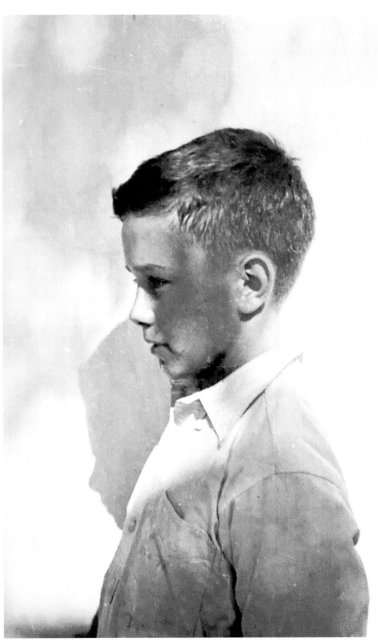
Zach as a schoolboy.

The class of 1951. The University of Cape Town's newly qualified medical doctors. De Beer is in the second row from the front, second from the right.

Winning Maitland, 1953.

The young candidate.

Wendy, Maureen, Debbie, Oupa Strauss, Zach and Zach junior, 1959.

The first session of the first republican House of Assembly, 5 June 1961.
De Beer is second in the third row on the right.
From: Parliament of South Africa collection

The Progressive Federal Party parliamentary caucus, 1977.
De Beer is standing at the back next to the lamp. Eglin is in front, second from the left, next to Suzman. Swart is behind Eglin's right shoulder.

Meeting the ANC leadership – Tertius Myburgh, Tony Bloom, Oliver Tambo, President Kenneth Kaunda, Gavin Relly and De Beer.

The Democratic Party parliamentary caucus, September 1989.

With Nelson Mandela and Tony Leon.

Mentor and friend, Harry Oppenheimer.

Zach and Mona.

Unless otherwise indicated, all photographs supplied by Wendy de Beer Furniss.

This led to the founding of the right-wing Conservative Party (CP) under Treurnicht's leadership on 20 March 1982.

Botha's reforms and the CP's vehement opposition to any changes to apartheid placed the PFP in a difficult position. This was evident in the 1983 referendum with its "Yes/No" option to the question "Are you in favour of the implementation of the Constitution Act, 1983, as approved by Parliament?". The PFP's stance was that the proposed tricameral constitution was a confidence trick that safeguarded apartheid and not the future as it would polarise whites and blacks, promoting conflict and dissatisfaction.[14]

De Beer, Oppenheimer and Tony Bloom were the only prominent businessmen to actively campaign for the "No" vote. Addressing meetings, he was adamant that the new constitution was an insult to blacks by asking whites to turn their backs on them. It furthermore swindled coloureds and Indians by bringing them into the parliamentary system in which they would have no power, he explained. In addition, it would give the President, elected by the majority party in the white chamber, too much power and the proposed constitution was nothing more than a new way to maintain domination and discrimination. He pleaded that white South Africans should vote "No" and let the NP go back to the drawing board and come back with something which really was a step in the right direction.[15]

Business leaders were deaf to this warning as they were receptive to Botha's message that he could not continue with reform if there was a "No" vote in the referendum.[16] While the NP had the full support of the Afrikaans-medium press and the state-controlled SABC, which gave the NP nearly 400 per cent more air-time than the PFP,[17] the usually Progressive supporting English-medium press was deeply divided. The *Sunday Times*, *The Natal Mercury*,

---

14 *Rand Daily Mail*, 1 November 1983.
15 *Rand Daily Mail*, 8 October 1983; Z 333, Speech in opposition to the proposed constitution. (In the possession of Wendy de Beer Furniss.)
16 *Rand Daily Mail*, 28 November 1983.
17 *Rand Daily Mail*, 1 November 1983.

the *Daily Dispatch*, *The Friend*, *Finance Week* and the *Financial Mail* urged a "Yes" vote, while *The Star* advised its readers to abstain.[18] The PFP lacked the financial means for an effective campaign. The NP, supported by big business, spent more money on full-page advertisements in the Sunday press on one day than the PFP had to spend on the entire campaign.[19]

Despite the Progressives' best efforts, the proposed constitution was accepted with an overwhelming majority of 66 per cent to the 34 per cent of "No" votes, of whom about 10 per cent were liberal protest votes. Tens of thousands of traditional Progressive supporters, up to 30 per cent of them, voted "Yes" as they saw the new constitution as a step in the right direction.[20] Slabbert became deeply depressed about his inability to convey to whites his fear for the future of the country.[21]

Slabbert's gloom was aggravated by the consequences of Botha's reforms as it unleashed pent-up forces in the black majority which could not be regulated from above. His reforms not only failed to satisfy black aspirations; they raised frustrated expectations. The result was a dramatic growth in anti-apartheid organisations, for example the United Democratic Front (UDF) formed in 1983 to oppose the tricameral parliament, and the escalation of black resistance. This in turn led to a revolutionary climate and an ever-increasing cycle of violence which Botha could not break. Despite the increasing brutality of security forces, the apartheid state lost control of numerous black townships. The harsh methods used by the security forces to deal with the uprising led to international condemnation and calls for punitive economic sanctions and disinvestment. The Progressives, with Helen Suzman in the lead and with the full support of De Beer, felt that this would reduce the country to a wasteland, and black people would be the most

---

18 E. McKenzie, "The 1983 referendum: The English press and the Progressive Federal Party campaign", *Kleio*, 1991, Vol. 23, pp. 85–96.
19 Slabbert, *The last white parliament*, p. 112.
20 *Sunday Times*, 6 November 2014.
21 Swart, *Progressive odyssey*, p. 165.

adversely affected by these measures.[22] This opposition to economic sanctions earned the party the hostility of anti-apartheid activists. Progressives were accused of being the tools of apartheid capitalistic oppressors.[23] In reality, the business community remained aloof from the Progressives – a situation Slabbert explained in the following terms:

> Their interest [big capital] were closely tied to government, to power. I never experienced business looking upon the PFP as a protector of their interests. How could we. We had very little power.[24]

In addition, black leaders increasingly questioned the bona fides of liberal politicians, accusing the PFP of being the "icing sugar on the system of oppression" or of keeping the "illusion of peaceful change".[25] The PFP came under increasing pressure from the UDF with the accusation that by being in parliament the party provided the apartheid state with legitimacy.

The rise in black resistance to apartheid, combined with the international isolation of the apartheid state, led to the PFP losing support in white parliamentary politics. Botha's reforms fuelled not just the rise of the CP, but also of the neo-fascist Afrikaner Weerstandsbeweging (AWB) under the leadership of the thuggish Eugene Terre'Blanche. The growth of the right-wing led to the marginalisation of the PFP. Enlightened voters, including a significant number of Progressive supporters, felt that as Botha was doing its best with reforms, they had to vote NP to support him against the reactionary CP and AWB. The NP adroitly exploited the Progressives' fear of the right-wing to win over the electoral

---

22 Z274, "Focus on sanctions" by Zach de Beer. Article for publication in SA Forum position paper. (In the possession of Wendy de Beer Furniss.)
23 Suzman, *In no uncertain terms*, p. 267.
24 D. Shandler, "Structural crisis and liberalism: A history of the Progressive Federal Party, 1981–1989 (MA, UCT, 1991), p. 87.
25 UFS, ACA, P.W. papers, File PS3/1/2, Frederik van Zyl Slabbert, 'Problems of a parliamentary opposition in South Africa', p. 7. (Paper delivered at a symposium in Bonn, Germany, May 1981).

base of the PFP. This was evident in the by-election in the Port Elizabeth constituency of Newton Park on 1 May 1985. In the 1981 general election, the PFP had failed with 1195 votes to capture the constituency from the NP, but in 1985 the seat seemed right for the plucking. But when the CP entered a candidate, the NP won the seat with ease. For Slabbert it was a devastating blow, making it clear to him that the PFP's stance on the necessity to negotiate with the ANC, and the party's exposure of police brutality, alienated white voters as the party was seen as only caring about black people. [26]

---

26 US, Slabbert papers, 430.X1, Unpublished memorandum (August 1986) by Slabbert on the reasons why he resigned as party leader, p. 8.

CHAPTER 18
Meeting the African National Congress leadership
1985

With South Africa trapped in a cycle of violence, De Beer became part of a delegation to meet the ANC leadership in Zambia in an attempt to bring about a peaceful solution. President Kaunda had suggested a meeting between South African businessmen and the ANC. He acted as the facilitator with Hugh Murray, editor of the respected business magazine *Leadership*, as the organiser in South Africa for a delegation to be led by Gavin Relly, chairman of AAC. The planned meeting could not be kept secret and on 6 September the *Financial Mail* broke the news, listing the names of prominent businesspeople who could be part of the delegation. An outraged Botha responded that to talk with the liberation movement was an act of disloyalty to the young soldiers protecting South Africa against the violence of the communist-dominated ANC.[1] Some businessmen, for example Anton Rupert, refused to be part of the talks. Oppenheimer also felt that the trip should be cancelled, but Relly insisted that it go ahead.[2] He led a delegation of seven to Zambia. They included corporate businessmen, De Beer, Tony Bloom of Premier Milling, the South African Foundation's Peter Sorour and journalists Murray of *Leadership*, Harald Pakendorf, editor of *Die Vaderland*, and Tertius Myburgh, editor of the *Sunday Times*.

The group departed from Johannesburg on Friday 13 September 1985 in a private Gulfstream jet and landed at an airstrip in

---

1 *Die Burger*, 9 September 1985. D. Pallister, S. Stewart, I. Lepper, *South Africa Inc. The Oppenheimer empire* (London, 1988), p. 275.
2 Butler, *Cyril Ramaphosa*, p. 208.

the Luangwa Game Park, 400 km east of Lusaka. After driving 40 kilometres – it was a stifling hot and humid day – they met the ANC group led by Oliver Tambo at Kaunda's Mfuwe presidential game lodge. Tambo took the meeting seriously and carefully prepared himself and his delegation by asking a number of questions on what the ANC "require from the monopolists", and "[w]hat do the big capitalists want?" He was determined to get big business to increase pressure on the apartheid government to create an atmosphere for talks with the ANC, and to encourage tensions between big capital and the apartheid regime:

> Nothing we do or say during the discussion must indicate that we are willing to bargain away their claims in return for some vague promises from the monopolists. We must ensure that they leave here determined to demonstrate to us that they are distant from Botha. Place before them a number of conditions to prove their bona fides.[3]

The Zambian president introduced the Relly delegation to the ANC delegates – Thabo Mbeki, Chris Hani, Mac Maharaj, James Stuart and Pallo Jordan. An icebreaker between the two groups was the fact that the Relly delegation was all dressed as for a safari with open-necked shirts, while the ANC delegation were in formal suits. This led to jokes about who most resembled revolutionaries and capitalists.

In the relaxed conversations that followed, De Beer spoke of the delegation's impression of events in South Africa and that there had been a retrogression in South Africa's human relations the previous 30 years. However, he said that recently it seemed to dawn on the government that there was only one South Africa. The dropping of the pass laws was significant in this respect, but he felt that the challenge of political power sharing remained untouched. He concluded by asking how much bloodshed there

---

3 M. Maharaj and Z.P. Jordan, *Breakthrough. The struggles and secret talks that brought apartheid South Africa to the negotiating table* (Cape Town, 2021), p. 104.

would be before this takes place, and what kind of a country will be left at the end?[4]

This led to an animated discussion on the influence of the SACP in the ANC, the use of violence, negotiations with the apartheid state, and the respective merits of private economic initiative versus economic justice.[5] The ANC made it clear that when in government it would pursue a mixed economy but that large business corporations would be nationalised. Tambo set out the ANC's socialist aspirations in the following terms: "We cannot leave the large corporations operating as they do. They represent tremendous wealth amid unspeakable poverty." He identified AAC as one of the three corporations which would be broken up if the ANC came to power. De Beer found the ANC's dated attachment to a nationalised economy rather shocking as he felt that these ideas belonged in the 1950s. He tried to persuade them that on practical grounds their economic plans would not work.[6]

Despite the frank exchanges and widely different views, the six-hour meeting was cordial. The businessmen left Zambia in a positive mood and they had reason to be. Mark Gevisser, Mbeki's biographer, is of the opinion that the meeting established a dialogue between South Africa's reigning industrialists and its future rulers about the future shape of South Africa. It was a dialogue that enlightened both sides and by 1994 there would be an unexpected consensus between them. He also was of the opinion that the meeting contributed to the transformation of the ANC into an advocate of liberal democracy.[7] Ultimately, the meeting was a significant moment in South African history as it was an icebreaker that paved the way for a succession of delegations to the ANC by cultural figures, academics and politicians.

---

4 L. Callinicos, *Oliver Tambo. Beyond the Engeli Mountains* (Cape Town, 2004), pp. 579–583.
5 H. Pakendorf, *Stroomop. Herinneringe van 'n koerantman in die apartheidsera* (Cape Town, 2018), pp. 155–156, 175–183; Sunday Times, 15 September 1985.
6 *Guardian*, 16 September 1985; *Rapport*, 18 February 1990.
7 M. Gevisser, *Thabo Mbeki. The dream deferred* (Johannesburg, 2007), p. 504.

Back in South Africa, Relly declared that he emerged from the talks "with a good sense that more talks might lead to some fruitful conclusion".[8] De Beer also expressed the hope that the talks would be followed by a further meeting with the ANC: "The future lies in our common South Africanism. We have a common interest in that." When pressed on the ANC's commitment to the armed struggle, he responded that he obviously did not support it, but that it was a product of being outlawed in 1960. A furious Botha did not share this view and accused the delegation of "showing signs of weakness to the enemies of South Africa".[9]

After the Zambian mission, De Beer was a prominent supporter of Slabbert's idea to create a national convention movement. The PFP leader had become desperate about the political violence in the country and developed the notion of such a movement to bring about constitutional reform to rescue South Africa from disaster. His idea was to bring together parties and organisations that were in favour of negotiations between the ANC and apartheid state. A co-sponsor of the proposed alliance was Chief Mangosuthu Buthelezi, leader of the KwaZulu Bantustan, as well as of Inkatha, a cultural movement for the Zulu that he turned into a mass movement. Buthelezi had used his position as a Bantustan leader to secure a power base. This meant that, instead of being a puppet of the apartheid state, he had to be treated with circumspection and respect by a wary NP leadership. He was "simultaneously needed and feared" by the apartheid state.[10] With time, Inkatha became a rival of the ANC and this led to violent clashes with the UDF.

Leading UDF activists like Allan Boesak and Bishop Desmond Tutu were supportive of the national convention idea, but three days before the official launch refused to be part of it. According to Slabbert, the UDF withdrew after the ANC claimed that the national convention movement would weaken revolutionary fer-

---

8 *The Star*, 14 September 1985.
9 *Guardian*, 16 September 1985.
10 S. Marks, *The ambiguities of dependence in South Africa. Class, Nationalism, and the state in twentieth-century Natal* (Johannesburg, 1986), pp. 116, 123.

vour and could be a sly strategy of the Botha regime. Although more than 150 people from the political, business, sport and academic world met on 21 September 1985 at the Sandton Sun Hotel in Johannesburg to discuss the possibility of launching a mass-based alliance to provide alternatives to government policies, nothing came of the initiative.[11] That he was not seen as part of the anti-apartheid struggle by the ANC leadership, whom he met in Lusaka in October 1985, was a chastening experience for Slabbert,[12] especially as the quality of the ANC leaders impressed him. He was particularly taken by the charming Mbeki who was keen that Slabbert should leave parliament.[13] The meeting with the ANC leadership brought home to Slabbert how out of touch parliament was with what was happening in South Africa.[14]

The final straw that broke the camel's back for Slabbert was the PFP's heavy defeats in the Port Natal and Springs by-elections at the end of October 1985. In Springs the party's total votes dropped to a paltry 14 per cent compared to the 36 per cent in 1981. Progressives voted for the NP candidate to keep the CP out. In Port Natal, where *The Natal Mercury* had urged Progressives to vote for the NP to support Botha's reforms against the right, the PFP candidate came a distant second.[15] On the same day the ultraconservative HNP, in an election agreement with CP, took Sasolburg from the NP, while the CP drastically reduced the NP's majorities in Vryburg and Bethlehem. These by-election results were an indication that the PFP would lose its status as the official parliamentary opposition to the CP in the next general election. After the disappointing by-election results, Slabbert, accompanied by Eglin, went

---

11 Grundlingh, *Slabbert. Man with a mission*, pp. 106–107.
12 F. van Zyl Slabbert, *Tough choices. Reflections of an Afrikaner African* Cape Town, 2000), pp. 101–103; J. Butler, R. Elphick, D. Welsh (eds.), *Democratic liberalism in South Africa. Its history and prospect* (Cape Town, 1987), p. 403.
13 A. Boraine, *What's gone wrong? On the brink of a failed state* (Johannesburg & Cape Town, 2014), p. 34.
14 F. van Zyl Slabbert, *The other side of history. An anecdotal reflection on political transition in South Africa* (Johannesburg, 2006), p. 46.
15 *The Natal Mercury*, 29 October 1985.

on a study tour to Australia and New Zealand. During their travels, he confided in Eglin that he considered resigning his seat and position as party leader as he felt that he was wasting his time in parliament.[16]

De Beer shared Slabbert's urgency that something had to be done about the crisis facing the country. Speaking in London on 7 November, he urged Botha to open negotiations with ANC leaders as there was the danger that if they were frustrated any longer, they could move to the left, as there were self-confessed communists in the movement's executive. He also urged British businesspeople to oppose sanctions and to financially support the Urban Foundation.[17]

In January 1986, the Relly delegation was once more in the news when Dr Fritz Leutweiler, the Swiss negotiator managing South Africa's international debt repayments, claimed in an interview that the businessmen that went to meet the ANC leaders in September regretted the talks. Fuel was added to controversy when Murray, who had played a leading role in arranging the meeting, expressed himself shattered about the recent acts of violence committed by the ANC.[18] In his response De Beer pointed out that he had never met Leutweiler and that the delegation had a useful visit: "We went there to learn something about these people and we did." On the question of ANC violence, he stated:

> It existed for a long time before the visit. The fact that it continues to exist after the visit makes very little difference to one's attitudes. I deplored the violence before I went to meet the ANC and I deplore it now.[19]

---

16 Slabbert, *The other side of history*, p. 45.
17 *Financial Times*, 8 November 1985.
18 *Die Burger*, 18 January 1986.
19 *The Star*, 19 January 1986.

CHAPTER 19
A shaken and demoralised party
1986–1987

On Friday, 7 February 1986, Slabbert announced his retirement from parliament in the House of Assembly. In an atmosphere filled with electricity, he emotionally explained his overwhelming feeling of absurdity in a parliament that ignored the conflict-ridden situation in South Africa. He said that the no-confidence debate was a "grotesque ritual in irrelevance" and that he was "trapped in a ridiculous political debate, while outside our country is bleeding". He then announced that as he could make no contribution to getting rid of apartheid, he had decided to resign from parliament.[1] Apart from Boraine, no other Progressive MP followed him out of parliament. De Beer was deeply disappointed with Slabbert's behaviour and concluded that he had merely cracked under the stress of frustration.[2] Ultimately, the overwhelming majority of Progressives remained committed to parliamentary politics. This feeling of solidarity in the PFP could not prevent Slabbert's resignation from being a fatal blow for the party. As Suzman puts it in her memoirs – who wants to vote or work for a party in which the leader declared parliament irrelevant?[3]

A badly shaken and demoralised Progressive parliamentary caucus, desperate for stability, asked Eglin to step in as acting party leader. For many in the PFP Eglin was an abrasive political retread that could not fill the gap left by the glamorous Slabbert.[4] Robin Carlisle, a President's Council member and a leading fundraiser,

---

1 House of Assembly debates, 7 February 1986, Col. 413–431.
2 De Beer – Wendy, 4 March 1986. (In the possession of Wendy de Beer Furniss.)
3 Suzman, *In no uncertain terms*, p. 255.
4 Swart, *Progressive odyssey*, p. 183.

felt that De Beer had the looks, charm, and eloquence to be the face of the party and asked that he made himself available for the leadership. De Beer turned down the suggestion as he had obligations to AAC. Also, he had no parliamentary seat.[5] The reality was that he had no desire to return to parliament. In an interview with B.M. Schoeman of *Finansies & Tegniek* (March 1985), he made it clear that in the three professions he had pursued – medicine, politics and business, it was the financial world that had given him the most satisfaction. Furthermore, he stated that he had no desire to return to politics: "Ek het steeds my belangstelling in die politiek, maar ek wil nooit weer terug Parlement toe nie." (I am still interested in politics, but I never want to return to parliament.) He was also adamant that he lacked the necessary ambition to be a party leader.

At the Federal Council meeting of 16 February 1986, Eglin was unanimously elected party leader. He did his utmost to revive the spirits of the devastated and bewildered party activists who found it difficult to come to terms with a much-loved and admired leader leaving them in the lurch.

Eglin had the additional challenge that some Progressive supporters felt that they had to vote for the NP to support Botha's reforms. Apart from implementing the tricameral parliament, Botha scrapped in 1986 the elected all-white provincial councils, replacing them with nominated multiracial executive committees. In addition, social amenities such as hotels, toilets, beaches, restaurants and libraries were opened to black people. He started to dismantle the cornerstones of apartheid. In 1985, the prohibition of mixed marriages and sex across the colour line was lifted. Black unions and their right to strike were recognised, while white job protection was abolished. Forced removals were halted, freehold rights extended to blacks in "white areas" and South African citizenship was restored to those who had lost it when their Bantustans became "independent".

By 1986 it was also formally admitted that the Bantustan system

---

5   Interview with R. Carlisle, 14 April 2020.

was not the answer to South Africa's racial problems. As Botha accepted the inevitability of black urbanisation and the permanency of urban blacks, influx control was abolished.

De Beer, who had little time for Botha as a person or a politician, was surprised by these reforms and felt that he deserved praise:

> If anyone had told me 12 months ago that the pass laws would be repealed by May 1986, I would have accused him of starry-eyed optimism. Yet that is just what has happened – and the repeal of the pass laws is only the most important of a number of positive changes that have been made.

However, he warned that these reforms were not enough. Only the total scrapping of apartheid would restore peace to the country.[6]

When an election was announced for 6 May 1987, the PFP was in a tight spot as most enlightened voters were content with the pace of Botha's reforms, and continued to view the PFP as a "boycott party". Eglin decided to form a "reform-minded alliance" with the NRP, which under the leadership of Bill Sutton had become more enlightened in its policies, to counter the negative perceptions of the PFP.[7] As a result, the party decided to contest 81 constituencies in a campaign dubbed "Operation Turbocharge". The PFP also decided not to oppose the candidates of the Independent Movement. This group consisted of three breakaway NP supporters: Dennis Worrall, South Africa's ambassador in Britain, had resigned in protest at the government's policies, and decided to oppose Chris Heunis, the cabinet minister responsible for constitutional matters, in the Helderberg constituency; Wynand Malan, MP for Randburg, had left the NP because of its refusal to scrap the Group Areas Act, it's handling of the security situation and because he believed in a South Africa with equal political rights for all; and Esther Lategan, who set out to oppose the NP in Stellenbosch as an independent.

---

6   *Spectrum*, 25 May 1986.
7   *Die Burger*, 15 April 1987.

Eglin, by standing back for the Independents to campaign, hoped to gain credit for placing the country ahead of his party, and ultimately hoped that the PFP would be seen as a catalyst for reform.

The Progressives' election manifesto advocated negotiations with the liberation movements and the calling of a national convention to create a new constitution in which all South Africans would have equal rights. As a prerequisite for negotiations, they campaigned that Nelson Mandela had to be released from prison, and the ANC, the SACP and the PAC had to be unbanned. The Progressive campaign lacked enthusiasm and failed to gain momentum. Eglin had managed to steady the party after February 1986, but he could not repair the damage done by Slabbert resigning. By leaving his post he did what the NP's demonisation of the Progressives could never achieve – undermine their belief in liberalism. His resignation implied a rejection of incremental change, the mainstay of liberal politics, and many Progressives as a result lost heart. In contrast to previous elections, the PFP found it difficult to attract volunteers to canvass voters and to put up election posters. Especially English-speaking university students refused to be involved in the election as they viewed the elections as irrelevant. Their boycotting of the elections would cost the PFP at least two seats. Even those Progressives who were involved lacked the missionary zeal of earlier campaigns. What struck the South African-born novelist Christopher Hope on his first visit to the country in 12 years to observe the election, was the atmosphere of sadness, the sense of failure and fear among the Progressives.[8]

The NP, against a background of ANC guerrilla activity with bomb blasts rocking Johannesburg, stay-away actions, strikes, and protests by students with ruthless efficiency created a perception of the Botha government as the only bulwark against revolutionary forces. At the same time the NP's attacks on the PFP convinced many voters that the party was soft on security, disloyal and unpatriotic, and that it could not be trusted with the reform

---

8   C. Hope, *White boy running* (London, 1987), p. 201.

process. The NP claimed that a vote for the Progressives would serve the interests of the ANC and communists.[9] In a number of newspaper advertisements, with headlines such as "Over my dead body would I vote for the ANC. So why vote PFP?", the Progressives were painted – in the words of Lenin – as "useful idiots" for the revolution.[10] The NP-supporting Afrikaans press also hammered on the PFP's alleged links with radicalism.

As proof of the PFP's close relations with the ANC, and their approval of revolutionary violence, the NP distributed a photo of Helen Suzman embracing Winnie Mandela with the caption of Mandela's controversial statement: "With our boxes of matches and our necklaces, we shall liberate our country."[11] (Ironically, while the NP bashed the Progressives for being too radical, the UDF accused them of being just a different shade of the NP for participating in the apartheid parliament.)[12] The NP was assisted in this onslaught by the SABC, which degenerated – in the words of the journalist Fleur de Villiers – into "statutory praise singing" of the government.[13] According to the Department of Journalism and Media studies at Rhodes University, the NP received 75 per cent of all screen time allocated to political parties.[14]

The NP's propaganda did much to undermine the PFP's alliance with the NRP and to deny the Progressives any benefits from supporting the Independent Movement. Many conservative English-speaking NRP supporters refused to be associated with the Progressives. At least 75 per cent of former NRP supporters in Natal voted for the NP.[15] Worrall, Malan and Lategan, fearful of alienating voters, also went out of their way to disown any links with the Progressives.[16] The NP effectively plugged into the feeling of many

---

9 *Die Burger*, 25 March, 21, 28 April 1987.
10 *Sunday Times*, 5, 26 April 1987 and 3 May 1987.
11 *Die Burger*, 5 May 1987.
12 *Cape Times*, 30 April 1987.
13 *Sunday Times*, 29 March 1987.
14 *Sunday Times*, 3 May 1978.
15 *Die Burger*, 23 April 1987, 13 May 1987.
16 *Pretoria News*, 28 March 1987.

whites that there had to be political reform as white survival could not just be secured through repression. Reform, however, had to be slow and controlled and not at the cost of the white minority. At the same time a perception was created of the Progressives as a hindrance to orderly reform because of the party's unreasonable opposition to Botha's reforms.[17] NP propaganda not only prevented enlightened Afrikaners from supporting the PFP, but also convinced some Progressives to vote NP. Here the concern about the level of violence in the country, especially the behaviour of the AWB, was a crucial factor. This extreme right-wing group propagated a race war to maintain Afrikaner supremacy, and did not hesitate to use strong-arm tactics to disrupt NP meetings. Fearful of the AWB and the reactionary policies of the CP, and feeling that only the Botha government could bring about reform, numerous Progressives decided to support the NP.[18]

And yet, despite the onslaught of the NP, the PFP remained confident that it would gain NP seats. In an interview with the BBC's Radio Four, De Beer predicted the NRP/PFP and Independents would gain as many as ten or a dozen seats.[19] The election result was a shock for De Beer and the Progressives. Of the votes cast, the NP captured 52,29 per cent (123 seats), the CP 26,62 per cent (22 seats), the PFP 14,03 per cent (19 seats), and the NRP 1,97 per cent (1 seat). The PFP-NRP alliance lost eleven seats to the NP; seven of the Progressives and four of the NRP. Even in Houghton, Suzman's majority was reduced. For De Beer the Progressives got hammered "as a result of one of the most ruthless and unscrupulous propaganda campaigns in history".[20] The high hopes for "Operation Turbocharge" were dashed by factors beyond Eglin's control – the legacy of Slabbert's resignation, and the high level of political

---

17 *Die Burger*, 4 and 13 May 1987.
18 D. Welsh, "The ideology, aims, role and strategy of the PFP and NRP" in D.J. Van Vuuren, L. Schlemmer, H.C. Marais, J. Latakgomo (eds), *South African election 1987* (Pinetown, 1987), pp. 81–100.
19 Z253, Transcript of an interview with BBC Radio Four's Today programme, 6 May 1987. (In the possession of Wendy de Beer Furniss.)
20 *Business Day*, 30 October 1987.

violence in the country. In contrast to the PFP's poor performance, the Independents attracted significant support. Malan won in Randburg, Worrall, a charismatic and effective speaker that held audiences spellbound, lost with 39 votes, and Lategan did well in Stellenbosch where the Progressives traditionally performed badly.[21]

The election result shattered the PFP's morale, leaving the party in a state of despair. Progressive morale suffered another blow on 19 August 1987 with an NP by-election victory in what had been a safe Progressive ward in the Johannesburg City Council.[22] These setbacks opened a latent fault line amongst Progressives – whether the focus had to be on maintaining liberal democratic values with vote-catching as a secondary emphasis, or to focus on power-politics to create a united opposition which could position itself to be an effective challenge to the NP.[23] In August 1987, the PFP suffered another blow with Jan van Eck, MP for Claremont, resigning from the party, claiming that the parliamentary caucus was too conservative. In October 1987, two more MPs, Peter Gastrow and Pierre Cronjé claiming that the PFP had ceased to be a viable political factor, joined Wynand Malan to form a new political party, the National Democratic Movement (NDM). The Independent Movement had split after the election with some bad feelings between Malan and Worrall, who formed the Independent Party. The reason was their conflicting approaches to politics. Malan wanted to focus on extra-parliamentary politics, he wanted to engage with the ANC and to draw it into negotiations, while Worrall with his focus on parliamentary politics wanted to keep his distance from the ANC and UDF.[24]

De Beer, who felt that in the wake of the defeat the Progressives had to close ranks and stand firm, was outraged by the behaviour

---

21 D. Worrall, *The independent factor. My personal journey through politics and diplomacy* (Wandsbeck, 2018), p. 178.
22 *Beeld*, 20 August 1987.
23 *Sunday Times*, 2, 9 August and 27 March 1988.
24 J. Momberg, *From Malan to Mbeki. The memoirs of an Afrikaner with a conscience* (Stellenbosch, 2011), p. 41.

of the defecting MPs and he condemned them publicly, while he also expressed his unhappiness with the Independent Movement's lack of gratitude to the PFP.[25] However, this did not prevent him from reaching out to Malan and Worrall for a possible merger with the PFP. The 1987 election had convinced him that many South Africans favoured liberal values but were not prepared to vote for the PFP. This was made clear to him when he and Eglin met Malan to discuss a possible merger between the NDM and PFP.

Malan rejected this offer out of hand as he felt that election politics was something of the past and had no meaning whatsoever. In addition, he felt that most Afrikaners would culturally never feel at home with the Progressives and that they viewed Progressives as affluent English-speaking liberals who took a superior attitude to Afrikaners, making them feel stupid. When De Beer challenged this perception, Jannie Hofmeyr, who had accompanied Malan to the meeting, attempted to explain the Afrikaner attitude to liberals with an anecdote, namely that his Afrikaner father was irritated by the way his English-speaking mother held her knife and fork, as he felt that it was her way to say "ons is beter as julle" (we are better than you). His father knew that this was not true but did not know how to tell her this. The Afrikaner perception of liberals could be wrong, but they still did not want to be associated with the Progressives.[26]

As a result, De Beer who was eager for the Progressives to break out of its support being limited to enclaves of upper-income English speakers, became determined to form a new party based on Progressive values to bring all enlightened South Africans together. Apart from reaching out to Malan, he became part of a three-man task force with Eglin and Errol Moorcroft, former MP for Albany, to contact Worrall on a possible merger.[27]

While De Beer was focusing on merger talks, there was a growing wave of unhappiness with Eglin's leadership. The *Sunday Times* (11

---

25 *Business Day*, 30 October 1987.
26 Correspondence with W. Malan, 28 March and 10 April 2022.
27 *Financial Mail*, 8 July 1988.

October 1987) reflected the attitude of many Progressives when it blamed the problems in the PFP on the absence of a truly inspiring leader. Carlisle, who had resigned as the party's Secretary-General, led a low-key revolt against Eglin as he felt that he should have taken responsibility for the defeat and resign.[28] The challenge for Eglin was that in the parliamentary caucus there was no undisputed leader-in-waiting to replace him. At the PFP's Federal Executive Committee meeting on 18 October 1987, there was some lobbying for De Beer to take over, but he made it clear that he was not prepared to put himself forward.[29]

Carlisle went to see him in Johannesburg in an attempt to change his mind. He left the meeting with the impression that De Beer did not want to be seen as the person knifing Eglin, but that he would not object if someone else was wielding the knife.[30] With the knifing metaphor Carlisle was referring to the old adage, "he who wields the knife, never gets to wear the crown". Two other Progressives' deputations also went to see De Beer. Douglas Gibson, chairman of the PFP in the Transvaal, accompanied by Ian Davidson, met him in his office at the AAC headquarters, on 44 Main Street, Johannesburg, urging him to come to the party's rescue. He listened with interest but was adamant that he would not challenge his friend for the leadership – creating the impression that he was not averse to the leadership, but also that he was not overeager.[31]

Tony Leon, the young and dynamic leader of the Progressives in the Johannesburg City Council, also went to see De Beer. He had high expectations of him, expecting a second political coming to save the PFP:

> I ... expected the 'old Zach' of party mythology to appear: the one-time boy wonder who apparently according to old Prog hands, had

---

28 *Sunday Tribune*, 24 January 1988.
29 Shandler, "Structural crisis and liberalism: a history of the Progressive Federal Party, 1981–1989", p. 226.
30 Interview with R. Carlisle, 14 April 2020.
31 Correspondence with D. Gibson, 31 March 2020.

blazed a trail of intellectual brilliance and charisma across the South African political scene in the 1950s and 1960s.[32]

De Beer did not reject Leon's approach outright, again creating the perception that he would be available with some cajoling. He joked that as an old dog he liked his stomach to be tickled.[33] That he had doubts about leading the PFP was understandable. He did not want to push Eglin out of the way as he wanted him to resign on his own accord with his dignity intact. Aware of how sensitive Eglin was of the criticism of his leadership, he had kept quiet about the deputations. Publicly he expressed full support for his friend: "I am Mr Eglin's strongest supporter, and as long as he wants the job, I will remain his supporter. If he is run over by the proverbial bus, then I will consider my position."[34]

However, De Beer's desire to prevent a bloody revolution had convinced him to re-enter the bear pit of parliamentary politics. Between 29 September and 2 October 1987, he attended an international conference on "South Africa in transition" in New York. In his paper "Building the liberal centre in South Africa" he acknowledged that after 40 years of trying to do so his attempts had been met with disappointing results, but that he would not give up on his efforts to create a liberal society.

> … I represent a significant number of South Africans who refuse to give up hope of a reasonably peaceful transition to democracy, and because the utter sterility of the alternative must surely become clearer as time goes on – thus winning recruits for the liberal centre.[35]

His sense of duty to the PFP also left him with no choice but to take over the leadership. As explained to Paul Bell in an interview for the *Leadership* magazine:

---

32 Leon, *On the contrary*, p. 191.
33 Interview with T. Leon, 3 April 2020.
34 *Sunday Star*, 12 June 1988.
35 Z244, "Building the liberal centre in South Africa". (In the possession of Wendy de Beer Furniss.)

> ... well, if you've an active member of the PFP since 1959, you've persuaded a lot of people to put their resources and their lives on the line. The time comes when you have to do it too. The duty falls on you. If your children have grown up, and you've got a few bob in the bank, how do you justify not doing that?[36]

De Beer was also determined to compensate for his refusal to contest the leadership back in 1979, and his hasty departure from parliament in 1980. That it was a nagging thought is reflected in a clipping he kept amongst his papers of the *Financial Mail* (8 July 1988), "Return of the prodigal Prog". The article wryly commented that the state of liberal opposition in the country was reflected in the fact that the frontrunner for the party's leadership was a man who had written his own political epitaph in 1980 as "He might have succeeded, if he'd had the will", and raised a number of questions on his proposed leadership:

> Can he pull the floundering party together? Can he unite the disparate opposition groups of the Left? Can he make a better job of his politics than he did last time round? If De Beer tackles the PFP the way he tackles his business problems, he could still emerge as a force in SA politics. It is his last opportunity.

---

36 P. Bell, "Changing the guard", *Leadership*, Vol., No. 3, 1988, p. 14.

CHAPTER 20
The leadership of a battered political party
1988–1989

In June 1988, Eglin, feeling that he had done his bit, announced that he was not available for re-election as party leader. He set out to find a replacement who was committed to the same principles and who could keep the party intact. He was surprised to hear through Bobby Godsell, a rising star at AAC, and in a subsequent exchange of letters with Oppenheimer, that De Beer was willing to succeed him. After a meeting with De Beer, he was convinced that he was the right person to lead the party and to achieve some realignment with Malan and Worrall.[1]

In contrast to 1979, De Beer had no doubts about his abilities or his will to lead the party. He knew exactly what the main characteristic duties of a party leader were, namely strong, principled beliefs, willpower and the ability to judge what can be achieved quickly and what must be held as long-term objectives. He saw it as his prime task to hold the party together, as the romantic ideal of a leader who issues a clarion call and wanders forward, alone regardless of the political consequences, would be of little real value. He was fully aware that the life of the leader of an opposition party was largely to attend meetings and to participate in conversations. Party members had to be listened to, they had to feel that they were taken seriously. He knew that the leader had to constantly evaluate the strength of feelings in the party. But equally important was that he had to present an image to voters with which they could identify. Ironically as a man blessed with great charm, he did not rate charisma highly. For him Clement Attlee, the British prime minister between 1945 and 1951, served

---

1 Eglin, *Crossing the borders of power*, p. 242–243.

as an example. He had little charisma but brought about enormous and lasting changes in British society because he fully understood his party and his people, and he also focused on what could be achieved rather than on the personal impact he could make. To be an effective leader, humility was a far more important quality than charisma, especially as humility reflected self-confidence and not self-importance.[2] Furthermore, De Beer felt that his business experience would be to the party's advantage:

> As for my speciality, I'm a marketing man, I have good interpersonal skills. I am the first person in a long time to enter the Parliamentary arena from a background of pretty senior business involvement. That will be reflected in what I say and do. We all play to our strengths.[3]

The announcement that De Beer would become party leader provided an immediate boost for the PFP. The feeling was that if a person of his stature was willing to be the leader there was still hope for the Progressives. At the PFP congress on 5 August, De Beer was elected unopposed as leader. In his acceptance speech, he spelt out his vision and priorities for the PFP and vowed to dedicate himself to the party and its liberal-democratic values:

> I am deeply honoured to be the leader of the Progressive Federal Party. I am under no illusions as to the difficulty of the task – but please also understand that I view it as vital to the future of South Africa, and that I will make any effort, run any risk and pay any price to achieve success in building a strong organisation to promote our values ...

He set out as first task to restore the party to full strength and health, and then to "bring together those who by inner conviction belong together" as many South Africans believed in the Progres-

---

2 Fragment of a book De Beer intended to write. (In the possession of Wendy de Beer Furniss.)
3 Bell, "Changing the guard", p. 14.

sive principles of equal human dignity, personal freedom, and the rule of law. This implied the PFP merging with other groups, and he addressed the concerns of the sceptics: "I believe that party loyalty is desirable and valuable. But, in the final instance, the highest value in politics is not loyalty to party, but loyalty to principle." He concluded his speech on a ringing note by quoting Franklin Roosevelt: "We simply must find the courage to give ourselves a chance. We have nothing to fear but fear itself."[4]

De Beer's first challenge as party leader was the lack of administrative support. As he informed Jani Allan of the *Sunday Times* in a wide-ranging interview on 24 July 1988:

> It is going to be difficult to operate without the enormous supportive infrastructure of a big business group. … I sit here with a highly trained secretary, technology, typing, duplicating, telexing … it increases your potential enormously. I'm going to be going down to the Post Office to buy stamps! That's the thing I'm dreading most.

To create a support system, he asked Mienke Bain, who was his personal assistant at AAC between 1980 and 1984 and had become a close friend (she resigned her position with the birth of her daughter), to become his assistant. She created an office in his Saxonwold home in Johannesburg and until his retirement in 1994, assisted him with administration tasks, dealing with his correspondence and typing his speeches – all written by himself. Owing to family obligations, she could not accompany him to Cape Town when parliament was in session. The party provided a parliamentary assistant.[5]

The biggest challenge for De Beer was to rebuild the morale of a shaken and demoralised party. Even if the PFP was not in its battered state, it would still have been a challenging task to be the leader of a small liberal opposition party. As Van Zyl Slabbert explained:

---

4   *Comment*, September 1988, "De Beer: The way ahead".
5   Interview with M. Bain, 30 April 2020.

> How does a liberal-minded party in opposition make progress when the Parliamentary terrain is dominated by an unaccountable executive authority that uses its power to rig the game totally in its favour and is threatened only by a growing party to its right that believes it is not rigging it well enough? ... Out there in the hustings of white politics it is getting tougher for liberals, not easier.[6]

To be the Progressive leader is a thankless and all-consuming task, a true test of character. Being in opposition year after year without any prospect of political power while your warnings fell on deaf ears was a demoralising experience for even the most committed liberal. It could lead to frustration, lethargy, and fractious behaviour, culminating in internal tensions. The newspapers that had lauded your appointment could turn on you in no time. As De Beer indicated in his *Progress* article of 1979, a person needed to be a superman to lead the PFP:

> He must give the impression of being a specially distinguished person, without however the slightest suggestion of elitism or snobbery. Preferably, he should not belong to a minority group of the population. He must know the game of politics, be a skilful strategist, have a sense of timing. He must have the confidence and admiration of the mass media. He must be seen to uphold clearly recognised principles. He must be like a lion when he faces the enemy, yet charming, affectionate, understanding and co-operative among his own people. He must be intellectually outstanding, temperamentally resilient, emotionally stable and physically tough. He must have great organising ability. He should have no great need for sleep, or for holidays; and should be able to tolerate much travel and entertainment. Not least, he must be married to someone who can put up with the extraordinary life he leads and remain loyal, cheerful and supportive.[7]

---

6 F. van Zyl Slabbert, "Rituals and realities", *Leadership*, Vol. 7, 3, 1988, p. 20.
7 Z375, Article for Progress by Dr Z.J. de Beer MP, 21 June 1979. (In the possession of Wendy de Beer Furniss.)

He would get this support from Mona.

Even before De Beer was elected, there already was doubt amongst the younger Progressives that his leadership could be a mistake. As Leon explains in his memoirs:

> De Beer had unfailing civility, great personal charm and warmth; he was possessed of a first-rate intellect and noblesse oblige acquired over 25 years in the Anglo American empire, however, his removal in 1961 from the political front line extinguished much of the fire in his belly. Assuming the leadership of a battered political party at the age of nearly sixty … was probably not the most rejuvenating step the PFP could muster.[8]

The day before the party conference elected De Beer as leader, Slabbert had sent him a telegram, "Jy slaan jou hand aan die ploeg op 'n moeilike akker in ons land. Baie sterkte." (You are putting your hand to a plough in a difficult time in our country. I wish you good luck.)[9] He indeed needed all the luck he could muster as his ideal to "bring together those who belong together" was viewed with suspicion by many in the PFP. For Marius Barnard, MP for Parktown, De Beer was a pleasant and an honourable man, but not a great leader. He was especially unhappy that he would not fight to maintain the identity of the PFP. This feeling was shared by John Malcomess, MP for Port Elizabeth Central, who warned that De Beer did not intend to lead the party, but to bury it.[10] Schwarz also felt that there was no need to form a new party, as it was up to the NDM and the IP to join the Progressives.

The reluctance of many Progressives to merge with the parties of Malan and Worrall was understandable. Until 1987 both had been members of the NP and critics of the PFP. The biggest part of Malan's career was to oppose the liberalism of the PFP. In the 1977

---

8 Leon, *On the contrary*, p.153.
9 University of Stellenbosch (hereafter US), 430.A.39, F. van Zyl Slabbert – Z. de Beer, 4 August 1988.
10 M. Barnard, *Defining moment* (Cape Town, 2011), p.298.

municipal election he defeated Ray Dunlee, the leader of the PRP Randburg council, and in the parliamentary election in November 1977, he won this PFP held seat. In the 1981 election, he retained the Randburg seat with a small majority over the Progressives. It was Progressive support that ensured his victory in the 1987 election.

In the early 1960s Worrall was a PP member, but later joined the NP and became an enthusiastic proponent of its policies. He was a favourite of Vorster, who made him a senator. On Vorster's instructions he fought the Durban North by-election in 1976 with the slogan "Support Vorster, vote Worrall". Although he was defeated, he was elected to parliament in 1977, winning a PFP-held seat in Cape Town before making his move to a high-profile diplomatic career in 1980. Many Progressives could not forgive him his past, and his condemnation of the "Prog image" as too anti-Afrikaner and unpatriotic went down badly.[11]

In an interview with the *Cape Times* (8 August 1988), De Beer attempted to allay Progressive concerns about any merger by emphasising that he had been part of two party mergers in the past, and that what the party stood for was more important than what it was called. Fortunately, one of his strengths was his ability to convey a case as he explained his definition of a brilliant politician to Jani Allan in a *Sunday Times* (24 July 1988) interview:

> A man who can go with very few errors to the root of any question and can describe in language which is easy for ordinary people to understand what it is that he's saying. Brilliance has to do with comprehension and then explanation. Capturing the essence. Being able to understand complex concepts and articulate them so that everybody can understand them.

The local government elections on 26 October was De Beer's first test as leader. The future of the party depended on its performance,

---

11   Suzman, *In no uncertain terms*, p. 275; Swart, *Progressive Odyssey*, pp. 135, 198–200.

especially as the NP was determined to annihilate the Progressives. Eager to secure the votes of Progressives to counter the growing CP, the NP repeated its 1987 tactic of portraying the PFP as unpatriotic, the "Packing for Perth" party. The result was a tough and bitter campaign. De Beer took the offensive by condemning the NP for impoverishing the country with its apartheid policies and again emphasised that a vote for the NP was a vote for creeping poverty.[12]

He addressed a succession of meetings to inform the public of his liberal political record and to lay down the major principles upon which the PFP had been built and for which it must fight, namely equal rights, personal freedom and the rule of law. At a meeting in the Johannesburg City Hall on 17 August to launch the PFP's campaign, he informed those present that the PP's first public meeting after its founding in 1959 was in the same hall. In his short speech at that meeting 29 years earlier, he had raised the same question he put to the conscience of each person present then: "Is the colour of a man's skin the measure of his worth?" He made it clear that the Progressives rejected any discrimination based on race:

> Scrap the Group Areas Act – open all South Africa to free settlement. Let every South African buy or rent, with his own money and a free market, that little piece of South Africa in which he wants to live. Leave it to ordinary preference and economic considerations to determine who lives where. No conflict, no cruelty, no forced removals, no deliberate overcrowding or slums. Personal Freedom, one of the great pillars on which this party is built – and on which South Africa should be built.[13]

Furthermore, he demanded that Mandela be released and the ANC unbanned.

---

12 *Beeld*, 26 October 1988.
13 Z5, Speech at the Johannesburg City Hall, 17 August 1988. (In the possession of Wendy de Beer Furniss.)

Seeing a good result in Johannesburg as crucial for the survival of the party (the election in the city was complicated by the presence of former Progressives standing as independents), De Beer made sure that the Progressive campaign under Leon's leadership was properly funded. He personally campaigned hard in the city. On election day he visited with Tony Leon the polling stations of all the marginal Johannesburg wards. Although the NP secured control of the City Council by winning 26 wards to the PFP's 18, the CP's 4 and three independents, it was a good performance for the Progressives as they had won an additional ward.[14] This softened the blow that the party had lost its majority in Sandton, as it had to share power with independent candidates. In Randburg and Midrand the Progressives did well. In East London the Progressive candidates defeated all their NP opponents, while in Cape Town the party consolidated its position.[15] De Beer was satisfied with the result:

> We in the PFP are pretty happy with the outcome; but our critics are quick to say that there's precious little reason for this happiness, and in a way they have a point. I suppose it's all right to confess now that many Progs had a real fear that the declining trend of the past two or three years would manifest itself once more. In other words, to have stopped the slide as we certainly did was in itself an achievement.[16]

The election result had boosted De Beer's standing in the party. His encouraging and appreciation of party activists endeared him to party members. (Jack Bloom, an unsuccessful candidate in Johannesburg, treasured his consoling note from De Beer so much that he reproduced it in his memoirs.)[17] However, although the results

---

14 Leon, *On the contrary*, pp. 147–148.
15 *Beeld*, 27 and 28 October 1988.
16 Z23, Z.J de Beer, *"Parturiunt montes – nascitur ridiculus mus"* (The mountains are in labour, and silly little mouse is born), Article written for *The Star*, 31 October 1988. (In the possession of Wendy de Beer Furniss.)
17 J. Bloom, *Out of step. Life-story of a politician politics and religion in a world at war* (Johannesburg, 2005), p. 33.

had boosted the PFP's confidence, the party was still in a tough spot. In Johannesburg the Progressives did well in terms of the number of wards it had won, but its overall 33 per cent of the vote in the city was down from its 47 per cent in the 1982 election. The PFP had lost support to the NP, which had pushed its share of the popular vote up from 28 per cent to 42 per cent.[18]

The PFP's growing but still limited success in reaching out to Afrikaners, as well as De Beer's sense that they were ready for the plucking as the NP was increasingly becoming like the old UP with a let-things-develop policy, convinced him of the necessity to reach out to Malan and Worrall to form a broader-based party. Merger talks gained momentum when Louis Luyt, a prominent and controversial businessman and chairman of the Transvaal Rugby Union, became involved. Concerned by the state of the country and the isolation of South African sport, as well as being annoyed by the government's criticism of his own attempts to talk with the ANC, he decided to act as a facilitator to bring about a unified opposition to the left of the NP. He initially placed his hopes on Slabbert to lead such a party, but after he made it clear that he did not want to be involved, he approached De Beer. Following his positive response, Luyt arranged a meeting at his Johannesburg mansion for the three opposition leaders on 18 August. Wimpie de Klerk acted as the facilitator. He was a highly respected former newspaper editor and the older brother of F.W. de Klerk, a senior government minister, and representing the so-called "fourth force", dissident former NP supporters. It was the beginning of a long process of occasionally acrimonious negotiations.[19] On 15 October, the party's Federal Executive mandated De Beer to reach out to the NDM and IP for a possible merger.[20]

The big challenge to bring these three parties together was the

---

18 *The Star*, 27 October 1988.
19 L. Luyt, *Walking proud. The Louis Luyt autobiography* (Cape Town, 2003), pp. 312–314; M. du Preez, *Louis Luyt. Unauthorised* (Cape Town, 2001), pp. 52–54.
20 *Sunday Times*, 20 November 1988.

antagonism between Malan and Worrall after their acrimonious break the previous year. The sniping between the representatives of the NDM and IP hampered the negotiating process. On 8 December, Eglin suggested that the two parties had to meet without PFP representatives to resolve their differences. The IP delegates (Worrall, David Gant and Jannie Momberg) and those of the NDM (Malan, Esther Lategan and Jannie Hofmeyr) went to a Cape Town steakhouse, Nelson's Eye, for a meeting. Assisted by flowing red wine and good steaks the meeting was according to Worrall such a success that Malan called out: "Kêrels, ons kan hierdie lot skaak!" (Chaps, we can hijack this lot!) There and then it was decided to form a new party with the two of them as the leaders and with De Beer as the party chairman.[21]

Malan's recollection of the dinner differs significantly from that of Worrall's. According to him the leadership issue arose after he had raised his concerns that Afrikaners could be alienated if De Beer was the leader of a new party. But personally, he had no desire to lead the party and had serious doubts about continuing with a parliamentary career. In addition, after his experience with the Independent Movement, he was determined not to work with Worrall as joint leader again, nor to serve under him should he be elected leader. It was in any case only the pressure from his fellow NDM MPs that had convinced him to participate in the merger talks. In the end he reluctantly allowed that a letter be written to De Beer offering him the party chairmanship purely to see if anything could develop out of it. But as he did not want De Beer to think that he was conspiring behind his back, he alerted him the next morning about the decision at Nelson's Eye. He advised him that personally he would not be part of this type of leadership and urged him to reject the offer.[22]

Publicly, De Beer took the news calmly, but most Progressives, especially Eglin, were offended, seeing it as an attempt to hijack

---

21 Worrall, *The independent factor*, pp. 189.
22 Interview with W. Malan, 28 March and correspondence 29 March and 10 April 2022.

the party. Salt in Progressive wounds was that the Nelson's Eye decision was leaked to the press before De Beer had received the letter with the offer. An outraged Luyt summarised the attitude of many Progressives when he told Worrall "[t]he President is busy sending the country to hell and you and your fellows behave like children."[23] Some of the tension was diluted on the evening of 13 December when Worrall and Malan went to visit De Beer. This led to a more relaxed meeting between them the next day at Luyt's home. Eglin, Tian van der Merwe, and the provincial leaders of the party – Roger Hulley (Cape), Roger Burrows (Natal) and Douglas Gibson (Transvaal) – accompanied De Beer. The meeting agreed that early in 1989 a new party, the Democratic Party, was to be formed on the principles of a true democracy, the removal of apartheid, the protection of cultural, language and religious rights and with the agreement that parliamentary and extra-parliamentary activities could not be separated. A Steering Committee was formed with De Beer as the coordinator.[24]

However, the leadership of the new party remained unresolved as De Beer made it clear that he viewed any idea of the three of them as co-leaders as unacceptable. He had reason to be concerned as the recent history of the Social Democratic Party (SDP) in Britain served as a warning that collective leaderships did not work. The party was formed in 1981 by the so-called "Gang of Four", namely Roy Jenkins, Bill Rodgers, Shirley Williams and David Owen, all breakaway politicians from the Labour Party, with colossal goodwill and public support. The continuing tensions between the four leaders made it difficult for those setting up a party organisation, as it led to duplication and unclear lines of command. The absence of a single leader hampered the momentum of the party.[25] In a note attached to a clipping "Take me to your leader" (*Financial Mail*, 16 December 1988), De Beer informed Wendy about events:

---

23 Worrall, *The independent factor*, pp. 187–190.
24 *Beeld*, 15 December 1988; *Cape Times*, 14 December 1988.
25 J. Campbell, *Roy Jenkins: A well-rounded life* (London, 2014), p. 570.

Fortunately, Malan and Worrall abandoned their silly 'invented troika' proposal after about twenty four hours. They then proposed that Willem de Klerk lead the new party. Willem declined. So for the time being I am the front runner on a very short lead.[26]

Tos Wentzel, political correspondent of *The Star*, who had inside information on developments, reported on 16 December that De Beer was likely to be the leader as he was the most capable of keeping all the elements in the new party together. Despite the uncertainty surrounding the leadership, the meeting of 14 December was an important breakthrough, and an emotional one for De Beer as it meant the end of the line for the Progressive identity. Eglin went home with him and they spent the evening talking with nostalgia about "the people, events, the trauma, the good days, the bad days, the successes and the disappointments that were all part of our long association with the PFP and the PP before it".[27]

---

26 De Beer – Wendy, 17 December 1988. (In the possession of Wendy de Beer Furniss.)
27 Eglin, *Crossing the borders of power*, p. 251.

CHAPTER 21
Parliament and the Democratic Party
January–September 1989

With the ideal for a new party settled, De Beer had to focus on his return to parliament. To make this possible, Nic Olivier had to step down as the party's only nominated MP.[1] He entered a parliament in which there was sense of urgency to deal with the challenge of a country in the grip of a black revolt and international isolation. Even the most conservative NP MPs knew that reforms had to take place. The presence of coloured and Indian MPs in the tricameral parliament played a crucial role in this. Victims of apartheid invaded the cosy and secure parliamentary club of NP MPs who had no idea of the practical effects of the policies they so enthusiastically supported. Listening during debates to incidents of racial humiliation, of forced removals and detention without trial, played a role in convincing them to accept the need for constitutional reform.

One of these MPs was F.W. de Klerk, who became increasingly convinced of the injustice of apartheid. As he described in his memoirs:

> White cabinet ministers had to report to the coloured and Indian houses on their activities. They were exposed to criticism and indignation over the injustices of apartheid. They were also taken to task over the remaining elements of discrimination. Sometimes government ministers were shouted down and often they had to listen to moving protestations and views they had never before experienced or heard directly. ... All this powerfully influenced my attitudes and philosophy. I came more and more to the conclusion

---

1   *The Argus*, 1 February 1989.

that there could be no solution without the removal of all forms of racial discrimination.[2]

De Beer was sworn in as an MP on 2 February 1989. His arrival was overshadowed by the news of Botha's resignation as leader of the NP. The President, recuperating from a stroke, had decided to separate the presidency from the leadership of the party. After narrowly defeating Barend du Plessis, the Minister of Finance, in a parliamentary caucus vote, De Klerk was elected party leader. De Beer had no high opinion of De Klerk, especially as he was at the forefront of trashing Eglin in the McHenry affair. He also viewed him as too conservative. His first speech as PFP leader was on 6 February during a joint sitting of all three houses in the Great Hall in response to De Klerk's opening address as the Acting President. He expressed his shock on the extent of government corruption, but did not find it surprising as the totalitarian nature of the apartheid system encouraged corruption, especially in the Bantustans. He then proceeded to explain the vision of the soon to be formed Democratic Party:

> Successful modern industrial countries have small governments, not huge ones. They are democracies, not semi-feudal oligarchies. They are deregulated; their people have equal rights and freedoms. They have free markets and free societies, not Group Areas Acts. This is the sort of society that South Africa needs and is not getting. It is racism that corrupts; it is racism that impoverishes. We want the normal democratic society to which I have referred. This party and the shortly to be born Democratic Party are committed to that sort of society.[3]

During the no-confidence debate in the cabinet, he condemned the government for not delivering the growth rate necessary to give the country much needed jobs and prosperity. He also attacked the

---

2 F.W. de Klerk, *The last trek: A new beginning* (London, 1998), pp. 96–97.
3 Debates of parliament, 6 February 1989, Col. 58.

failure to deliver on the promise of a clean administration and the lack of progress in bringing about a new constitution to provide full citizenship for all South Africans. He again pleaded that without democracy there will never be peace in the country:

> As long as the majority of South Africans are denied normal civil rights, there will be no consent of the governed. The government will as now continue to be by force majeure. As long as this goes on there will be no peace, prosperity or real security, only strife, corruption and creeping poverty.[4]

For the rest of the session he continued to hammer on the levels of government corruption and the faltering state of the economy. However, it was difficult to make his mark, as parliament was in the grip of a free-for-all fight between the CP and NP. The CP MPs viewed the slightest deviations from Verwoerdian apartheid as a threat to white survival. The result was bitter and emotional clashes with the NP and the Progressives being reduced to spectators. James Selfe, the PFP's Director of Communications and Marketing, felt that De Beer, after his long absence, was out of his depth:

> It was as if he had returned to Parliament in 1961 after some sort of a time-warp. Zach therefore conducted himself in 1988 as he would have in the 1960s. He used to berate the caucus for its (lack of) "attendance in the House", at a time when what happened in the House was largely irrelevant. He expected reporters still to take down his comments verbatim in short-hand. He spoke both English and Afrikaans with a plummy accent, and, while he might have won some arguments "in the House", failed spectacularly to command the attention of Parliament as a whole, or, more seriously, to build a genuine emotional connection with his electorate. He also misunderstood how completely politics had changed while he had been hibernating.
>
> Still more was to come: he failed to appreciate that, while he

---

4 Debates of parliament, 10 February 1989, Col. 357.

delivered erudite speeches in "the House" on the need to negotiate a common future, talks were already taking place between the NP government and the ANC that would set South Africa on a trajectory that he had no conception of.[5]

Selfe's comments are not without merit but is too harsh. It was a challenge for De Beer to find his parliamentary feet again, but he did find them. He impressed Dr Pieter Mulder, CP MP for Schweizer-Reneke, as a good and measured speaker with arguments based on reason. Although not a streetfighter in the class of Eglin, he could use sarcasm and humour with effect to convey his message.[6] In addition, his focus on parliament did make sense. The main task of the PFP remained the conversion of the NP to abandon apartheid. Trapped between the NP and CP, it was near impossible to command the House, but he was listened to. He also developed into a polished television performer when given the opportunity to spread the Progressive message to the broader public.

Outside parliament the arrangements for the founding of the Democratic Party proceeded although the leadership issue remained unresolved. De Beer's aspirations took a blow on the eve of the Steering Committee meeting of 12 January 1989. The NDM and IP released a press statement "that in the interests of presenting to the electorate a new party with a new personality, it would be inappropriate for any one of the PFP, NDM or IP leaders to head the new party". Avril Howes, the IP's Transvaal regional director, bluntly stated that De Beer was "one man they will fight tooth and nail".

The two smaller parties hoped to convince Wimpie [Willem] de Klerk to accept the leadership.[7] They were determined that the new party should not be seen as the PFP in drag because of its image as anti-Afrikaner, and of being "unpatriotic". Schwarz was outraged by the "holier than thou attitude" by these former NP

---

5 Correspondence with J. Selfe, 4 April 2020.
6 Correspondence with Dr P. Mulder, 17 March 2021.
7 *Business Day*, 11 January 1989.

MPs.[8] Swart viewed it as sickening,[9] while Suzman struggled to control her anger: "... I am a bit fed up with the derogatory way in which the newcomers – all the Johnny-come-latelys who are now anti-Nat – have been referring to the PFP, which after all have been fighting the Nationalists for the past 30 years."[10] For De Beer, who was proud of his Afrikaner identity and whose entire political career was motivated by his desire to save his fellow Afrikaners from themselves, the attitude of NDM and IP must have been hurtful but his response was a laconic: "I note the statement and await developments with interest." [11]

After Wimpie de Klerk once more rejected any suggestion of him being available, the Steering Committee decided that the leader would not be elected at the founding congress but at a later one. At a PFP garden party, De Beer made it clear that he was the right person to lead the party, "... the party will need the very best leader it can get – someone of proven ability, of mental and moral and physical strength, someone of unquestionable loyalty to the principles we are fighting for."[12] In this he was supported by many Progressives, who pushed a "Zach-or-die" strategy.[13] According to Jannie Momberg, a prominent IP member, the stalemate on the leadership led to Luyt offering himself as compromise leader. This led to the three leaders, desperate to keep Luyt out, accepting a triumvirate leadership.[14]

De Beer realised that he had no choice but to agree to this decision:

---

8   Shandler, "Structural crisis and liberalism: A history of the Progressive Federal Party, 1981–1989", p. 224.
9   Suzman, *In no uncertain terms*, p. 275; Swart, *Progressive Odyssey*, pp. 135, 198–200.
10 Wits, Helen Suzman papers, M62.28.1.1, H. Suzman – D. Clark, 7 June 1089.
11 *Cape Times*, 11 January 1989.
12 Z113, De Beer's speech at the Garden Party, 14 January 1989. (In the possession of Wendy de Beer Furniss.)
13 *Sunday Times*, 15 January 1989.
14 Momberg, *From Malan to Mbeki*, p. 45.

> The present situation appears to be that there is no candidate in sight other than the three present leaders. There is a suggestion doing the rounds – and I would expect to hear more of this during the next week or two – about a triumvirate leadership in some form. My own judgement, on purely practical grounds, is that this is simply not viable except as a very temporary expedient.[15]

Fully aware what the sacrifice of the Progressive identity meant to many, he was meticulous in keeping the PFP's Federal Council informed of developments, even getting Luyt to address the Council on the benefit of the merger.[16] On 28 January 1989, the Federal Council mandated him to negotiate a merger on the basis of a joint leadership, but on the condition that a single leader had to be elected in August at the party's first congress.[17] The Steering Committee met on 4 February in Cape Town and after a six-hour meeting decided the party would be launched in Johannesburg on 8 April, and that it would be jointly led by De Beer, Malan and Worrall. De Beer swallowed his pride and in the *Leadership* (March 1989) argued that in a period in which the new party had to consolidate its various elements by laying sound foundations, the triumvirate had an advantage as every member would feel directly represented by his own man. The time to switch to another leadership would be determined by the party in congress.

The merger placed considerable stress on De Beer's longstanding relationship with Suzman. She felt that compared to the rag-tag groupings of Malan and Worrall, the PFP was the only financially solvent one, with significant grassroots support, and that they in effect were hijacking the party. For her De Beer's claim to the leadership of any merger was beyond question. Personally, she felt that he had been very weak in the negotiating process as he should have made the leadership issue non-negotiable and that it was

---

15 Wits, PFP/DP papers, D2, De Beer's letter to senior PFP members, 16 January 1989.
16 Luyt, *Walking proud*, pp. 315–316.
17 *The Argus*, 30 January 1989.

crazy to enter a general election without a single leader. She had no doubt that Worrall, whom she couldn't stand, had his "beady eyes fixed on the job", and the longer a leadership election was delayed the better were his chances.[18]

On 23 February in East London, De Beer, Malan and Worrall spoke together for the first time in front of a big crowd. All three spoke optimistically about the prospects of the new party. For De Beer the party would fight for a path to peace and security through a common patriotism that would put South Africa first – and not blackness or whiteness – and the acceptance of the full human dignity of all South Africans.[19] He confided in Wendy that the few weeks before the new party was formed had been hectic and that he was exhausted, but he also knew that in the year ahead he had to get the party off the ground, get elected leader of the party by September/October, and had to fight in the upcoming election in order to become the official opposition. After the election, he said, he would start looking around for a successor as he ideally wanted to retire by 1993.[20]

Right up to the founding of the new party he had to soothe the doubts of Progressives. In an opinion piece for *Sunday Times* (2 April 1989), he made it clear that the values for which he had always stood would be safe in the new party and that there was a significant number of South Africans interested in the party – who never before contemplated joining the Progressives – and that the public response was more positive than anything he had previously experienced. On 7 April 1989, the PFP disbanded at the Johannesburg College of Education. Despite the expectations of a stormy dissolution, the conference – attended by 500 people – was a nostalgic event. Marius Barnard was the only delegate to vote against the motion. De Beer received strong applause when

---

18 Wits, Helen Suzman papers, Ma 8.2.1, H. Suzman – G. Waddell, 2 June 1989.
19 *Daily Dispatch*, 24 February 1984.
20 De Beer – Wendy, 23 March 1989. (In the possession of Wendy de Beer Furniss.)

he made it clear that the dissolution of the PFP was an end and a beginning:

> Some of us have been involved in the same process for the dignity of the individual for many years. We have done that in whatever party we belonged to and we will continue to do it the Democratic Party ... I ask you to see today as a very important milepost.[21]

That the leadership issue bothered most Progressives was reflected in the enthusiastic support for a motion by Leon that the DP should elect a leader before the coming election. De Beer responded that he was extremely keen for the post and that he would run for that office, but that he would also serve loyally under anyone who was chosen.[22]

The next day at the same venue, the Democratic Party (DP) was launched. The event was attended by 1500 delegates and observers. In an atmosphere of American-style razzmatazz, the blue and yellow rising sun logo of the party, symbolising a new dawn was unveiled. De Beer in his speech set out his ideals for the new party:

> This party has a new vision for the future of the country. Ours is a vision of one nation: a nation of 37 million South Africans; a nation united by common goals, not divided by racist laws; a nation built on the foundation of freedom, whose people take charge of their own lives, seek their own paths to personal progress, and together build a society which enshrines the very best in human experience, namely the dignity of the individual person; a nation governed by all its people, for all its people: in a word, a democratic nation. ... When the Nats say that those who oppose them are ipso facto allies of the ANC, they lie. And when the ANC says that those who oppose apartheid but do not join them are fellow-travellers of the Nats, they lie also.[23]

---

21 *The Star*, 8 April 1989.
22 *The Star*, 8 April 1989.
23 Z105, De Beer's speech at the founding conference of the DP, 8 April 1989. (In the possession of Wendy de Beer Furniss.)

For Leon it was a worthy, but rather flat speech, while the one by Worrall, although light on content, was a barnstorming one that set the hall alight.[24]

The DP had the challenge that 150 days after its founding it would have to face a general election in September. The NP and its supporting press immediately went on attack to portray the party as weak on security, unpatriotic and untrustworthy.[25] On 10 April, De Beer was elected parliamentary leader of the DP. (Malan would be in charge of political contacts, and Worrall of marketing and public relations.) According to Suzman, who had announced her retirement from parliament, a daunting task awaited him as the newly formed DP parliamentary caucus was deeply divided:

> I'm rather sorry I won't be in the post-election caucus to see how he [Tony Leon] and Harry the Black [Schwarz] get on together. Already there is going to be considerable friction since Harry hates van Eck, and Peter Soal can't stand Peter Gastrow, and so on and so forth.[26]

On the 10th during the budget debate, De Beer delivered his first speech as a DP MP setting out the vision of the new party:

> ... of one nation, a nation of 37 million South Africans, a nation united by common goals, a nation built on the reality of freedom, whose people take charge of their lives, seek their own paths to personal progress and together build a society which honours ... dignity of the individual, a nation governed by all its people, for all its people: in a word, a democratic nation. We shall work creatively for these values and we shall fight against all parties and groups which oppose them. Racial discrimination is a denial of all these aims. So is the employment of violence as a political weapon. Therefore we reject both the right and the left.[27]

---

24 Leon, *On the contrary*, p. 155.
25 *Beeld*, 10 and 11 April 1989.
26 Wits, Suzman papers, Ma 8.2.1, Suzman – Waddell, 2 June 1989.
27 *The Argus*, 11 April 1989.

In the debate on the State President's vote, he set out the DP's goals on how to create a democratic society, namely by sharing political power with a common voters' roll, scrapping the Group Areas Act and the Reservation of Separate Amenities Act, and opening educational institutions for all.[28]

> We offer instead to South Africa the vision of a free, democratic nation based on justice ... a country where every person's task is to love his or her own life, to produce, to consume, to progress and to build an ever greater, more open society. All it takes is the courage to stop thinking in racist terms, and to think instead in democratic ones.[29]

In this period, as Worrall points out in his memoirs, De Beer used his position as parliamentary leader to stamp a clear liberal-democratic identity on the party.[30]

Outside parliament he started addressing a succession of public meetings with Malan and Worrall to convey the DP's message and to raise funds. They were met with vast and enthusiastic crowds, more than 2000 in the Cape Town City Hall (11 April), 1400 in the Feather Market Hall in Port Elizabeth (25 April), and 1800 people in the Durban City Hall (2 May).[31] To Wendy he described his fellow leaders as "formidable platform performers".[32]

Photographs of the three leaders at these meetings show them smiling happily together, but there were some tensions. De Beer felt that while his two fellow leaders got all the publicity, he as the parliamentary leader was doing all the hard work. Malan, he complained to Wendy, was hardly ever in parliament.[33] According

---

28 Debates of parliament, 13 April 1989, Col. 5301.
29 Debates of parliament, 17 April 1989, Col. 5489.
30 Worrall, *The independent factor*, p. 197.
31 *Cape Times*, 12 April 1989; *Eastern Province Herald*, 26 April 1989; *The Daily News*, 3 May 1989.
32 De Beer – Wendy, 22 June 1989. (In the possession of Wendy de Beer Furniss.)
33 De Beer – Wendy, 18 May 1989. (In the possession of Wendy de Beer Furniss.)

to Gant, Malan, who focused on extra-parliamentary associations, was nervous that a too close a relationship with De Beer with his Progressive and AAC background might harm his efforts.[34] However, Malan – although conceding there were some tension between him and Worrall – is adamant that he had no problems with De Beer as he viewed him as a decent person with integrity, and that it was easy to get on with him. His only criticism was that De Beer lacked political passion with his "end of history" approach to the values of the individual and the financial market and his notion that the battle of ideas was over and people around the world would embrace liberalism. Privately he felt that De Beer did not really belong in politics as he was more of a corporate manager who was only in a leadership position because the PFP's financial sponsors wanted him to keep the parliamentary caucus together. But ultimately, he got on well with De Beer and felt that with his own agenda of negotiation between the "system and struggle", he could reckon on his integrity.[35]

De Beer's relationship with Worrall was more complicated. It started back in the early 1950s when Worrall as a UCT student was the leader of the UP youth in the Cape Peninsula and De Beer was the newly elected MP for Maitland. Although De Beer on occasion picked him up at his home on a farm near Durbanville to accompany him to Worcester where he was to address a UP meeting, their relationship was a formal one. While his relationship with De Beer remained distant, the young Worrall developed a lifelong friendship with Eglin. De Beer, according to Leon, did not like Worrall as he was influenced by old Progressives who had a low opinion of him.[36] This could have been a factor as Suzman, for example, could not forget or forgive that he had joined the NP in the 1970s. However, as De Beer's philosophy was that if you have nothing nice to say, it's better not to say anything at all, he kept his

---

34 Correspondence with D. Gant, 5 April 2020.
35 Interview with W. Malan, 28 March and correspondence 29 March and 10 April 2002.
36 Interview with T. Leon, 3 April 2020.

true feelings to himself.[37] He had a good working relationship with Worrall, but they would not become friends. Whereas Eglin and his wife had regular social dinners with the Worralls, De Beer only did so once and then in his capacity as a party representative.[38]

A serious source of strain amongst the three leaders was the growing unhappiness amongst old Progressives with NDM and IP members who attempted to be nominated as DP candidates for PFP-held parliamentary seats. Only three of the sitting DP MPs in Cape Town did not face a nomination contest.[39] Selfe felt that there was an orchestrated attempt by Malan and Worrall to unseat former Progressives in their Cape Peninsula seats.[40] As a result, many Progressives felt that those who had kept the liberal opinion alive during the dark years of the 1960s and 1970s were being pushed aside by the latter day converts. Esther Lategan's unsuccessful challenge of Ken Andrews for the Gardens nomination – a seat he had won from the NP in 1981 – defeating the cabinet minister Dawie de Villiers, and narrowly won against a fierce onslaught in 1987, created a fair amount of bitterness amongst former Progressives.[41] This bitterness was reflected in Swart's refusal to support Worrall when he contested the nomination for Berea, a seat Swart had turned into a Progressive fortress. Worrall for his part noted that he had no help from De Beer in Berea. But De Beer would have invited trouble by involving himself in the contest as it could only have deepened the latent divisions in the party. Worrall eventually secured the Berea nomination with a narrow majority.[42]

These events placed enormous strain on De Beer, and he found it exhausting. To Wendy he confided that "leadership level life is one long muddle" as he neither trusted nor had any confidence in his

---

37 Interview with M. Bain, 30 April 2020.
38 Correspondence with Dr D. Worrall, 22 and 27 March 2022.
39 *Cape Times*, 13 June 1989.
40 Correspondence with J. Selfe, 29 May 2020.
41 D. Welsh, "The Democratic Party. Developing a political culture", *Indicator South Africa*, Vol. 6, No. 3, Winter 1989, p. 16.
42 Worrall, *The Independent factor*, p. 198: Correspondence with Dr D. Worrall, 22 March 2022.

co-leaders, and that his life consisted of combat and intrigue. He ended his letter jokingly in an Afrikaans term traditionally used by the NP: "Wat 'n mens alles vir volk en vaderland opoffer!" (What one will sacrifice for the people and the fatherland!)[43]

These internal divisions and tensions bolstered his determination to contest the election with himself as the leader. The 1987 British parliamentary election had shown that collective leaderships can do more harm than good. The electoral alliance of the Liberal Party and Social Democratic Party was fatally handicapped by the dual leadership of David Owen and David Steel. What could happen to a party led by three leaders? De Beer approached Luyt at his Ballito vacation home in Natal to secure his support for him to be the leader. The rugby supremo refused to become involved as he felt that the leader would not be picked but would emerge.[44] This left him determined to work his way around pettiness and problems to get the party running.[45] His diplomacy and tact ensured the troika's efficiency and party unity.

---

43 De Beer – Wendy, 22 June 1989. (In the possession of Wendy de Beer Furniss.)
44 Luyt, *Walking proud*, p. 318.
45 Interview with M. Bain, 30 April 2020.

CHAPTER 22

The shattering of the political mould
September 1989–February 1990

By avoiding any public fallouts, the DP maintained its political momentum. In early June 1989, the party scored a stunning victory in a Johannesburg City Council by-election in the Linden ward. The ward with an electorate evenly divided between Afrikaners and English speakers had been won by the NP in October 1988 with the PFP securing only 36,74 per cent of the vote. Eight months later the DP polled 56,86 per cent.[1] On 18 June, De Beer boosted the momentum of the party with an impressive SABC television interview. In an effort to portray the Democrats as soft on security, the interviewer was provocative and aggressive. De Beer handled the situation with great aplomb and made it clear that the party, if in power, would unban the ANC and SACP and would release Mandela unconditionally to participate in negotiations for a new constitution. He was so impressive that the *Cape Times* (20 June 1989) dedicated a leading article, "Dr De Beer scores", praising his appearance, while *The Star* (20 June 1989) published a cartoon of him as David slaying the SABC Goliath.

The strong public support for the DP and the enthusiasm among party members pleasantly surprised De Beer. In his old constituency of Maitland there were six aspirant Democratic candidates even though the NP had a 3500-vote majority in the 1987 election.[2] The DP launched its election campaign on 22 July with 98 candidates. De Beer predicted that with the high level of inflation, taxation and unemployment, the economy would be a major issue in the

---

1 *Business Day*, 9 June 1989.
2 De Beer – Wendy, 22 June 1989. (In the possession of Wendy de Beer Furniss.)

election, and that the medicine for the country's economic sickness was political and not economic.³ On 24 July, he was nominated as the DP candidate in Parktown. The seat was available as Barnard had decided to retire. Parktown, although contested by the NP, was such a safe Democrat seat that he could focus on the party's national campaign. The Botha government was on the back foot with the escalating violence and the government's inability to cope with a stagnated economy, while the corruption and greed of leading NP politicians fuelled anger and frustration amongst voters. Botha's image as a finger-wagging bully also alienated a growing number of voters. Surveys showed that the NP would not achieve an outright majority and that there could be a hung parliament. To gain traction, the NP started a poster campaign of a benevolently smiling De Klerk as a "man of action". De Beer was dismissive, proclaiming that although De Klerk had good manners, he was not the courageous reformer the country needed so badly.

> I will say that FW de Klerk is one of the most cautious politicians I have ever encountered. His instinct is always to try to please everybody and to avoid commitment to any irretrievable action.⁴

On 14 August, the NP campaign received a boost when the friction between a cantankerous and ill Botha and his cabinet culminated in his resignation and replacement by De Klerk as President. In contrast to the abrasive and bullying of the "big crocodile", De Klerk immediately portrayed himself as a man of the future, a competent and amiable administrator. His foray into Africa to meet Mobutu Sese Seko of Zaire and Kenneth Kaunda of Zambia provided him with the opportunity to act presidentially, and to make potential DP voters think twice about where they would put their cross on the ballot paper.

Realising that it was near impossible to win back hard-core CP supporters, the NP turned its focus on the DP to prevent en-

---

3   *Sunday Times*, 23 July 1989.
4   *The Star*, 24 July 1989.

lightened and floating voters from supporting the party. De Klerk portrayed the NP as the champion of moderate and sensible reform compared to the radicalism of the DP, who intended to hand over the country to a black majority government.[5] NP propaganda painted the DP as a puppet of the UDF and Cosatu, the alleged internal wing of ANC/SACP alliance. In a debate organised by the Johannesburg Junior Chamber of Commerce and Industry, André Fourie, NP MP for Turffontein, claimed that "A vote for the DP is inevitably a vote for an SACP/ANC government". When those present burst out laughing, an irate Fourie told Mona de Beer to "go and laugh outside". Her husband calmly replied that the DP was prepared to consult with the ANC, but that it could not co-opt with a liberation movement as it did not share the same political beliefs.[6]

Ironically, while the NP attempted to portray Democrats as the useful idiots of the liberation movement, the perception amongst black activists was that the DP by participating in parliamentary politics was collaborating with the apartheid regime. When De Beer was scheduled on 31 July to debate Slabbert and Steven Friedman of the Institute of Race Relations at Wits on the relevance of parliamentary politics, protesting black students prevented the meeting from taking place as he was seen as part of a racist system.[7]

This did not prevent the NP from placing an advertisement in the press that depicted the three DP leaders as blind mice being manipulated by the anti-apartheid movement.[8] De Beer responded that this attack was just another version of the NP's tried and tested "swart gevaar" (black peril) tactics. He said that if the DP was a puppet of the anti-apartheid movement, former SADF senior officers, namely General Bob Rogers, former chief of the SAAF, as well as General Wally Black, former Chief General Operations, would not be DP candidates.[9] This did not prevent Gerrit Viljoen, Minister of

---

5   *Die Burger*, 4 and 6 September 1989.
6   *The Star*, 9 August 1989.
7   *Business Day*, 1 August 1989.
8   *Sunday Times*, 13 August 1989.
9   *Sunday Times*, 27 August 1989.

Constitutional Development, in a television debate with De Beer to condemn the DP for undertaking to unban the ANC and SACP, and to release Mandela. For him the unconditional negotiations with these groups without the renunciation of their methods of resistance would render negotiations meaningless. De Beer countered that by excluding organisations that represented a large segment of the population from negotiations would make such a process meaningless, because the outcome would be rejected by the majority of the population.[10] His calm and analytical approach did much to neutralise the NP's attack that to negotiate with the ANC would be treason.

Despite De Beer's concerns, the troika functioned well in the campaign. Malan had a standing amongst "verligte" Afrikaners, while the charismatic Worrall was a brilliant orator who attracted vast crowds to his public meetings. In his final meetings he was able to attract 1500 and 1200 supporters respectively compared to the 700 for De Klerk's final meeting.[11] De Beer had a good campaign. He crisscrossed the country to address public meetings, but it was his cool and polished television appearances combined with his unflappability and gravitas that did much to enhance the DP's campaign. On 31 August he was impressive in a televised debate with Barend du Plessis. He pointed out to viewers that apartheid was the root cause of high government expenditure, poor productivity in industry and the outflow of capital; all factors harming the economy. The only solution was to bring all South Africans together into one harmonious nation, with a just government. Du Plessis had no choice but to agree that this was the only solution for the country's economic ills.[12]

The election campaign was a last nostalgic electoral get-together for Suzman, Eglin and De Beer. On 31 August, they addressed 400 people at a public meeting at the Greenside Primary School in Johannesburg. De Beer praised Suzman's courage and honesty.

---

10   *The Star*, 23 August 1989.
11   Worrall, *The independent factor*, p. 200.
12   *The Star*, 1 September 1989.

Many, many times I and others have been tempted to patch over cracks, to hide issues behind clever words, to seek short-term formulae to tide us over. Many, many times we have been challenged by Helen's clear and steady visions. We have been forced back to face reality, and to do what is right and accept the consequences. For this among many things, I am deeply grateful.[13]

On the eve of the election on 6 September, the Democrats had momentum as it had encouraged a feeling amongst a growing number of voters that significant constitutional reform had become a necessity. Democrats expected to win between 28 and 35 seats. De Beer predicted a total of 30 seats. He entered polling day – a bitterly cold one – in a confident mood. This confidence was justified as the party gained 12 seats from the NP, securing a total of 33. (Maitland was not one of them.) The NP won 93 seats. The DP furthermore increased its majorities in the seats the PFP had won in 1987. In Parktown, De Beer won comfortably with 8864 votes to the 2800 of B. Ginsberg, his NP opponent. In terms of the popular vote, the Democrats secured close to 20 per cent compared to the 14 per cent of the PFP in 1987. The party had made significant inroads into Afrikaner middle-class urban constituencies, winning in North Rand, a constituency with a majority of Afrikaner voters. For De Klerk it was a warning that the "verligte" vote, formerly a solid base of support for the NP, could no longer be taken for granted. However, the DP failed in its mission to become the official opposition as the CP won 39 seats, attracting 31,45 per cent of the vote with its support mainly amongst farmers in the Free State and Transvaal and working-class Afrikaners on the Witwatersrand and in Pretoria.

Publicly De Beer proclaimed that a significant portion of the electorate had swung towards the perception of South Africa as one nation and that there was enough encouragement for the party to fight onwards to the day when it will become the government

---

13 *The Star*, 1 September 1989; Greenside speech, 31 August 1989. (In the possession of Wendy de Beer Furniss.)

of South Africa.[14] Privately in a letter to Relly, he took a more sober note by pointing out that despite the enthusiasm generated by the so-called "fourth-force" nothing had come of the dramatic breakthrough among Afrikaners. He summarised the success of the DP in the following terms: "It is difficult not to conclude that, when it comes to voting support, the DP is only a warmed-over PFP – but a greatly reinvigorated one."[15]

De Beer was surprised when De Klerk in his comment on the election noted that when the votes cast for the Democrats were added to those earned by the NP, it was close to a seventy-per-cent support for orderly reform and renewal amongst white voters,[16] He expressed his hope that De Klerk was right, but made it clear that he did not share the President's confidence in the desire of NP voters to accept constitutional reform.[17]

On 11 September 1989, De Beer was elected as the DP parliamentary leader by the caucus for the period leading up to the party's conference in Durban on 7 October.[18] This did not signify support for his leadership of the party. An opinion poll amongst Democrats showed that only 33 per cent wanted him as leader, compared to the 48 per cent that backed Worrall. Malan was lagging behind by 19 per cent.[19] In addition, there was a feeling that the troika was a success and had to continue.[20] This perception was the strongest amongst Democrats who had not been previously aligned with the Progressives. This group feared that if De Beer should become the leader, it could damage the image of the party amongst Afrikaners. De Beer was fully aware of this sentiment as he informed Relly: "There will no doubt be a determined attempt at the Congress to

---

14 *The Star*, 7 September 1989.
15 De Beer – Relly, 9 September 1989. (In the possession of Wendy de Beer Furniss.)
16 A. Ries, E. Dommisse, *Leierstryd* (Cape Town, 1990), p. 257.
17 Z40, Z. de Beer, The 1989 election and the next five years, 28 September 1989. (In the possession of Wendy de Beer Furniss.)
18 *Beeld*, 12 September 1989.
19 *The Star*, 2 September 1989.
20 *Sunday Times*, 10 September 1989.

cling to the troika so as to avoid a former PFP leader – but we shall see."[21]

To counter such a step, he set out to convince party members that the troika could not be a permanent arrangement and that the time had come to elect a single leader. Also, that every other party anywhere in the world find it desirable to have a single leader. The multiplicity of decisions to be taken on a day-to-day basis by the troika, combined with logistical problems, were simply too great to continue. He made it clear that he would serve under anyone whom the congress elected. Malan had no concern about serving under De Beer as he was privately adamant that he would not serve under Worrall,[22] who could win a possible leadership contest. Publicly he opposed a single leader as it was still necessary for the DP to develop its own identity separate from the identities from which it had grown. A single leader would stamp his own personality on the party to the possible detriment of the growth of the party. Worrall was also adamant that it was in the party's interest to retain the troika.[23]

Jannie Momberg, the newly elected MP for Simon's Town, a former NP and IP member and an outstanding organiser, led the campaign to maintain the troika. Crucially Tian van der Merwe, the popular MP for Green Point, joined him. As a PFP candidate in the 1987 election, he had hung on to his seat with a 39-vote majority. Under DP colours, his majority increased to 1823 votes. To avoid any possible hint that the party was the PFP in new colours, he fully supported the troika.[24] Leon, the newly elected rumbustious MP for Houghton, led the campaign for a single leader who should be able to make the snap decisions which politics require on a daily basis and could accept the responsibilities of office.[25] He was supported by many old Progressives.

---

21 De Beer – Relly, 9 September 1989. (In the possession of Wendy de Beer Furniss.)
22 Correspondence with Wynand Malan, 10 April 2022.
23 *Sunday Tribune*, 24 September 1989.
24 Momberg, *From Malan to Mbeki*, p. 62.
25 *Business Day*, 29 September 1989.

It was a deeply divided group of delegates that arrived at the Royal Hotel in Durban on 7 October. De Beer in his conference address warned the delegates not to overestimate the party's achievement in the election as no massive breakthrough was made into the ranks of its political opponents. The election result was more a case of consolidating natural supporters. But he predicted that the party's growth would be more thrilling than the phase that had just ended.[26] He then called for a single leader, as the failure to dispense of the troika would be a sign that unification was incomplete. The subsequent debate on the leadership exposed old party alliances as former Progressives pressed for a single leader. Leon, in supporting the motion, delivered what he conceded in his memoirs was a reckless and ill-judged speech that was unhelpful to De Beer.[27] He was so barracked that Schwarz had to intervene to remonstrate with the delegates. Leon provocatively responded: "I have been heckled by Nats before." Van der Merwe argued that a collective leadership was best suited to South Africa's needs and provided the party with much more appeal.

After a two-and-a-half-hour debate, the 543 delegates voted to maintain the troika with 330 votes to 213. Malan and Worrall expressed their happiness with the vote. For Worrall it demonstrated that the old identities had fallen away, while for Malan the decision transcended internal divides, that the concept of a white knight leading the party was out for a long time to come. De Beer tactfully responded that he regretted the decision, but that it was more important to serve the party in whatever way was best.[28] However, former Progressives who felt that they have been shoved aside by former NP supporters who were only interested in the PFP's money, organisation and safe parliamentary seats, made no effort to hide their anger and frustration.[29] Schwarz was outraged and

---

26 De Beer's opening address to the conference, 7 October 1989. (In the possession of Wendy de Beer Furniss.)
27 Leon, *On the contrary*, p. 176.
28 *Sunday Tribune*, 8 October 1989.
29 *Sunday Tribune*, 8 October 1989.

in the *Star* of 15 October 1989 made it clear that he was offended that repenting former NP supporters who had helped to make apartheid laws, are telling him after decades of opposing apartheid to be ashamed of his old Prog identity. On 25 November at the DP's National Council meeting in Pretoria, leadership responsibilities were divided amongst the three leaders. De Beer would be the parliamentary leader, Malan was responsible for extra-parliamentary consultations, and Worrall for the expansion and development of the party.[30]

Despite the leadership differences, De Beer approached the new parliamentary session in 1990 with political momentum, determined to put pressure on the NP to bring about significant reforms. As he informed Relly in September of 1989, he did not expect any drastic reforms from the government: "Given that De Klerk is by nature a very cautious person, I think business would be well advised to assume that there will be very little early change in the South African situation."[31]

He was unaware that De Klerk had realised that white domination had become untenable and morally indefensible.[32] The country was in the grip of a low-level civil war with internal unrest, strikes, the guerrilla warfare of the ANC, and the rise of right-wing violence. South Africa was turning into a wasteland. In addition, sanctions and disinvestment were paralysing the economy. It was obvious that to continue with apartheid would be catastrophic. The implosion of communism and the decline of the Soviet Union provided an opportunity to negotiate a peaceful settlement with the anti-apartheid liberation movements.

De Beer went to Cape Town in January 1990 to condemn apartheid and to propagate liberal principles. This planned approach was overturned when at 09:30 on 2 February he was handed a

---

30 Wits, PFP/DP papers, Ab2.2.11, National Council Minutes, 25–26 November 1989.
31 De Beer – Relly, 9 September 1989. (In the possession of Wendy de Beer Furniss.)
32 *Beeld*, 14 February 2015.

copy of De Klerk's presidential opening address he would deliver at 11:00. De Klerk's dramatic speech terminated the outlawing of the ANC, PAC and South African Communist Party (SACP), and led to the release of political prisoners, including the unconditional release of Nelson Mandela.

As the President neared the end of his speech, De Beer turned to Eglin sitting next to him and said: "I have a feeling that the things we have fought for are actually going to happen." Eglin responded: "Yes, from here onward the process takes over."[33] In retirement, De Beer would proclaim the election result of 1989 as the highlight of his political career as the Democrats had helped to push De Klerk into his reforms.[34]

David Welsh, in his study on the rise and fall of apartheid, concurs because the DP and its Progressive predecessors with their sustained criticism of apartheid had an impact on a growing number of whites encouraging them to embrace reform.[35] For Eglin the DP had pushed De Klerk over his own Rubicon as he viewed the election result as a mandate for a new leader with fresh ideas to establish a common system for black and white.[36] De Klerk had opened his address with the statement that "[t]he general election of 6 September 1989 placed our country irrevocably on the road to drastic change."[37]

De Beer's faith in parliamentary politics had been vindicated. But he had to face the challenge that De Klerk's speech had shattered the mould of South African politics. In the words of Leon: "De Klerk had metaphorically detonated a political explosion of such thermonuclear intensity that its after effects are still being

---

33 Z152, De Beer's report back meeting to the Parktown constituency, 8 August 1990. (In the possession of Wendy de Beer Furniss.)
34 The O'Malley Archives, Nelson Mandela Centre of Memory, O'Malley's interview with Zach de Beer, 8 November 1994, https://omalley.nelson mandela.org/omalley/index (accessed 28 August 2019).
35 Welsh, *The rise and fall of apartheid*, p. 386.
36 H. Giliomee, *The last Afrikaner leaders: A supreme test of power* (Johannesburg, 2012), p. 297.
37 Leon, *Opposite Mandela*, p. 18.

felt today, thirty years later."³⁸ With De Klerk's speech the DP had lost the reason for its existence as South African politics had become a bipolar struggle between the NP and the ANC. Leaving the chamber, Pieter Mulder told a DP MP that his party was in deep trouble as "F.W. het jul beleid gesteel" (F.W. has stolen your policy).³⁹ On the afternoon of 2 February 1990, De Beer sent a note to the stunned DP MPs that they should not panic about De Klerk's speech as there was still work for the party to do and they had to hold the President to his commitments.⁴⁰

---

38 T. Leon, *Future tense. Reflections on my troubled land* (Johannesburg, 2021), p. 78.
39 Correspondence with Dr P. Mulder, 17 March 2021.
40 Correspondence with T. Leon, 8 March 2021.

CHAPTER 23
A new political mould
February–August 1990

After 2 February it was an odd experience for De Beer not to attack the NP: "Some of us have been fighting the Nats consistently for 40 years, and it would be foolish to deny that the habit dies hard."[1] However, in his speech to parliament on 5 February, he rose to the occasion by being adamant that the DP was not in mourning because the NP had taken over its policies. He made it clear that he found it a delicious coincidence that the speaker before him was Gerrit Viljoen, who a few months earlier had lambasted him for urging the unbanning of the ANC and SACP. He congratulated De Klerk on his speech which had created more hope for South Africa than had been evident for 40 years.

> Since I first came to parliament 37 years ago I have witnessed the rise, the development and the growth of apartheid and then its failure and its decline. I hope I have now seen the beginning of the end.[2]

He rejected as ridiculous the notion that the DP had become irrelevant:

> When one has fought for one's values and one's policy for years and others then become converted to them, how on earth does that make one irrelevant?[3]

And he said that as it would be difficult to arrive at a non-racial

---

1 Z176, De Beer's speech at a Parktown fundraising function for the DP, 12 May 1990. (In the possession of Wendy de Beer Furniss.)
2 Debates of parliament, 5 February 1990, Col. 71.
3 Debates of parliament, 5 February 1990, Col. 71.

democracy, the Democrats would cooperate with anyone who moved in that direction. But emphasised that the party would not sacrifice its independence as its most important work was still to come.[4] It was a speech that rose to the occasion. Momberg, no admirer of De Beer, thought it was a particularly good one.[5] An opinion shared by Freek Swart, the parliamentary correspondent of *Die Burger*.

When the CP introduced a motion of no-confidence in the cabinet, De Beer gave the DP's full support for change and reform as De Klerk had stopped the rush down the Gadarene slope of apartheid. However, his support was on condition that the NP brought about significant reform and scrap all apartheid legislation.[6] In an article, under the headline "The racism battle must still be won" in the *Sunday Times* (11 February 1990), he emphasised that the DP would have to work hard to keep pressure on the NP to maintain the momentum of reform, and to contribute to the negotiating process between the NP and the ANC:

> The Democratic Party is about to play the most important role of its life in contributing to the creation of a single, just and therefore harmonious nation. Our clear future vision based upon our own history equips us for the task. We look forward to it intensely.

However, he could not counter the growing doubts amongst Democrats about the party's role, relevance, and future. *Die Burger*, which had resented the Democrats' morally superior attitude to the NP, gloated in the party's predicament, proclaiming that it had become irrelevant.[7] Doubts about the future of the party were promptly reflected in its finances. After the election, the party was approximately R1 million in debt to its bank, while it needed R1,75 million a year to function. The party had to urgently find

---

4 Debates of parliament, 5 February 1990, Col. 72.
5 Momberg, *From Malan to Mbeki*, p. 66.
6 Debates of parliament, 9 February 1990, Col. 387–391.
7 *Die Burger*, 9 February 1990.

R3 million to keep going.⁸ In February the "Democratic Future Fund" – instituted in 1989 to raise R20 million over three years with debit orders to build the DP into a political force – had to be suspended as the party needed this money to pay off election bills and to keep its offices running.⁹ This led to intense discussions on the so-called "Gastrow options".

Peter Gastrow, the DP MP for Durban Central, had set out four possible directions for the party to follow:

- Closer move to the government in a supportive role.
- Closer move to the ANC.
- A formal alliance with the ANC.
- An independent identity in the traditional opposition role.¹⁰

Personally, Gastrow made no secret of the fact that he preferred closer ties with the ANC:

> If the DP, with its present support base, were to join the ANC to assist in making democracy and a future economy work, it could make a contribution way out of proportion to the numbers that it brings into the ANC.¹¹

The growing doubts about the future of the DP was fuelled by the seemingly unstoppable growing level of political violence in the country. Fatalities were caused by black people who continued to protest against white minority rule, but also because of the rivalry between the ANC and Inkatha. In 1990, the movement became a political party, the Inkatha Freedom Party (IFP). Behind the scenes, the NP was secretly funding the IFP and provided covert military training for Inkatha recruits. Although the IFP was open to all, it was

---

8   Wits, PFP/DP papers, National Council minutes, 25 and 26 November 1989.
9   *Frontline*, Vol. 8, No. 6, February 1990, p. 3.
10 *Sunday Times*, 18 February 1990.
11 P. Gastrow, "Towards a convergence of democrats?", *Die Suid-Afrikaan*, April 1990, p. 17.

used by Buthelezi to mobilise ethnic nationalism. This intensified the conflict with ANC supporters, especially on the Witwatersrand. In 1990, a total of 3699 deaths in political violence were recorded, an increase of 163 per cent from the previous year. To show his concern about the violence, De Beer attended on 10 November the funeral of the 13-year-old Wandisile Nomaxhayl, who had been killed in Khayelitsha.[12] Many felt that with the NP, ANC and Inkatha as the main political players vying for political power, and with the CP and AWB attempting to maintain the apartheid state (there were 52 acts of right-wing violence, including murder),[13] the DP had become irrelevant.

On 7 March 1990, Strauss died of a heart attack while on a visit to Cape Town. Over the years De Beer had maintained contact with him. Shortly before, in December 1989 and January 1990, he had taken Wendy and her family, including Strauss, on a vacation to the Pilanesberg Game Reserve.[14] As a forgotten figure, his death, apart from short and superficial newspaper announcements, went unnoticed. And yet, Strauss's philosophy that a public figure had no right to place personal happiness before duty and responsibility, or to indulge in self-pity,[15] had a profound effect on De Beer. These were character traits that he needed after 6 June when the DP suffered a crushing defeat in the Umlazi by-election.

In September 1989, the NP had won this lower-middle-class seat of which 80 per cent of the voters were English speaking, with 6149 votes against the DP's 3314 votes, and the CP's 2429. After 2 February, there was no possibility that the DP could erase this majority. However, Worrall felt that the Democrats had to contest the seat to bolster the perception that it was the party of the future, promoting a democratic culture as the NP with its apartheid policies lacked the credibility to do so.[16] De Beer had his doubts

---

12 *Sunday Times*, 11 November 1990.
13 Welsh, *The rise and fall of apartheid*, pp. 388, 397.
14 Correspondence with Wendy de Beer Furniss, 28 April 2020.
15 P. Meiring, *10 politieke leiers. Manne na aan ons premiers* (Cape Town, 1973), p. 180.
16 *Sunday Times*, 3 June 1990.

because the party lacked the funds to fight the seat,[17] but in the end he went along with Worrall.[18] The Durban newspapers, the *Daily News* (28 March) and *The Natal Mercury* (25 April), fearing that the CP could win the seat if the reformist vote was divided, urged the Democrats to withdraw. The result was a devastating blow for the DP as it's support was reduced to 982 votes compared to the 5762 of the NP, and the 5215 of the CP. As had been warned by the local press, the DP had nearly delivered Umlazi to the CP.[19]

In parliament the NP took great pleasure in the DP's poor performance and the knock to Worrall's reputation. J.C. Matthee, NP MP for Durban Point, read a private letter from Rory Riordan, Director of the Human Rights Trust, to Worrall. (The letter was erroneously forwarded to an NP fax machine in parliament.) Riordan warned that to participate in the by-election would be a disaster for the DP and for the prospects of Worrall's leadership and that, whatever the result, any DP involvement in Umlazi could only cause considerable loss of donor and voter support for the Democrats. Worrall, according to Matthee, had been on an ego trip since his return from London, and that at Umlazi it had smashed into the ground like a meteor.[20] Worrall, outraged by the way his private mail was used, angrily responded that it was not his decision alone to contest Umlazi – it was taken after a healthy debate in the party.[21] Worrall had reason to be angry about being scapegoated as the by-election defeat had harmed his reputation. For "Dawie", always a shrewd observer of parliamentary ups and downs, the "Worrall factor" had taken a terminal blow.[22] It was indeed the case as he increasingly disengaged from politics, focusing more on his Omega company.[23]

---

17 Wits, PFP/DP papers, Ab2.2.11, Minutes of the National Council, 25–26 November 1989.
18 Interview with T. Leon, 3 April 2020.
19 *The Natal Mercury*, 7 June 1990.
20 Debates of parliament, 14 June 1990, Col. 11858–11859.
21 Debates of parliament, 15 June 1990, Col. 11969–11999.
22 *Beeld*, 16 June 1990.
23 Correspondence with D. Worrall, 27 March 2022.

After Umlazi the consensus amongst political observers was that there was no place for the Democrats in the political system.[24] De Beer did his utmost to rally the party by emphasising that the pro-reform vote of the NP and DP had clearly exceeded the anti-reform vote of the CP.[25]

During the Appropriation vote for the President, he firmly linked the DP to the reform movement by defending De Klerk against the CP's accusation that he exceeded the mandate he had received from the electorate in 1989. He conceded that the accusation had merit, but that the President's reforms came closer to meeting the requirements of all the people of South Africa as distinct to the requirements of a privileged minority. For the relatively minor offence of exceeding his election mandate, De Klerk could be easily forgiven. The DP voted with the NP.[26]

The battered DP received some solace when on 14 June the party against all expectations won a ward from the NP in a Randburg city council by-election, and in doing so secured control of the city.[27]

Only 21,98 per cent of the registered voters in the ward went to the poll, and the DP candidate had a 48-vote majority. It was not an indication of support on the national stage, but De Beer used this victory to boost the party's position when he set out the Democrats' approach to future by-elections. He declared that the party would not oppose the NP if it would favour the CP. The DP would furthermore abandon its emphasis from "going for power", Worrall's favourite slogan, to supporting the negotiating process between the NP and the ANC. (De Beer met Mandela with Worrall and Malan on 23 February 1990 in Orlando West, Soweto, and would develop a good relationship with him.) Until the outline of the constitutional process was clearly visible, he emphasised, the DP would not surrender its independence or integrity. If the

---

24 *Beeld*, 8 June 1990.
25 *The Natal Mercury*, 8 June 1990.
26 Debates of parliament, 11 June 1990, Col. 11275.
27 *Beeld*, 14 June 1990.

Democrats wanted to join any other organisation, they had to do so right away.[28]

Among all the pessimism on the future of the DP, there was some optimism as parliament started to repeal apartheid legislation. On 12 June the Discriminatory Legislation Regarding Public Amenities Repeal Bill was debated. As the last remaining member of the 1953 parliament, De Beer apologised to parliament that he as a young politician had espoused support for the so-called proven South African tradition of social segregation: "I am sorry that 37 years ago I still supported the principle of social segregation." He expressed the hope that South Africans with the scrapping of the Act would use the opportunity and use their rights of free association to get to know one another better, and would learn to work together."[29]

With all the changes taking place, he felt that the DP had reason to be optimistic. Addressing a DP youth symposium in Port Elizabeth on 8 July, he quoted Dickens's *Tale of Two Cities*. That it was the "best of times and the worst of times" for the Democrats. But that the party was in a unique position to contribute to the negotiating process. In doing so, the DP had to maintain its identity, integrity and independence.[30] Three days later his optimism took a knock when Malan resigned as co-leader, as an MP, and as a member of the party. In an interview with Padraig O'Malley, an Irish journalist with an interest in South Africa's transition to a democracy, Malan stated that after 2 February the DP was suffering from its own success and had become irrelevant.[31] Malan, who since 1987 had doubts about continuing his parliamentary career, had the highest opinion and respect for De Klerk and he felt that as the President was setting out to achieve a peaceful transition of power to all South Africans, there was no need for him to remain in parliament any longer. After being informed by Malan of his resignation, De

---

28 Debates of parliament, 15 June 1990, Col. 11928–11930.
29 Debates of parliament, 12 June 1990, Col. 11454–11455.
30 *Beeld*, 9 July 1990.
31 The O'Malley Archives, Nelson Mandela Centre of Memory, O'Malley's interview with Wynand Malan, 10 July 1990, https://omalley.nelsonmandela.org/omalley/index (accessed 28 August 2019).

Beer made no effort to change his mind, as he understood that he was determined to leave politics. However, he did advise him to stay on for a few months to improve his pension. Malan responded that his pension would play no role in his decision.[32]

It is possible that the pension suggestion was an effort to keep Malan in parliament longer. According to Soal, his resignation was a great disappointment for De Beer.[33] It had the potential to have the same destructive impact as Slabbert's resignation in 1986 – to demoralise supporters, and to question the continued existence of the party. It also left the Democrats to deal with a difficult by-election. (In September 1989, Malan had won Randburg with a majority of 1714 votes.) Frans Lourens, chairman of the NP in the constituency, immediately announced that the party would contest the seat as the DP had no right to a continued existence.[34] When the CP announced its intention to also contest the seat, it left the DP in an impossible position.

On 12 July, in an interview with O'Malley, De Beer conceded that the DP was facing a crisis and again quoted Dickens:

> The Democratic Party, I always quote Charles Dickens' novel *Tale of Two Cities*, it begins by saying, "They were the best of times, they were the worst of times", and for the DP this is true today. It is the best of times for us, particularly for the old people like myself because we fought for these things hopelessly for nearly 40 years and suddenly they are all happening. But it is the worst of times because the strategic decisions the Democratic Party has to make are nearly impossible.

The option he wanted to pursue was that of a gadfly that prodded and urged De Klerk to get rid of the rest of apartheid, and to play a leading role in the negotiating process between the apartheid government and the ANC. Once the shape of a new constitution

---

32 Interview with W. Malan, 28 March 2022.
33 Interview with P. Soal, 11 April 2020.
34 *Beeld*, 12 July 1990.

became visible, the DP would re-evaluate its political options.[35] But by then the reality was that most of his energy was expanded on the struggle to maintain party unity with the growing divisions between the pro- and anti-ANC factions.

In August, Leon targeted what he termed as ANC fellow-travellers in the party by launching a scathing attack on the ANC/SACP for economic illiteracy and meaningless populism. This led to Van Eck, Momberg and Gastrow accusing him of sabotaging the party's relationship with the ANC and alienating black people. In his memoirs, Leon points out that it was left to De Beer in his droll way to pick up the pieces: "Tony Leon is a young man with a strong mind and a rich vocabulary, but all his criticism of the ANC seems to contain substance."[36] However, Leon felt that De Beer, whom he referred to as "kindly but conflict-averse", was too accommodating to the ANC fellow-travellers.[37] The reality was that De Beer was in a difficult situation, as many Democrats were starry-eyed about the ANC and Mandela. And coming down too hard on the ANC admirers could weaken the party by forcing this group into the arms of the liberation movement.

---

35 The O'Malley Archives, Nelson Mandela Centre of Memory, O'Malley's interview with Zach de Beer, 12 July 1990, https://omalley.nelsonmandela.org/omalley/index (accessed 28 August 2019).
36 Leon, *On the contrary*, p. 190.
37 T. Leon, *Opposite Mandela, Encounters with South Africa's icon* (Johannesburg, 2014), p. 34.

CHAPTER 24
Party leader
September–December 1990

With the DP in crisis, it was decided that a party leader would be elected at the national congress in Johannesburg on 7 and 8 September. De Beer promptly announced his candidature. Worrall stood back for Tian van der Merwe, whom he viewed as one of the most intelligent, politically committed people he knew, with the personality to go with it.[1] At the age of 43 years, the handsome and popular Van der Merwe created the image of youthful dynamism. One of his supporters was Selfe, who had serious doubts about De Beer's leadership abilities:

> Whether it was because of some inherent shyness, his early triumphs or because of his experiences at 44 Main Street, he was one of the most arrogant, self-satisfied and pompous people I have ever met. He expected to be hero-worshipped. He was unfailingly polite but condescending to people whom he regarded as inferior, and in particular, the professional staff of the Party, awkward in company he could not dominate, and completely out of touch.[2]

When tired, stressed and exhausted, De Beer could occasionally appear patronising and arrogant, but this was certainly not the norm. Ultimately, Selfe's criticism reflected not so much De Beer's character flaws, but the deep generational divide in the DP. Many of the younger Democrats viewed the old Progressives of the 1959 generation, even Suzman, with some disdain as being stuck in the 1960s and 1970s – or in their enclaves of Parktown, Houghton

---
1 Worrall, *The independent factor*, p. 196.
2 Correspondence with J. Selfe, 4 April 2020.

and Sea Point – out of touch of a changed South Africa in which extra-parliamentary politics had become more important. This perception was shared by Gastrow, who felt that Van der Merwe was the right person to pull the DP into the more relevant direction of extra-parliamentary activities, which De Beer opposed.[3]

Leon, although the leading figure amongst the younger and impatient members, felt unable to support Van der Merwe as he was uncertain about his vision for the future alignment of the party. On the eve of the conference, Van der Merwe had stated that he would actively seek joint projects with parties like the ANC so that the DP could exert influence. He viewed him as chronically disorganised. At the same time Leon, who was fond of De Beer and acted as his campaign manager, had deep misgivings about his "chairman of the board"-type of leadership, as well as doubts about his leadership mettle:

> ... by 1990. At the age of 62, the fires which had apparently burned once so bright within him had all but extinguished. Instead, he seemed redolent of a past age offering very little promise for the future. It was not known generally, as well that he was ill: on medication for high blood pressure, and declining.[4]

Health-wise De Beer had to deal with atrial fibrillation, an irregular and often rapid heartbeat that commonly results in poor blood flow and brings about fatigue. His medical condition caused him some discomfort and concern, but he was not worsening. With the necessary medication, he could fulfil his duties as party leader. By cycling early in the mornings in the streets of Camps Bay, Clifton and Sea Point, he ensured that he remained fit.[5]

De Beer, in his pitch to the 500 conference delegates, partly written by Leon and Bobby and Gillian Godsell, gave an overview

---

[3] Interview with P. Gastrow, 31 March 2022.
[4] Leon, *On the contrary*, p. 191.
[5] Z 193, De Beer's answers to a questionnaire for the *Habitat* magazine, 19 February 1990. (In the possession of Wendy de Beer Furniss.)

of his public career and his years of service to the principles of liberalism. He also emphasised his distrust for both the ANC and NP as custodians of liberal and democratic values, and stated that he was a defender of the DP's status as an independent party:

> But if any of you are looking for a leader who will lead you either into the ANC or the National Party as these organisations exist now – get yourselves another candidate. I am not about to damage, dissolve or destroy the Democratic Party. Nor am I about to turn it into an "agterryer" [henchman] of either the Nats or the ANC.

On a personal note he addressed the concern that he could be a bit too distant:

> I've lived the South African life, as a doctor in the slums, as a director in the boardrooms, as a politician among people. You may find me a little stiff and formal at times – but there is nothing false or self-conscious in my vision for our party and our land. My vision for the D.P. is not to be a me-too party, providing a chorus of approval for the Nats or the ANC or whoever. It is to be a pathfinder, with original thinking and the guts to say unpopular things when necessary.[6]

Van der Merwe made a plea for the party to move away from its conventional role by engaging in joint political action with groupings in black communities. He believed that the DP had to seek a closer degree of cooperation with the ANC. A DP MP privately informed Anthony Johnson, the *Cape Time*'s political correspondent, that it was a Hobson's choice between the two candidates, "between sudden death and a malingering malaise".[7] The congress decided by 274 votes to 195 to elect De Beer – a much narrower victory margin than expected. For Anne-Marie Mischke, the political correspondent of *Rapport*, the main reason for De

---

6   Z147, Candidate's speech, 7 September 1990 (In the possession of Wendy de Beer Furniss.)
7   *Cape Times*, 8 September 1990.

Beer's victory was his forty years of dedication to the principles of liberalism. According to her, his speech – emphasising his struggle against apartheid – had an emotional impact on the conference. Some of the delegates told her that although they favoured closer ties with the ANC, they had voted for De Beer as they felt that Van der Merwe lacked his experience and status.[8]

In his acceptance speech, De Beer set out a vision that the party had an important role to play in shaping the country's emerging democracy. He said that he had no other objective in life but to build a truly democratic South Africa. To achieve this goal, he re-iterated the sentiments he uttered on becoming the PFP leader: "For this I will fight any force, travel any road, suffer any pain." To achieve a truly democratic country, this "most sacred ideal", he felt strongly that the party had to retain its rugged independence during the negotiation process, as he would not leave democracy only in the hands of the ANC and the NP.[9] To ensure the future of the party his objective was to move away from the confines of whites-only politics to secure all-race support.[10]

After the speech, a stormy debate erupted about the future of the party. The Hillbrow constituency, with Lester Fuchs, a close friend of Leon, as its MP, submitted a motion that the DP remained a separate party with the ability to criticise the NP and ANC openly and publicly. The Sandton constituency, with the pro-ANC David Dalling as its MP, urged the party to negotiate joint strategies with the ANC.[11] The result was a vitriolic clash – interrupted by catcalling and boos from delegates – between Dalling and Schwarz, two old friends and allies since their days as Young Turks in the UP. The conference decided to retain the Democrats' status as an independent and distinct political force. Another acrimonious debate followed on whether the party should allow dual membership with other parties and organisations. The debate reflected the deep divide in the

---

8 *Rapport*, 9 September 1990.
9 *Cape Times*, 10 September 1990.
10 *Sunday Times*, 9 September 1990.
11 *Cape Times*, 7 September 1990.

parliamentary caucus as Schwarz and Leon vehemently opposed it, while Gastrow, Van Eck and Cronjé were its leading supporters. It was eventually decided not to allow dual membership without the consent of the National Council.[12] It was a bruising conference, but the DP had not split as had been predicted.

De Beer's first challenge as party leader was the Randburg by-election. In London, on his way to Glasgow to attend his son's wedding, he ran into Barend du Plessis, leader of the Transvaal NP, who was on his way to the USA. They came to an agreement that the DP would not contest Randburg, but that in future by-elections a seat would be defended by the party that had won it in the 1989 general election.[13] However, De Klerk refused to approve the agreement. De Beer went with Gibson to visit him in his presidential office in the Union Buildings in Pretoria. De Klerk, according to Gibson, was smug in his stated determination to reject any agreement between the two parties. That De Beer was shaken by the encounter was evident on his arrival at his Saxonwold home. He poured himself the biggest glass of whiskey Gibson had ever seen.[14] It was possibly this encounter that contributed to him referring to De Klerk in private as "Tricky Frikkie".[15] In the end the DP had no choice but to withdraw its candidate.[16]

Salt in De Beer's wounds was that the highly respected journalist Hennie Serfontein, who in the 1970s as an investigative journalist at the *Sunday Times* had exposed the influence of the secretive Afrikaner-Broederbond, used Randburg to launch a scathing attack on him and the Democrats.[17] He accused the DP of being

---

12 *Beeld*, 8 and 10 September 1990.
13 *Beeld*, 26 September 1990.
14 Interview with D. Gibson, 1 April 1994.
15 The O'Malley Archives, Nelson Mandela Centre of Memory, O'Malley's interview with Zach de Beer, 8 November 1994, https://omalley.nelson mandela.org/omalley/index (accessed 28 August 2019), and a marginalia on page 17 of his copy of Steven Friedman's *The long journey. South Africa's quest for a negotiated settlement*. (In the possession of Wendy de Beer Furniss.)
16 *Beeld*, 28 September 1990.
17 *Vrye Weekblad*, 5 October 1990.

like the old UP, a party of the past, divided and racist because of its ANC-bashing which was hysterical and more savage than the NP's attacks on the ANC in the elections of 1987 and 1989. The DP had become such a joke that not even the NP wanted anything to do with it. The attack was over the top, but it did reflect the attitude of many in the press – and in intellectual circles – that to criticise the ANC was racist and supportive of apartheid. It was an accusation that would gain momentum as the 1994 election approached. That Serfontein's attack irked De Beer was reflected in him keeping the clipping on file and underlining the accusation of racism.[18]

The NP, with Democrat support, secured an easy victory over the CP in Randburg. Publicly, De Beer put on a brave face, proclaiming that he was not unduly perturbed about losing Randburg as the party was preparing itself for the democracy lying ahead.[19]

The DP's political clothing being stolen by the NP.
From: Cape Times, 6 November 1990

---

18   Clipping in the possession of Wendy de Beer Furniss.
19   *Sunday times*, 7 October 1990.

But the harsh reality was that the by-election highlighted the party's declining status. Between May and September, support for the Democrats had dropped by 4,6 per cent, while its ailing image aggravated the difficult task of raising money to maintain party structures.[20] With the NP seen as the party of reform, donors felt that their money would be more effectively used if it was given to De Klerk.

Under these challenging circumstances De Beer would spend many hours late into the night with Eglin to analyse the political situation and discuss strategies for the way ahead. He increasingly relied on his friend's opinion and advice, and concurred with him that the DP had to focus on being a facilitator in the peace process.[21]

> Trust has to be built so that negotiations can go forward. It is perfectly understandable that trust between the Nats and the ANC is difficult to establish. In all this, with many of the leading actors proclaiming the need for a democratic solution, there is one organisation on the scene – admittedly not the largest or the strongest – whose commitment to democracy is beyond doubt, which has earned the trust if not always the agreement of people on all sides. This is the Democratic Party.[22]

This approach led to some tension in the caucus as Leon was convinced that a purely facilitating role would be self-immolating for the DP. For him De Beer was too deferential to Eglin, behaving as a junior partner, with the result that he was too passive on the future role the party should play.[23] (Andrew disagrees as he is of the opinion that De Beer did not allow Eglin to usurp his leadership.)[24] But then Leon was unimpressed with the party's leadership. He found the parliamentary caucus stifling and resented that a system

---

20 *Sunday Times*, 30 September 1990.
21 Eglin, *Crossing the borders of power*, p. 262.
22 *Sunday Times*, 9 April 1990.
23 Leon, *On the contrary*, p. 189.
24 Correspondence with K. Andrew, 6 April 2020.

of seniority determined where you sat in the House, when you could make a speech and determined portfolio appointments. For him some of the DP frontbenchers were exhausted volcanoes and counted for less than their years of service.[25] His preferred approach was to create a South African version of the Namibian Democratic Turnhalle Alliance (DTA), a moderate, multiracial party that secured 30 per cent of the popular vote in Namibia's first parliamentary election. With this significant vote, the DTA secured a pivotal role in negotiating Namibia's constitution. To become the South African version of the DTA, the DP had to be neither pro-black or anti-white, or vice versa, but to be the champion of individual rights from which economic liberalism naturally flows.[26]

However, De Beer's main task was to counter the demoralisation amongst Democrats and to keep the party going. At the Free State party congress in Harrismith on 6 October, he confronted this defeatist attitude:

> ... people are questioning our future role: we are asked what there is still for us to do. Should we not fold our tents and tip-toe away, they ask. Now this is great nonsense. ... No-one has a clearer duty than we do to fight for our principles – and we shall fight for them till they are achieved. And if we lose support, we will fight to regain it, but will not be diverted from our duty.[27]

He used the death of Steytler in October to bolster his case. In an emotional obituary he reminded his fellow Democrats of the courage it took to be a liberal more than 30 years earlier, that their idealism had prevailed, and that they had to continue with the DP to ensure that liberal-democratic values should be part of the new constitution:

---

25 Leon, *On the contrary*, p. 176.
26 *Frontline*, Vol. 8, No. 6, February 1990, p. 5.
27 Z140, De Beer's speech to the congress, 6 October 1990. (In the possession of Wendy de Beer Furniss.)

> He [Steytler] believed implicitly that our principles would win in the end because they were right. He was impatient with matters of strategy and tactics. Just keep belting out the truth. "Zach"', he said to me once, "you and I will never be in power; but we will live to see other people applying our policies." He did, thank God. ... Thirty years ago, some of us might have lacked courage, had it not been for Jannie. Now, we must carry on without him. We can, because of him.[28]

His efforts to revitalise the DP took a knock in November when the party lost one of its heavyweights with Schwarz's resignation on being appointed as South Africa's ambassador to Washington. He was a volatile personality, but an outstanding parliamentarian, especially on financial affairs, with a reputation as a fighter. In addition, Neil Ross, the party's national director also announced his resignation.[29] Fortunately, the NP by then had agreed with the principle that parties in support of reform and transition should not oppose each other. Gibson would be elected unopposed to parliament as Schwarz's replacement for Yeoville.

In October and November, De Beer in an attempt to secure support and funds for the DP, went on a tour of 36 cities and towns to introduce himself to supporters, and to keep them up to date with the party's role in creating a new South Africa.[30] On 14 November, after six weeks on the road, 12 flights on South African Airways, three flights with a private aircraft, travelling one thousand kilometres by car and speaking at more than hundred gatherings, he returned home.[31] At the National Council meeting of 24 and 25 November, he reported that the floating vote gained during the election had disappeared, but that the hard core of the party was healthy. He admitted that the past year had been a very difficult

---

28 Z126, Steytler obituary, 31 October 1990. (In the possession of Wendy de Beer Furniss.)
29 *Sunday Times*, 4 November 1990.
30 *Beeld*, 2 October 1990.
31 Z119, De Beer's summary of his tour, 15 November 1990. (In the possession of Wendy de Beer Furniss.)

one for the DP struggling to establish a role in the new South Africa, but assured them that as the Democrats sat in the middle of South African politics, it was well placed to build bridges to promote convergence to bring about a stable government.[32]

---

32 Wits, PFP/DP papers, Ab2.2.11, National Council, 25–26 November 1990.

CHAPTER 25
A kind of political concussion
1991

The DP entered the 1991 parliamentary session with the intention of pushing for the rapid dismantling of the apartheid state. De Klerk pre-empted De Beer by announcing that all remaining apartheid acts would be repealed. The CP was outraged. Before storming out of the chamber, they accused De Klerk as a traitor and the executioner of the Afrikaner.

De Beer was shocked by their behaviour. But he had his own challenges as Van Eck, Cronjé and Momberg had joined a protest demonstration by the ANC instead of attending the opening ceremony.[1] In his response to the presidential address, De Beer was supportive but demanded that something had to be done about the high level of violence in the townships, and the lack of confidence in the police amongst black people. He also raised concern about the poor economic conditions, as well as the shortcomings in the educational system. The only solution was to get a multiparty conference off the ground as a matter of urgency and to speed up the process of negotiations in which the Democrats could play a leading role:

> ... we in the DP find ourselves positioned between the NP and the ANC. We agree with the ANC that black people cannot readily accept the legitimacy, as distinct from legality, of the present government. We agree with the NP that the present Government simply cannot vanish from the scene. For there to be a legal continuity, it must continue to exist.
>
> So we conclude that steps must be taken forthwith to arrange the

---

1 *Beeld*, 2, 4 and 8 February 1991.

effective participation in the governing process of representative black people so that legitimacy can be improved.[2]

At a press briefing on 7 February, he ruefully pointed out that he was the "representative of a rather strange animal in South African politics, a party whose success threatens to be its nemesis", but that he was positive about its future. On a question where he saw himself in five years, he responded:

> Oh well, if I'm alive and if I'm active, I'll be somewhere in the government. ... I believe there's going to be a centrist coalition of parties which will include at least portions of the present ANC, portions of the present NP, at least. And if that is so, then people like us will be swept up somewhere in the middle of it.[3]

However, he felt that it was too early to form any such centrist coalition. On 3 June he set out his vision of the DP by addressing the demands that the party should be part of an equivalent of the Namibian DTA, a centre-right block against the ANC. For him, this option could possibly tear South Africa down the middle with competing forces on the left and right. The only option for the party was to follow its own path, propagating a liberal-democratic constitution:

> The DP cannot claim to be among the largest of South Africa's political movements, but our record shows that we have pretty consistently had a clear view of the future. Today I believe we are entitled to call upon other leaders to listen to and examine the case we are putting.[4]

During the parliamentary session, De Klerk proceeded with legislation to repeal the pillars of the apartheid state, namely the Land

---

2 Debates of parliament, 4 February 1991, Col. 107–108.
3 Z239, Transcript of the press briefing, 7 February 1991. (In the possession of Wendy de Beer Furniss.)
4 Debates of parliament, 3 June 1991, Col. 11191.

Laws of 1913 and 1936, the Group Areas Act, and the Population Registration Act. De Beer was fulsome in his praise of the President:

> These are giant steps towards the democratic values we support, and the realisation of human dignity in South Africa, which to us is the highest ideal.[5]

And yet, it was a difficult parliamentary session for the Democrats as De Klerk and the NP claimed all the credit for the gradual dismantling of the apartheid state, ignoring the DP's Progressive predecessors' opposition to discriminatory laws. The party also suffered a blow on 19 May 1991 with Tian van der Merwe's death in a car accident. He was a diligent and courageous MP who had raised the party's profile in extra-parliamentary circles and was seen as De Beer's successor.[6] The growing belief among some of the DP MPs that the party could not survive in a changed political environment furthermore darkened the mood in the caucus.[7] De Beer had had enough of this pessimism and in a meeting in Yeoville on 32 July, he lashed out at the Democrats who seemingly had a kind of political concussion:

> Many of our people have been sitting still and transfixed, like so many rabbits staring at a cobra with its hood and its head high and swaying. Over and over again, we have heard the question: is there a role for the DP? This is the moment for me as the leader of this party to say to all it members and supporters: for heaven's sake snap out of your trance, and get on with the task of building our party, especially among people of colour, where we are much weaker than we should be.[8]

---

5   Debates of parliament, 12 June 1991, Col. 12579.
6   *Cape Times*, 20 May 1991.
7   *Beeld*, 22 June 1991.
8   Z216, Speech at the Yeoville constituency, 31 July 1991. (In the possession of Wendy de Beer Furniss.)

However, after 9 August the sense of pessimism in the DP deepened when De Klerk addressed a public meeting in the Western Transvaal town of Ventersdorp and the AWB went on the attack. In the subsequent violent clash, three AWB members were killed while 48 people were injured, including six police officers. This convinced many Democrats that they had to support De Klerk as the only person who could bring about a non-racial democracy. An already bruising year for De Beer became more difficult in October when he had a health scare with a transient ischemic attack (a mini stroke), which did not cause permanent damage but served as a warning of a potential stroke. As a result, he had to adjust his blood pressure medication.[9]

There was no let-up regarding divisions in the DP in the caucus which became toxic. On 6 November 1991, Robin Carlisle, MP for Wynberg, tabled a motion of no confidence in Dalling as the chief whip for attending an ANC fundraiser in Stellenbosch. The motion was debated at a special caucus meeting at the Johannesburg International Airport. Dalling, in his defence, pointed out that he had attended the meeting with his wife, an ANC member, and with the sanction of De Beer. The debate led to a vitriolic clash between Leon and Kobus Jordaan, MP for Umhlanga, who leaned towards the pro-ANC group. De Beer eventually calmed the meeting. After four hours of arguing, the Carlisle motion was replaced with one stipulating that party members should not attend fundraising activities of other parties.[10] The meeting achieved nothing but to raise the tension levels among MPs, leaving them demoralised on the eve of the annual party congress. It fuelled the gloom in the caucus that the party was fading into obscurity.[11]

This sense of despondency deepened on 14 November with the DP's defeat in a Johannesburg City Council by-election in Ward 16 at the hands of Sam Moss, a former PFP mayor and provincial councillor for Parktown. (Ward 16 straddled the constituencies of

---

9   Interview with Wendy de Beer Furniss, 17 November 2021.
10 Momberg, *From Malan to Mbeki*, p. 86.
11 *Sunday Times*, 10 November 1991.

Parktown and Houghton, the heartland of DP support, and was a symbol of great emotional value for former Progressives. In 1972 it was the first ever municipal ward to be captured by the PP and was the Progressives' safest seat in any local government.) Local reasons had played a crucial role in the DP's defeat, but Moss credited as an important reason the DP's close ties with the ANC. This led to Leon holding Dalling responsible for the defeat.[12] For De Beer, the defeat in his own backyard was humiliating. In June 1989, the DP's victory in the Linden ward reflected a party with momentum, while the Ward 16 defeat signified a party in terminal decline.

At the National Council meeting of 14 November, De Beer made it clear that the constant dissension and infighting had given the impression that the party had no future. The Democrats had to work at building an image of being well-organised, disciplined and effective. The protagonists on the left and right had to approach one another in a spirit of loyalty to the party and to each other.[13] During the discussion on the party's image and where it was going, Leon and Dalling tore into each other. Both the pro- and anti-ANC sections then leaked information on the clash to besmirch the other side. At the national congress on 16 and 17 November at Sea Point, De Beer, after his re-election as leader, laid down the law, demanding that Democrats do not demonstrate their affection for other competing organisations and air the party's dirty linen in public as it humiliated him and damaged the party. He viewed his re-election as a mandate to deal more harshly with the factions in the party. He felt that those whose loyalty was not to the DP had to leave, while he was adamant that the party had to retain its own identity, integrity, and independence. He highlighted the DP's role in playing a mediating role between the NP and the ANC.

His speech made an impact, and the conference voted with a big majority to retain its independence. This placed the pro-ANC

---

12   *Die Burger*, 15 November 1991; Beeld, 15 November 1991.
13   Wits, PFP/DP papers, Ab2.2.11, National Council minutes, 14 November 1991.

MPs on the back foot, and in the election for party chairmanship, Andrew easily defeated Momberg.[14] The conference was a success for De Beer, but Leon felt that he could have done more to offer the party a road map into the future,[15] especially as negotiations for a future South African constitution were about to start. However, the biggest challenge for De Beer was to keep the party unified and afloat. The financial situation of the DP was so dire that the party could not even afford to hold two National Council meetings that year.[16]

To add to De Beer's woes, Boris Wilson's memoir, *A time of innocence* – a severe condemnation of liberals – was published. The title was based on a quotation by G.K. Chesterton: "As much as I ever did, more than I ever did, I believe in Liberalism. But there was a rosy time of innocence when I believed in Liberals." Wilson used the book to settle personal grudges. The belief that his political career was frustrated and undermined by liberals who were jealous of him is a central theme in the text. He paints a picture of himself as the solitary defender of South African liberal ideals surrounded by jealous, opportunistic and self-serving so-called liberals. He emphasises that he became disillusioned with parliament as he believed that liberals could achieve nothing there and that the NP was using it and the presence of the Progressives to give the impression that South Africa was a democratic state. He felt he had to resign as an MP in 1961 as he had unwittingly become a tool of the apartheid machine and that his presence in parliament was an exercise in futility.

Furthermore, he questioned the integrity of Eglin and De Beer by accusing them of political immaturity and selfishness, and of being too ambitious to become the leaders of the PP. For him De Beer was a politician driven only by the desire to become the leader of a political party, in the process sacrificing the PFP and liberalism

---

14 *Sunday Times*, 17 November 1991; *Die Burger*, 16 November 1991.
15 Leon, *On the contrary*, p. 201.
16 Wits, PFPO/DP papers, Ab2.2.11, National Council meeting, 16 November 1991.

to lead the DP. He claimed that the AAC through Harry Oppenheimer and his former son-in-law, Gordon Waddell, influenced the PP and fuelled the perception that the Progressives represented the interests of big business. As the ANC was determined to deny liberals any credit for their role in the anti-apartheid struggle, *A time of innocence* could not have appeared at a worse time for De Beer. Wilson's accusation that liberals, by being in parliament, provided credibility to apartheid, as well as Slabbert's resignation in 1986, would be used as proof of liberal collaboration with apartheid.

Against this background, multiparty negotiations started on 21 and 22 December to set out the principles of a democratic South Africa at the Convention for a Democratic South Africa (Codesa) in the World Trade Centre in Kempton Park. Five working groups were appointed to investigate matters such as the principles of a new constitution, arrangements for an interim government, and the future of the Bantustans. De Beer was appointed as the chairman of the Steering Committee that was in charge of the daily management of the convention. The committee of eight individuals was drawn from the delegates. It was responsible for maintaining Codesa's momentum and for settling procedural disputes within working groups. The ANC's Mac Maharaj headed the committee's secretariat. The Steering Committee would play a leading role in steering the convention.[17] In his opening speech to the convention, De Beer set out his goals and vision for a future South Africa:

> Our task is to write the constitution which will enable those who come after us to be proud citizens of a free South Africa commanding respect in the community of nations. We are deeply conscious that we have to approach this task not writing as it were on a clean slate, but dealing with a human society which is the product of centuries of wrong. Much is rightly said of the terrible harm that was done in the name of apartheid: but we dare not pretend that injustice began in 1948. The distortions caused by race and sex discrimination

---

17   S. Friedman, *The long journey. South Africa's quest for a negotiated settlement* (Johannesburg, 1993).

have been present for centuries. Their impact is there for all to see in the life of our people today. ... One of the great tasks Codesa must fulfil is to produce a constitution which prevents abuse of power by government. ... Those who have come to Codesa to pursue party political aims without regard to great national interest will be cursed by generations to come. Those who have come prepared to subordinate all narrow interests to the general good will have a place among the heroes.[18]

The opening was marred by a row between De Klerk and Mandela about who was to blame for the violence in the country. Fortunately, the clash did not end the negotiations. A bigger threat was the rivalry between the IFP and the ANC. Buthelezi increasingly felt that the ANC and NP had seized control of the negotiating process, marginalising the interests of the Zulus, and that Codesa was threatening his KwaZulu powerbase. He was determined to be a third and equal partner in the negotiation process.

Despite the truculence of the IFP and the growing violence in the country, De Beer remained positive about the negotiations. In an article for *Leadership* magazine (Vol. 11, No. 1, 1992), he pointed out that the NP and ANC had accepted that bargaining for power was better than fighting for it, and that the big game was power, not ideology; and that they were pragmatists, not dogmatists. In addition, the NP had adopted the policy of the DP which it once had vilified, while the ANC, which once only had sneers for white liberals, increasingly spoke their language.

---

18   Z201, Speech delivered to the opening of Codesa, 20 December 1991. (In the possession of Wendy de Beer Furniss.)

CHAPTER 26
The Liberal crusader
1992

With the start of the 1992 parliamentary session, it was decided that parliament would only sit three days a week to enable MPs to attend Codesa. De Beer would play a limited role in the negotiating process as he focused on preparing the Democrats for the coming election. Eglin led the DP's negotiating team consisting of Andrew, Leon and Dene Smuts.[1]

In his opening address to parliament, De Klerk urged people to show fortitude, perseverance and determination on the path to a new South Africa. De Beer responded positively: "He may know that the Democrats will continue to show these qualities."[2] To put pressure on the government to hasten with reforms, as well as to bolster the standing of the DP, he introduced in the House of Assembly on 31 January a motion of censure in the cabinet: "We accept that the NP is serious about establishing a democracy, although we are critical about many things that it is saying and doing along the way – hence the motion of censure."[3] He said that it was unacceptable that the government was still maintaining the old apartheid system of "own affairs". Maintaining four departments of education and health meant excessive government spending. Furthermore, he censured the government for not restoring confidence in the economy. Apartheid had harmed the economy, and the only way to encourage economic growth was to bring about a new constitution.[4] De Klerk responded dismissively that it did not suit De Beer to be so emotional.

---

1 Eglin, *Crossing the borders of power*, p. 296.
2 Debates of parliament, 27 January 1992, Col. 111.
3 Debates of parliament, 31 January 1992, Col. 449.
4 Debates of parliament, 31 January 1992, Col. 448–453.

After the Potchefstroom by-election on 19 February in which the NP lost the seat to the CP, De Klerk was far more collegial. A jubilant Treurnicht demanded a parliamentary election. De Klerk responded by calling a referendum for 17 March in which whites had to indicate whether they supported the reform process. An hour before the announcement, Barend du Plessis was running around in parliament searching for De Beer to inform him of developments and to plead that his support would be needed.[5] Fearing that if the CP should win the referendum, it could unleash a civil war, De Beer promised his support, but on the condition that the referendum had to be about a new democratic dispensation through negotiation, and not about parties or personalities.[6]

The DP set out to run its own distinctive campaign with posters, pamphlets and cinema advertising. On 3 March, De Beer shared a platform with De Klerk in the Cape Town City Hall to address more than 2000 people. This led to some unhappiness in the party. Momberg, who until 1987 was an NP member, loathed his former party with the passion of the convert and refused to appear with De Klerk.[7] Eglin was unhappy, as Democrats were determined to vote yes, and he felt that a shared platform with De Klerk could only dilute the DP's identity.[8] At the meeting De Beer was, according to the *Cape Times* (4 March 1992), at his statesmanlike best. He was candid about the probability of opposing De Klerk in the future, but gracious also to acknowledge De Klerk's role for leading the country from a past that was slowly but surely killing South Africans. The referendum was the most important vote ever for whites, with the choice between the hope of a continued existence and the certainty of total disaster. That he stood shoulder to shoulder on the same platform with a life-long political opponent emphasised the critical nature of the campaign, which simply had to be won.[9]

---

5   *Sunday Times*, 5 April 1992.
6   Debates of parliament, 21 February 1992, Col. 1457.
7   Momberg, *From Malan to Mbeki*, pp. 88–89.
8   Eglin, *Crossing the borders of power*, p. 274.
9   *Cape Times*, 3 March 1992.

De Beer then proceeded to tour the country to address a succession of DP public meetings. As it became clear from public opinion surveys that the "Yes" vote would secure a majority, he warned against complacency and apathy as it could result in a low majority, which could erode the negotiating process.[10] He was such a convincing voice that the *Beeld* (16 March) published his message urging voters to vote for themselves, their children, and the country. That same evening he addressed a public meeting in the Johannesburg City Hall, declaring that a "No" vote would be a declaration of war against the majority of South Africans.[11]

In a high turnout of 85 per cent, the "Yes" campaign secured 1 924 186 votes (68,6 per cent) and the "No" vote 875 619 (31,2 per cent). In parliament, De Beer described the referendum as a truly unforgettable experience in which the voter was the real hero. He reached out to the CP, wishing the party the best in its difficult time and urging the Conservatives to participate in Codesa, as they were needed to create a non-racial South Africa. He then made it clear that in the wake of the referendum there was no possibility of the DP giving up its independence, "we are comfortable in our role as patriotic, liberal, democratic opposition. We shall play that role constructively here and at Codesa."[12] However, he had little time to enjoy the victory as the referendum brought the DP no benefits but strengthened the perception that the party had become irrelevant. This intensified the divisions in the party. Momberg, feeling that the Leon camp was gaining momentum, informed Van Eck on 31 March that he had broken emotionally with the DP and was determined to join the ANC.[13]

On 1 April, both Leon and Dalling submitted memorandums to the parliamentary caucus on the future of the party. For Leon the party faced a bleak future as its support had shrunk alarmingly amongst whites with no growth of support in the black commu-

---

10 *Cape Times*, 9 March 1992.
11 *Beeld*, 17 March 1992.
12 Debates of parliament, 20 March 1992, Col. 2464.
13 Momberg, *From Malan to Mbeki*, p. 89.

nity. In addition, the differences and attitudes in the party made it impossible to enter an alliance with another political party, and he was of the opinion that this issue could tear the party apart.

The inability and unwillingness to create an alliance with the ANC or the NP meant that the option of a new party had to be considered. Leon proposed that the party disband and form a new centrist one with the NP under the leadership of De Klerk. A new party without the discredited past of the NP, but with the powerful leadership of De Klerk, and a commitment to a fundamental liberal democracy would be an attractive and a practical alternative. With the DP driving the creation of a new party, it would give the NP the incentive to disband. This would be "reverse take-over" of the NP. Dalling proposed an alignment or association with the ANC. De Beer, Eglin, and Andrew wanted the DP to retain its independent status. According to the *Sunday Times* (5 April 1992), the meeting ended inconclusively, leaving MPs more divided than before.

In this period, De Klerk approached De Beer with an offer of a cabinet seat as the Minister of Finance to replace Du Plessis who had retired on account of ill health. This was accompanied with an offer that their respective parties should form a united front in the upcoming negotiations with the ANC. Rejecting the offer, he told De Klerk that he had been unable to secure the support of the caucus.[14] It was a lie, as he had kept the offer to himself. He only mentioned it to Wendy in confidence months later.[15] Leon would only hear about the offer years after the event.[16] Facing an irrevocably divided caucus, it made sense for De Beer to keep the offer to himself. It could only deepen internal divisions, even encouraging the pro-ANC group to leave the party.

As the leader of a party threatened with extinction, there was no possibility of him accepting the offer as he was determined to

---

14   In his memoirs *Hermann Giliomee: Historian* (p.161) Giliomee refers to "a reliable source in the NP government" in discussing this offer. In an email to me on 18 November 2021 he confirmed that this source was De Klerk.
15   Interview with Wendy de Beer Furniss, 17 November 2021.
16   Correspondence with T. Leon, 18 November 2021.

maintain the DP as an independent liberal voice. He was a crusader for liberalism.

On 15 April, the tensions in the DP caucus took a dramatic turn when De Beer suspended Van Eck (Constantia), Momberg (Simon's town), Cronjé (Greytown) and Rob Haswell (Pietermaritzburg South) for discussing with the ANC the possibility of joining the movement and representing it in parliament. Following their suspension, they promptly joined the ANC. Mandela was reluctant to accept them as he did not want to jeopardise his good relationship with De Beer.[17] (Their good relationship would not be damaged. In August, Mandela invited him with Leon and Andrew for dinner at his Houghton home. The new recruits to the ANC were not mentioned.)[18]

On 21 April, Dalling, who was hospitalised after a heart attack, also joined the ANC. The five MPs justified their decision on the grounds that the DP was unwilling to move closer to an alliance with the ANC.[19] The *Eastern Province Herald* (17 April) confidently predicted that after these defections, the DP had no real future on the national stage.

On 22 April the five DP defectors took their seats as independents on the parliamentary cross benches. Cronjé, on behalf of the group, explained to parliament why they had joined the ANC. De Beer then set out the reasons for the continued existence of the DP: The party was founded on immutable principles, freedom, human dignity and equality under the law, and the Democrats had an important role to play to bring about a new South Africa. There was a need for the DP and its principles if freedom and dignity and equality under the law were to thrive. The Democrats had an unbroken record of upholding equal rights and would be able to work together with the majority of South Africans as they emerge from the oppression of apartheid.

He conceded that the party would face a struggle to survive in

---

17 Momberg, *From Malan to Mbeki*, pp. 90–92.
18 Leon, *Opposite Mandela*, pp. 32–39.
19 *Beeld*, 22 April 1992.

the upcoming election, but that the Democrats were willing to face this challenge:

> And so, while there are a few of our people who seek salvation in the big battalions, the vast majority of Democrats believe that we have a duty to uphold our principles and values in the new South Africa. In the end, if it must be said of us that we committed some errors of judgement in framing strategy and tactics, then so be it, but it shall never be said of us that we sacrificed principles for expediency or truth or personal advantage. [20]

Die Burger described it as a dignified speech. But more importantly, he gave a clear direction for the struggling DP. Cronjé was unimpressed and predicted that as the DP was unable to adapt to changing circumstances it was inevitable that it would go the way of the dinosaur.[21]

The departure of the five dissidents brought peace and stability to the Democrat caucus, and a confidence to stand up as guardians for liberalism and economic freedom.[22] De Beer felt that the DP had found its feet again:

> The DP has in the meantime taken a grip on itself and decided with great firmness and clarity what it wants to do. Whether it can do it is another matter. Having got rid of five gentlemen who joined the ANC the DP have been able to achieve unanimity in its party structures in favour of a drive to establish a viable liberal democratic party which can sit in a central position on the spectrum, to the right of the ANC and to the left of the Nats. A human rights party, a classical liberal party, which will go for 10% or 15% of the electorate, which looks to be just possible if things go well, at worst for 5% which seems to be the probable cut-off point in a proportional representative

---

20   Debates of parliament, 22 April 1992, Col. 4858.
21   C. Louw, "Parlement se man van die daad", *Die Suid-Afrikaan*, June/July 1993, p. 16.
22   *Sunday Times*, 26 April 1992.

system, and would then see itself playing in the future the same role the FDP has played in modern Germany. A relatively small but very influential party because of its position on the spectrum. That's what we shall go for, I think, there is no doubts about that.[23]

At Codesa, negotiations proceeded in fits and starts, but by 15 May 1992 it was deadlocked. The ANC decided to withdraw from the convention to proceed with a mass action campaign in order to paralyse the country and to force the government out of power. De Beer blamed the NP for the breakdown. That after the referendum the government resorted to a sort of ostentatious arrogance, and its approach to negotiations was crude and outdated. The result was that the ANC met NP aggression with counteraggression. He then called on all South Africans who believed in human rights and in social market economics to come together and to mobilise for a new democracy and to build a strong grouping of the centre, capable at least of restraining the authoritarianism of the ANC and the NP.[24] Dr Tertius Delport, Deputy-Minister for Constitutional Development, accused him of ignorance and of not playing a constructive role in the negotiating process, as the DP had limited itself to be a facilitator.[25]

The ANC's campaign of mass action started on 16 June. The next day South Africa was shaken by the news of a massacre in the Boipatong township south of Johannesburg. Zulu residents of the Kwa Madala hostel, who were supporters of the IFP, attacked the residents of Boipatong and the Slovo Park informal settlement, killing 45 people and injuring 22. For the next few months, mass protest action dominated the political stage. On 7 September 1992, South Africa was shaken by another slaughter when soldiers of the Ciskei Bantustan army opened fire on ANC protesters at Bisho, killing 29 demonstrators and injuring hundreds.

---

23 The O'Malley Archives, Nelson Mandela Centre of Memory, O'Malley's interview with Zach de Beer, 17 July 1992, https://omalley.nelsonmandela.org/omalley/index (accessed 28 August 2019).
24 Debates of parliament, 8 June 1992, Col. 10444–10448.
25 *Beeld*, 9 June 1992.

This led to the DP doing something that was not normally part of its political armoury: organising a protest march. On 15 September, De Beer led a march of 400 liberals in support of peace and negotiations through the streets of Johannesburg. The group was led by a vehicle playing John Lennon's "Give peace a chance".[26] The Bisho massacre, and the fear of economic collapse, ended the mass action and led to the Record of Understanding between the government and the ANC which enabled negotiations to be resumed. This agreement was repudiated by Buthelezi as he felt the IFP was being sidelined with most of the provisions of the agreement, namely that the hostels of migrant labourers had to be fenced off while the carrying of "traditional" weapons was banned, were aimed at Inkatha.[27]

To discuss the political situation, parliament met on 12 October 1992 for a special sitting. The meeting took place with the country in the grip of endemic violence and a sustained economic downturn. Because of a split in the CP and the fact that six MPs of the coloured Labour Party had joined the DP, it had become the biggest opposition party in parliament. (The CP remained the largest opposition party in the House of Assembly.) The original purpose of the sitting was the premise that the negotiations would have reached an advanced stage, and that legislation had to be introduced for the appointment of multiparty committees that would work with the cabinet overseeing the government before the elections. Because of the events at Codesa, the legislation had to be put on ice.

De Klerk attempted to indicate the direction in which the country was moving. In his response, De Beer expressed empathy for the President's difficult position, but pointed out that the shocking condition of the economy was the reason why a political settlement had to be reached urgently. He urged the government to continue with bilateral negotiations with the ANC – it could not be allowed that the increase in violence delay a political agreement.

---

26 *Beeld*, 16 September 1992.
27 Welsh, *The rise and fall of apartheid*, pp. 451–454.

Codesa had taught him that only when the ANC and NP agreed, could negotiations proceed.[28]

The year 1992 was an exhausting and challenging one for De Beer. The future of the DP remained uncertain while the first fully democratic election was looming. The party continued to lose support to the NP, while earlier in the year the DP had arranged its first house meeting in Soweto in a modest matchbox house in one of the poorer parts of the township. Only seven people pitched to listen to De Beer. It was a warning of how difficult it would be to attract the support of black voters.[29] Then there was the difficulty of raising election funds. By the end of 1991, the party still had to pay a quarter of its 1989 election debt. In a National Council meeting, De Beer warned that the party would have to raise a great deal of money to accomplish its goals.[30]

---

28 Debates of parliament, 12 October 1992, Col. 11964.
29 Bloom, *Out of step*, pp. 41–42.
30 Wits, PFP/DP papers, Ab2.2.11, National Council, 12 November 1992.

CHAPTER 27

The marginalisation of the Democratic Party
January–June 1993

De Klerk's opening address for the 1993 parliamentary session differed little from those of the previous two years, namely it was an overview of the political situation and the proposed reforms and negotiations he intended to pursue. It left De Beer in a position that he found it difficult to say anything original:

> Mr Speaker, Elizabeth Taylor's seventh husband is supposed to have remarked on the eve of their wedding day that he knew what was expected of him, but the problem was how to make it interesting. I feel rather like that today.[1]

He proceeded to give his support to De Klerk's efforts and to express his appreciation that the NP and ANC had given their full support to the concept of a government of national unity. However, he did urge the government to immediately get rid of the Bantustan policy. This was in response to De Klerk's claim that their future would be determined by constitutional developments. The apartheid state over the years had adapted the name of its policy of territorial segregation. Initially, they were termed reserves, then Bantustans, which became homelands, and ended as national states. For De Beer they remained Bantustans and he condemned it as a tragic, farcical policy that encouraged corruption and brought only poverty and oppression to black people. He pointed out that the continuation of the Bantustans were proof that apartheid was

---

1 Debates of parliament, 1 February 1993, Col. 76.

not dead.² With an eye on the coming election, his attack was an effort to portray the NP as a party under which state corruption had flourished and had become so vast that it was a serious threat to economic and political stability.

Any hope of his message resonating with the wider public was deflated with the announcement of Mike Tarr, the DP MP for Pietermaritzburg North, that he had joined the IFP. He informed parliament that in Natal there was politically place only for the ANC and Inkatha, and that he could not side with the ANC.³ De Beer was hurt and surprised by the defection. To O'Malley he described Tarr as "very loyal and straightforward, a bit stupid and ox-like but salt of the earth sort of guy".⁴ He quickly had to shake off his disappointment when on 5 February he had to participate in the CP's no-confidence vote in the cabinet. While not supporting the CP, he condemned the government for maintaining racist and territorial segregation with the Bantustan policy, its failure to control violence and crime, its inability to prevent corruption and malpractice, and accused the cabinet that it had no remedy for the negative economic growth.⁵

However, De Beer's parliamentary performance could not counter the harsh reality that Tarr's defection confirmed the DP's marginalised status. Concerns about the future of the party led to Eglin, Andrew and Gastrow attending discussions on 2 February in Portugal with Slabbert, Dr Oscar Dhlomo, Director of the Institute for Multi-Party Democracy, Rev. Stanley Mogoba of the South African Council of Churches, and Prof Mamphela Ramphela of the UCT on the possibility to form a new centrist party.

De Beer made it clear that he preferred the continued existence of the DP.⁶ Nothing came from the talks in Portugal, but the survival

---

2   Debates of parliament, 1 February 1993, Col. 78–79.
3   Debates of parliament, 4 February 1993, Col. 392.
4   The O'Malley Archives, Nelson Mandela Centre of Memory, O'Malley's interview with Zach de Beer, 16 August 1993, https://omalley.nelsonman dela.org/omalley/index (accessed 28 August 2019).
5   Debates of parliament, 5 February 1993, Col. 434–435.
6   *Beeld*, 27 February 1993.

of the party remained in doubt. De Beer was in a no-win-situation. He was in the difficult position that whatever he did to raise the party's profile made no difference. If he criticised the government, he was condemned as unreasonable. (De Klerk made some show of his hurt after De Beer's Bantustan attack.) But on the other hand, any praise and support of De Klerk and the reform process bought the DP no benefits as it bolstered the NP. And yet, he never stopped giving credit to De Klerk for his reforms and his attempts, however fumbling, to dismantle the apartheid state.

On 30 March, he addressed parliament about the high anxiety amongst people because of the appalling crime rate, unemployment and the general sense of depression. He told the House that good liberal democrats asked him every day whether there is still hope and that his response was:

> We must, therefore, all accept that what was done on 2 February [1990] was absolutely right, even though it came many years later than it should have done: that the ugly events we see around us were to a large extent predictable because a badly distorted society has to find its way to normalcy, and that we must not lose our heads but be patient and very determined in pressing on to a settlement.[7]

During the appropriation vote on the Presidency, De Beer pointed out that there had been a great deal of evidence that the performance of De Klerk left much to be desired. That he had made a horrible mess of the appointment of the board of the SABC and of the arrest of 72 alleged PAC members – of whom only four were charged on minor charges – but that these were forgivable flaws:

> However, the major question with us is not the ham-handedness or mismanagement. It is whether the hon. the State President is still trying to lead South Africa to an open society based upon equality, liberty, and the rule of law. No matter how ineffectual he may sometimes be, we think he is still trying to do that. Because of our long-

---

7   Debates of parliament, 30 March 1993, Col. 3848.

standing devotion to those values, the open society, equality, liberty and the rule of law, we shall not oppose this vote.[8]

However, he did not hesitate to point out the dark past of the NP. During the debate on the Constitution Amendment Bill to abolish the President's Council, he emphasised that the sole purpose of the President's Council was to ensure the NP's domination of the tricameral parliament. For him the lesson to be learnt from the history of the unlamented President's Council was that the future political system had to be straightforward and transparent.[9]

On 1 April 1993, constitutional negotiations – now called the Multiparty Negotiating Process (MPNP) – restarted at Kempton Park. The CP was present as part of the Concerned South Africans Group (Cosag), which consisted of the IFP and the Bantustan leaders of Bophuthatswana and Ciskei. These negotiations were based on a two-phased constitutional process: Any decisions adopted at MPNP would have to pass through normal parliamentary channels to become a law. An interim constitution would be drafted at Kempton Park. A parliament would be elected in 1994 which would then become a constitution-making body to produce the final constitution. The constitution would finally be certified by a constitutional court.[10] The procedure adopted for the negotiation process entailed that specific problems would be referred to technical committees, which would work out solutions for consideration by the MPNF. If deadlocks should emerge, the major parties would deliberate privately to try and reach consensus.

On 10 April, Chris Hani, a leading ANC and SACP member, was assassinated by Janusz Walus, a right-wing extremist, with the assistance of Clive Derby-Lewis, a former CP MP. According to Prof. David Welsh, who acted as Eglin's advisor at Kempton Park, this assassination had given the country a glimpse into the abyss and was a spur to speed up negotiations. On 3 June, the negotiators at

---

8   Debates of parliament, 2 June 1993, Col. 9770.
9   Debates of parliament, 9 June 1993, Col. 10597–10600.
10 Welsh, *The rise and fall of apartheid*, pp. 438, 440.

MPNP set the election date for 27 April 1994. By then the IFP had refused to attend the constitutional talks as its demand for a federal system that would have given virtual autonomy to KwaZulu-Natal had been refused. Buthelezi also opposed the election of a parliament with constitutional-making powers as he knew that the IFP would be a minority party. The constitution, according to him, had to be drawn up by experts and ratified by a referendum, while he demanded outside arbitration to determine the status of the Zulu king.[11]

Buthelezi was engaging in brinkmanship and there was the fear that his disruptive behaviour could scupper the negotiating process, and eventually the election. The tension surrounding constitutional negotiations led to intensified violence and bloodshed between IFP and ANC supporters. Another threat to negotiations came from the white far-right. In July, after the setting of an election date, the CP withdrew from the MPNP. On 25 June 1993, right-wing anger with developments at Kempton Park led to an invasion of the World Trade Centre by AWB thugs who vandalised the building. It was an event that did much to dismay many conservative Afrikaners, and to discredit Terre'Blanche's AWB and the CP. One of those disgusted with the AWB thugs was General Constand Viljoen, a retired former SADF chief and a highly respected figure in white conservative circles.[12]

With South Africa's first democratic election approaching, the DP faced a coordinated attempt by the NP and the ANC to deny the party any credit for bringing apartheid to an end. For the NP to secure black, Indian, and coloured support, it had to diminish the DP's role and portray itself as the party responsible for the dismantling of apartheid. Here its decades-old propaganda of portraying liberals as high on ideals, but powerless and ineffectual muddlers in practice, paid off. Especially amongst white voters who feared an ANC majority, the perception remained that liberals

---

11 T.R.H. Davenport, *The transfer of power in South Africa* (Cape Town, 1998), p. 44.
12 Welsh, *The rise and fall of apartheid*, pp. 427–428, 482–485, 500–502.

were weak, untrustworthy, and opportunistic hypocrites who were financially so comfortable that they could escape the consequences of the collapse of apartheid. The Democrats found it difficult to counter the continuously repeated claim in the Afrikaans press that the DP was such a small party that it could play no significant role on the national stage.[13]

In the ANC, the DP's long history of opposing apartheid through its Progressive predecessors, and the vindication of its liberal principles, was resented. For the ANC to credit the Democrats for the peaceful transition to a democratically elected majority government would be to disparage the history of its long and heroic struggle against white oppression. During the long anti-apartheid struggle, socialists, Marxists and black nationalists scorned liberals as agents of capitalism, maintainers of white privilege and underminers of the revolutionary struggle. The DP was beyond the pale for participating in the apartheid state's parliamentary system, criticising the ANC's armed struggle, international sanctions, and the disinvestment campaign. For doing so, the democrats were labelled as racist agents working to blunt the freedom struggle. The resignation of Slabbert as PFP leader, and the memoirs of Wilson, fed this narrative. The DP's claim of opposing apartheid was rejected with derision.

To counter the gloom in the party, De Beer did his utmost to push a positive message in the National Council meeting of 8 and 9 May. He was adamant that the research showing that the DP would not do well in the election could be discounted, since the popularity of the NP and De Klerk had already declined considerably. There was the possibility of attracting at least 10%, if not 15%, of the electorate. To achieve this vote, the party had to spread the following message:

The DP would have to stress all the factors in its favour, its human rights record, its non-racialism, its recognition as an individual centrist party, its stance against corruption and its social market economic policy, but first and foremost it would have to succeed

---

13 *Beeld*, 10 September 1993.

in getting the message of proportional representation across to voters, and the fact that the DP were the party best equipped to accelerate the process of nation-building.

He sent council members away with the message that there was no substitute for hard campaigning, and that they had to realise that it was not only the party's survival that was at stake but also that of South Africa.[14]

His optimism was not shared by many Democrats as they found it difficult to spread the party's message. On 7 August 1993 at Orange Farm in the Vaal Triangle, delegates at a DP meeting were attacked with stones, and one Democrat was doused in petrol by youths carrying petrol bombs. The attack was justified on the grounds that the Democrats who had "enjoyed the luxury of apartheid" should not expect to seek support among apartheid's victims. The ANC spokesman, Ronnie Mamoepa, exonerated the attackers, accusing the DP of vilifying the liberation movement by criticising the ANC.

De Beer was outraged and condemned the incident because democracy was being trampled by bullies. He vowed that the DP would return to Orange Farm.[15] While struggling to secure support amongst black people, the DP continued to lose support amongst white voters, while some of its representatives jumped ship. In September 1993, six of the party's city councillors in Randburg and Sandton joined the ANC.[16]

---

14 Wits, PFP/DP papers, ab2.2.11, National Council , 8 and 9 May 1993.
15 *Sunday Times*, 22 August 1993.
16 *Beeld*, 10 September 1993.

CHAPTER 28
Fighting for survival
July–December 1993

In this period a feeling developed in the parliamentary caucus that De Beer lacked the energy and dynamism to lead the party. These concerns were fuelled by opinion polls showing that the DP failed to register more than two per cent nationally, and only six per cent among white voters. De Beer, as leader, ran behind his own party in the polls. According to Bob Mattes, a lecturer in political studies at UCT, this was astonishing as the DP had so little support to begin with.[1]

With De Klerk and Mandela, as well as Buthelezi dominating news, it was difficult for leaders of smaller parties to make an impression. Although De Beer was highly regarded across political divisions in parliament and at the MPNP, he made no impact on the wider public. Among some DP MPs, a perception developed that De Beer's main strength – his calm and unflappable attitude to challenges and problems, as well as the ability to soak up frustrations and never to be seen as too excited about anything – was a weakness. For them it created the perception of him being phlegmatic and indifferent with an unwillingness to fight for the DP and its cause.[2] Gibson, although fond of De Beer, was furthermore irked by his cultivated image of a weary elder statesman when he was not that old, encouraging the perception that he enjoyed the status of being party leader, but not the reality of being one.[3]

There was a growing concern amongst some in the caucus that

---

1 B. Mattes, "The campaign thus far", *Die Suid-Afrikaan*, March/April 1994, p. 15.
2 Interview with T. Leon, 3 April 2020.
3 Correspondence with D. Gibson, 31 March 2020.

the state of his health was hampering his leadership. During debates after lunch in parliament, he would occasionally fall asleep in his parliamentary bench. Worrall who sat close to him in parliament was amused at his frequent dozing during debates.[4] Soal, who sat behind him, would kick his bench to wake him. De Beer would then politely thank him. This led to NP MPs jokingly referring to him as Zzzach.[5]

By 1993, De Beer was exhausted as the demands of leadership in a small party were continuous and never-ending. In addition, the years of negotiating the cross currents of the troika and the divisions in the party had taken its toll.[6] His occasional nodding off in parliament was because he would have a glass of wine during lunch, and the wine together with his heart medication made him sleepy. On the other hand, the anecdotes about his dozing during debates are exaggerated as Pieter Mulder has no memory of any such incident.[7] However, when he fell asleep at a DP caucus meeting at the end of the parliamentary session, concerns about his leadership increased.[8] His appearance also contributed to these worries. At a party function he arrived in Stokie slippers (he suffered from gout) and his suit appeared too tight (as he had gained weight), creating the perception that he was past his shelf life as party leader.[9]

De Beer's leadership was not above criticism, but the main reason for the discontentment with him was the sense of gloom in the caucus that the DP would be annihilated in the coming election. According to Roy Jenkins, who led the small Social Democratic Party in the British political system dominated by the much larger Conservative and Labour parties, "[t]he lively hope of success is always a good healer for a party and a prop to the position of its

---

4 Correspondence with Dr D. Worrall, 22 March 2022.
5 Interview with P. Soal, 11 April 2020.
6 Correspondence with J. Selfe, 4 April 2020.
7 Correspondence with Dr P. Mulder, 17 March 2021.
8 Correspondence with J. Selfe, 4 April 2020.
9 Interview with D. Gibson, 1 April 2020.

leader."[10] For the DP there was no "lively hope of success" and this frustration and angst was taken out on De Beer.

Fuchs, a tempestuous and headstrong person – Carlisle viewed him as "an excitable young man with a somewhat messianic image of himself" – was convinced that De Beer was not physically up to the leadership, and that his heart was not in it anymore. He was of the opinion that if the DP wanted to secure any success in the coming election, the dynamic Leon had to be the leader. He went to visit De Beer at his Johannesburg home and requested him to stand aside for the young Hillbrow MP. Fuchs acted on his own initiative and did not discuss his plan with Leon, who was surprised to hear about it.[11] He promptly distanced himself from Fuchs and in parliament announced that he would personally endorse De Beer for another term as leader at the party's upcoming congress.[12] Leon, according to Selfe, was by then in two minds whether he should become the leader as it was evident that the DP would get a drubbing in the election. It would be better to remain the heir apparent, and to make his move after the election.[13]

De Beer told Fuchs that he had taken advice from his friends in the party and that they had advised him to stay on as leader. He was determined to lead the DP in the 1994 election. To resign before the election would leave the party in a crisis as there was no obvious successor: Worrall had faded from the political scene, Eglin had no interest in a third stint as party leader, while Leon was young, inexperienced and seen as too impatient and abrasive.

De Beer had the highest opinion of Leon's ability and talents.[14] He was always kind and encouraging to him, but once told him that he "suffered from divine discontent". Leon ruefully conceded that it was an accurate diagnosis of his impatience and always striving for the next best thing.[15] His abrasiveness convinced MPs such as Soal

---

10 R. Jenkins, *Baldwin* (London, 1987), p. 122.
11 Correspondence with T. Leon, 4 January 2022.
12 Debates of parliament, 20 September 1993, Col. 13319.
13 Correspondence with J. Selfe, 4 April 2020.
14 Interview with Zach de Beer junior, 22 April 2020.
15 Leon, *The accidental ambassador*, pp. 248–249.

and Jordaan that he should not be party leader. Less outspoken, but equally determined to keep him out of the leadership, was Eglin who felt that he lacked judgement on people and issues.[16]

The feeling amongst most DP MPs was that De Beer's statesman-like gravitas was needed for the party to compete with Mandela and De Klerk. *The Argus* concurred that in a crucial moment in political history it would be unfortunate to have De Beer fading from the scene as his dignity, common sense, gravitas, acumen and wise counsel was needed. To deal with the criticism of younger MPs, the newspaper recommended that the DP's upcoming congress in October elected a deputy leader because De Beer needed a backup, while the party had to plan for the future. However, to Wendy he made it clear that he did not want a deputy,[17] and nothing came of this suggestion.

To stamp out any rumours about his leadership, he announced that he would like to retire after the elections in April 1994 and that his decision would be influenced by the circumstances at the time, and after him assessing whether he would do the job better than anyone else: "I am quite well aware that if I hang on and hang on until I get gagga then there has to be some crisis to remove me. That you will have to leave to me to judge."[18]

In an interview with the Afrikaans opinion paper *Vrye Weekblad* (29 September 1993), Leon affirmed that De Beer had credibility and high standing in wider society and that the whole issue surrounding his leadership was not an attempted coup, but a discussion on leadership styles to which De Beer had been open, and that there was no demand that he should resign. Leon also used the interview to set out his ideas on what the DP's strategy should be in the coming election. He argued that the party's greatest achievement – being a facilitator between the ANC and the NP – had become a handicap as the party had lost its identity.

---

16 Eglin, *Crossing the borders of power*, p. 309.
17 Note with the clipping of the *Argus* to Wendy de Beer Furniss, no date, in her possession.
18 *Sunday Times*, 19 September 1993.

His solution was an aggressive stance to expose the weaknesses of other parties.

De Beer, at a parliamentary caucus meeting to clear the air about his leadership, conceded that his performance was unsatisfactory but that he would improve. He offered to go anywhere or do anything the party required from him. On hearing this, Carlisle leaped up and said: "Well Zach, you must lead and we will follow. But if you simply carry on as before you will lead us over a cliff."[19] Carlisle is of the opinion that in this period De Beer came over as a sad person as the realisation had kicked in that he was not cut out for the top leadership and that his reach exceeded his grasp by quite a wide margin.[20] Irene Menell, a close friend of Suzman and the Oppenheimers who often socialised with De Beer, also felt that although he was highly intelligent, charming and tough, he was limited by his own insecurities, namely, a sense of guilt as he was ambivalent about the demands of his ambition and whether he was "doing the right thing".[21] It would have been human for De Beer after the harrowing experience of listening to the MPs expressing criticism about his leadership to have doubts about his abilities and to appear melancholy. In 1979, Eglin had found the same experience shattering and it took some time to rebound. The criticism of his leadership left De Beer dispirited. It would take self-discipline, courage and a strong sense of duty to face the daunting task of leading the DP into the election. However, he would rise to the occasion.

A special parliamentary session did help to lighten his mood. On 21 September 1993, parliament convened to enter into law the Transitional Executive Council (TEC) Bill. The Bill was based on an MPNP decision to create a multiparty executive to help run the country until the election, with the government in a form of power-sharing. The TEC ended three centuries of white rule as the government could no longer govern on its own and had to do so

---

19 Leon, *On the contrary*, p. 218.
20 Correspondence with R. Carlisle, 14 Aril 2020.
21 Correspondence with I. Menell, 16, 18 and 21 August 2021.

in tandem with the TEC. For De Beer it was a moment of joy: "For forty years those of us who fought against apartheid wondered whether it would be replaced within our lifetimes."[22] The Bill was passed despite the rowdy behaviour of CP MPs accusing Roelf Meyer, the NP's chief negotiator, of being a despicable traitor, and that parliament had become a rubber stamp of events settled in Kempton Park.[23] The TEC, with two representatives from each of the MPNP contingents, had its first meeting on 7 December with Eglin and Andrew representing the Democrats.

That De Beer had taken the criticism of his leadership seriously was evident at the DP's national conference in Sea Point on 2 and 3 October. The 550 delegates unanimously re-elected him as leader. In his opening address, which he labelled the most important speech he would ever make, he set out the DP's approach to the coming election: That the main task of the party was to prevent the ANC, intolerant to other parties with communists among its leaders, to secure a two-thirds majority to write the new constitution. He was convinced that for most voters, the NP with its history of trampling of human rights and racism, was an unacceptable alternative to the ANC. Many South Africans who were concerned about an ANC majority would never vote for the NP but would turn to the DP with its history as a passionate defender of human dignity:

> We must fight on our claim that we, not the others, own democracy. It is we who have upheld human rights – we, not the ANC, stone-throwers of Orange farm; we, not the Nats whose servants killed [Steve] Biko and [Neil] Aggett …[24]

He made it clear that although the battle against apartheid had been won, the danger to human dignity was still amongst South Africans. To play a leading role in the new South Africa, the party had to win enough votes to earn positions in the cabinet of

---

22 Debates of parliament, 21 September 1993, Col. 13389.
23 *Beeld*, 22 September 1993.
24 *The Star*, 4 October 1993.

a government of national unity. To fight what he termed as the "mother of all elections" he undertook to take the leadership of the fundraising campaign on his own shoulders.[25] De Beer had not only buried the controversy surrounding his leadership but also succeeded in shedding the image of the party as an intellectual debating society for wealthy whites. A growing number of black people were part of party structures and played a leading role at the conference. Furthermore, he created a more muscular image of the party as the upholder of human rights in South Africa.[26]

At the same time, the DP was boosting its image at the MPNP. Under Eglin's skilful leadership the Democrat team punched above its weight and was instrumental in ensuring agreement on a powerful Bill of Rights, and a constitutional court.[27] De Beer's role in the final negotiations in Kempton Park did not go down well with his negotiating team. On 17 November 1993, on the evening before the final vote on the interim constitution, he became involved in a horse-trading deal that fuelled their perception that he was politically out of touch. Dene Smuts was leading the argument that a single ballot would diminish the degree of democracy as it would deny voters the right to vote for one party at national level and another one at provincial level. The ANC insisted on a single ballot, claiming that a double ballot would confuse first-time voters. At the same time, Leon was involved in negotiations to oppose executive appointments of Constitutional Court judges, as he feared that it would politicise the court. He wanted the judges to be appointed by the Judicial Service Commission. He felt so strongly about this that he told De Beer that he was minded voting against the interim constitution when it came to parliament for ratification.

De Beer responded that he supported the proposed constitution and would advise the party to do so as well. Under pressure from the DP's negotiating team, he held a press conference on the eve-

---

25 *Sunday Times*, 3 October 1993: *Cape Times*, 4 October 1993.
26 *Financial Mail*, 8 October 1993.
27 P. Waldmeir, *Anatomy of a miracle. The end of apartheid and the birth of the new South Africa* (London, 1997), p. 228.

ning of 16 December to express his disappointment on the appointment of Constitutional Court judges, but he made it clear that the party would not walk away from the negotiations.[28] He also telephoned Mandela and De Klerk to express his concern about the issue of the judges, and requested its urgent reconsideration. Cyril Ramaphosa as the ANC's lead negotiator, knowing that his party would concede the role of the Judicial Service Commission in these appointments, collared De Beer – who was not in the know about this development – with an offer that in exchange for a single election ballot the Constitutional Court judges would not be executive appointments. De Beer agreed to this, justifying his decision as follows: "It was a question of time. We were afraid that we might lose on both issues. To us, it was more important to secure the constitutional court and fight the second ballot at a later stage."[29]

However, Leon felt that De Beer had blinked, and that the DP was complicit in a disgraceful dilution of democracy. Eglin claimed that he felt "unclean" and condemned it in parliament as a shabby deal.[30] However, this compromise made possible – two hours before sunrise on 18 November – the approval of the final document. The interim constitution made provision for a five-year Government of National Unity (five per cent of the total vote would secure parties a place in the national government), a common citizenship, the incorporation of all the homelands, and the demarcation of nine provinces. The Constitutional Assembly, which would be the parliament elected in April 1994, would draft the final constitution, and a two-thirds majority was required to approve it. An excited De Beer urged those present that morning in Kempton Park not to rest until a full democracy was implemented.[31]

Parliament met on Monday 22 November to discuss the state of the negotiation process. The session immediately degenerated

---

28 *Beeld*, 17 November 1993.
29 *Sunday Times*, 17 April 1994.
30 Leon, *On the contrary*, p. 221–226, 229.
31 *Beeld*, 19 November 1993.

into a free-for-all as the CP accused the NP of selling out white people. De Beer argued that the interim constitution had flaws and shortcomings and that there was still much to be done to improve it and that a constitution is not an end in itself, but a means to an end – an open, free, just and prosperous society. People had to develop habits of lifestyle and patterns of social intercourse to create such a society. He emphasised that South Africa had to work on achieving national unity. He concluded his speech with the hope that those elected on 27 April 1994 would make further improvements to the constitution.[32]

On 17 December, parliament met to ratify the Constitution of the Republic of South Africa Bill. The debate started in a calm atmosphere as seemingly even the CP realised that the end of the road had been reached. De Beer, although objecting to the single ballot for the national and provincial elections and the fact that the federal provisions were inadequate, expressed his joy and appreciation:

> We in the DP support this constitution. We support it strongly and with joy in our hearts, because it does go a very long way to giving effect to equal rights, personal freedom and the rule of the law, the great objectives that we have pursued for many, many years.[33]

Five days later he reiterated his gratitude on what had been achieved:

> South Africa is a very different place from what it was when this Parliament first met. The barriers of race are falling all around us. The principles of democracy, as it has been generally understood in the world of our time, are becoming established in our country. There is much to be grateful for.[34]

---

32 Debates of parliament, 22 November 1993, Col. 13818–13822.
33 Debates of parliament, 18 December 1993, Col. 15529.
34 Debates of parliament, 22 December 1993, Col. 16264.

The Bill was finally passed on 23 December. Outraged CP MPs, with their supporters in the public gallery, sang "Die Stem", and yelled at the NP benches that they were traitors. From the public gallery, a young man yelled at De Klerk: "Ek hoop u straf is nie so groot soos u sonde nie. U is 'n verraaier" (I hope your punishment is not as great as your sin. You are a traitor). In reaction, ANC and Labour Party MPs yelled "Amandla" with raised fists.[35] With the acceptance of the interim constitution, Worrall announced his retirement from parliamentary politics, resigning his seat in January 1994 to pursue a career in the private sector. De Beer expressed his regret, but made no attempt to persuade him to change his mind.[36]

For De Beer, the year had ended on a positive note. The DP was united with a clearly defined sense of purpose. He had a good party conference that had settled the concerns surrounding his leadership. Crucially, the interim constitution included every political principle he had fought for since the founding of the PP in 1959. This was a track record and an achievement with which he could face the electorate. The DP-supporting *Financial Mail* (10 December 1993) was confident that the party could secure at least 60 seats in the 400-seat National Assembly. De Beer made it clear that he would be extremely disappointed if the Democrats obtained less than seven per cent of the total vote and that the party could get more than 10 per cent,[37] securing him a place in the Government of National Unity.

---

35 *Beeld*, 23 December 1993.
36 Worrall, *The independent factor*, pp. 211–212.
37 *Cape Times*, 19 April 1994.

CHAPTER 29
A gruelling campaign
January–April 1994

De Beer was fully aware that in an "uhuru [independence] election" with the ANC being led by Mandela, the DP would struggle to attract black voters while some of the party's policies were not attractive to them. The Democrats, for example, opposed quotas as part of affirmative action for black people, as well as land distribution as property ownership was the basis of prosperous state. The DP supported a land policy based on a willing-buyer-and-willing-seller basis. The championing of the free market was an additional obstacle to attract black votes as many felt that private enterprise would benefit the big corporations such as the AAC. De Beer was accused that he had financially benefitted from apartheid while verbally opposing it. This claim of hypocrisy came from the investigative journal *Noseweek* of July 1993 under the heading "Dr De Beer: Dr Zackyll and Mr (take you for a) ride?", claiming that as an AAC director, he had few qualms for accepting huge and profitable contracts for the construction of apartheid facilities.[1] In retirement, he conceded that the accusation had merit and that it was difficult to counter, as it reflected the complex and ambiguous position of the businessman in the apartheid state.

He was of the opinion that the Democrats would only be able to attract black voters in the next general election with the growth of a middle class and the awareness that free-market economies outperformed state-run economies, and if the ANC failed to deliver the goods.[2] The DP decided to focus its campaign on

---

1   D. O'Meara, *Forty lost years. The apartheid state and the politics of the National Party, 1948–1994* (Randburg, 1996), pp. 363–364.
2   *The Natal Mercury*, 8 and 9 March 1994.

white, coloured and Indian voters. De Beer was confident that the Democrats' record of defending human rights combined with its image as a party of principle and policy, and not of power and personalities, would secure electoral support amongst these groups.

However, the DP had a considerable obstacle: the dismal financial state of the party. There were concerns that the party could run out of money before election day. The poverty of the party meant that the party's campaign only started in February 1994. De Beer confided in *The Natal Mercury* (9 March 1994) that the Democrats had only a fraction of the resources of the ANC and the NP. For example, the ANC had an election fund of R150 million.[3] The Democrats' entire budget was only marginally bigger than the R11 million the ANC had earmarked for its poster campaign. The party's coffers were so empty that there were months that De Beer had to sign a personal cheque to pay Mienke Bain. However, by then his personal assistant's admiration for him was so immense that she would have worked for free.[4]

But when it came to an election campaign, money was essential for propaganda purposes and the salaries of full-time organisers. The Democrat campaign lacked election offices, vehicles and organisers. The party had to rely on volunteers as well as privately owned vehicles to put up posters and distribute pamphlets.[5] This resulted in an amateurish campaign with no advance work for rallies. Consequently, unscripted appearances were common for De Beer with the potential of disastrous consequences.

As the main objective of the Democrats was to prevent the ANC from securing a two-thirds majority, which would enable the movement to write the final constitution, the DP's election manifesto, "Protecting you from the abuse of power", positioned the party as the natural watchdog to protect the rule of law and human rights:

---

[3] Welsh, *The rise and fall of apartheid*, p. 539.
[4] Correspondence with M. Bain, 30 April 2020.
[5] *Cape Times*, 16 March 1994; *The Natal Mercury*, 7 April 1994.

One golden thread runs right through the document. This is the unique shining belief of the Democrats in the supreme worth of the individual human being and in his or her essential dignity. Whether we are dealing with human rights. Or with economic solutions, with the rooting out of racism or the framing of the constitution, these are the values which guide and inspire us.

In contrast to the DP's long history of efficient opposition by its Progressive predecessors, the NP with its oppressive past would not be able to be a vigilant watchdog of liberal democratic values. According to Leon, the NP would be a "toothless chihuahua".[6] Voters were furthermore reminded that the NP politicians were propagating policies for which they had vilified the DP only five years earlier.[7]

From the opening shots of the election campaign, De Beer had to face the challenge that the Democrat's message was marginalised as the media news cycle, especially on television, was dominated by the jockeying for power between the ANC and NP. In fact, the election was a presidential race between Mandela and De Klerk with no interest in De Beer. To secure a distinctive niche, De Beer did his utmost to portray the DP as the champion of the free market with the message that South Africa could only become a prosperous democracy if there was an opportunity to generate wealth on own initiative. Nicky Oppenheimer, Harry's son and the deputy chairman of AAC, addressed a public meeting to praise the party's policies.[8] At a news conference in Cape Town on 11 April, he proclaimed that neither the ANC nor the NP fully supported the principles of the free market, and that the DP would protect them in parliament.[9] Addressing UCT students the next day, he lambasted the NP as a profligate and interfering party that had stifled private enterprise.[10]

---

6 *The Pretoria News*, 10 March 1994.
7 *The Natal Mercury*, 11 March 1994.
8 *Sunday Times*, 3 April 1994.
9 *Cape Times*, 12 April 1994.
10 *The Argus*, 13 April 1994.

However, De Beer's championing of the free market brought the Democrats little support as the ANC had adapted its stance on nationalisation. In January 1992, in an attempt to attract foreign capital to South Africa, Mandela at an international meeting at Davos, Switzerland, ditched the concept of the nationalisation of key industries.[11] After this, big businesses, with the exception of the AAC, accepted that it could do business with a future ANC government and saw no need to support the Democrats, or even the NP.

The DP was also marginalised by the desperate attempts to convince the IFP and the CP to participate in the election. As part of this process, parliament met at the end of February 1994 to approve the Constitution Amendment Bill and the Electoral Amendment Bill. These Bills made provision for separate ballot papers for the national and provincial parliaments as well as for the roles of traditional leaders when provinces adopted their own constitutions. KwaZulu-Natal was obliged to make room for the Zulu monarch. For the CP, provision was made for a Volkstaat Council to pursue the establishment of a homeland for Afrikaners. De Beer supported both Bills.[12] Despite these concessions, the CP and the IFP still refused to participate in the election.

On 11 March, South Africa was shaken by the so-called Battle of Bop, the bloody collapse of the Bophuthatswana Bantustan. To counter resistance to his regime, Lucas Mangope, the apartheid-appointed Bantustan leader, had requested right-wing support. This led to the intervention of AWB thugs and resulted in indiscriminate shootings and bloodshed, ending with the South African Army ousting Mangope and taking control of Bophuthatswana. The chaos of the day convinced General Constand Viljoen to register the newly formed Freedom Front (FF) to participate in the coming election. In doing so, he led the bulk of ultraconservative Afrikaners into constitutional politics and the new South Africa,

---

11 N. Ferguson, *The square and the tower. Networks, hierarchies and the struggle for global power* (St Ives, 2017), p. 312.
12 *The Natal Mercury*, 1 March 1994.

isolating the CP and AWB and the possibility of any significant right-wing uprising. Mandela praised Viljoen as one of South Africa's greatest politicians.[13]

Buthelezi and the IFP remained aloof while the violent conflicts between the ANC and Inkatha supporters increased. On 28 March, a total of 53 people died when the IFP marched on the ANC headquarters in Johannesburg. To maintain law and order, De Klerk declared a state of emergency in Natal on 31 March. Against this violent backdrop, the NP encouraged the perception that the DP was a minor and irrelevant party and that a vote for the Democrats would be a wasted one. Posters with "Only the NP can stop the ANC" were plastered on thousands of trees and lampposts. Hernus Kriel, Minister of Law and Order, proclaimed at a public meeting in East London that since there were no policy differences between them, there was no reason for the NP and DP to oppose each other. The Democrats had to join the NP.[14] De Klerk used this as an excuse to avoid a television debate with De Beer, claiming that it would serve no purpose.[15]

De Beer did his utmost to reach out to the Democrats' target groups. He criss-crossed the country to address public meetings with the promise that the party would protect human rights issues with tooth and nail. He had some colourful experiences along the way. In Worcester in the Western Cape a pensioner was determined to take off his pants to show him his scar from a recent operation.[16] In Phoenix, an Indian suburb north of Durban, he mingled with minibus taxi drivers, hawkers and street vendors, and had to submit himself to a head grip of the wrestler Gama Singh while posing for a photograph.[17] However, his campaign lost some momentum when on 20 March he announced that he could possibly retire from politics after the election. "I'm 65-and-a-half,

---

13 *The Pretoria News*, 22 April 1994.
14 *The Natal Mercury*, 11 March 1994.
15 *Sunday Times*, 17 April 1994.
16 *Cape Times*, 16 March 1994.
17 *Sunday Times Extra*, 13 March 1994.

I'm old enough to retire, but it depends on the election results, it depends on the composition of the cabinet, it depends on the rules of the cabinet."

He added that although Leon was second on the DP's national election list and a "thoroughly outstanding politician", it was by no means certain that he would take over the leadership.[18] The "retirement syndrome" – as it was referred to in party circles – distracted from the DP's message because journalists were then more interested in who would succeed De Beer. A senior party figure complained to Brian Pottinger of the *Sunday Times* (17 April 1994): "It drives me out of my mind when a leader goes around saying he is contemplating resigning depending on the outcome of the election."[19]

Although the "retirement syndrome" was a distraction, it was a minor one compared to the difficulty of reaching out to voters. Denied television exposure, it was a challenge to connect with white, coloured and Indian voters, but even more so a near impossibility to connect with black voters as the party was effectively prevented from campaigning amongst them. Because of the violence in Natal, big parts of the province were no-go areas for the Democrats. After death threats, the DP decided not to campaign in the Transkei as ANC and PAC activists disrupted the party's meetings.[20] At an electoral information meeting at the University of South Africa on 19 April, students were outraged when De Beer stated that he had always opposed apartheid. When he pointed out that he was one of the handful of PP MPs who had been courageous enough in 1960 to vote against the outlawing of the ANC, the students contemptuously howled him down.

This intolerance was also present at the University of the Western Cape (UWC) where the SRC refused to allow the Democrats to address meetings on the campus as they only allowed "parties

---

18 *Sunday Times*, 20 March 1994.
19 Leon, *On the contrary*, pp. 240, 244.
20 A. Reynolds, *Election '94 South Africa. The campaigns, results and future prospects* (Claremont, 1994), p. 113.

of the oppressed".[21] ANC supporters chased Leon off the Good Hope College's Khayelitsha campus.[22] At UCT, ANC supporters also attempted to disrupt his meeting. Leon warned that with this behaviour a new tyranny was facing South Africa.[23] De Beer challenged Mandela to control his followers and to allow free speech.[24] The ANC leader urged his supporters to be tolerant of other parties, but the message did not always percolate down to grassroots level. When the DP attempted to address a meeting in Kommetjie near Cape Town, two Democrats were stabbed and an IEC observer assaulted, while the party's pamphlets were destroyed.[25]

Leon was eventually allowed to address students at UWC but was howled down and forced from the platform. He fled the campus in a vehicle with spinning tyres as he was pursued by a mob throwing stones and tins at him.[26] On 14 April, while touring KwaThema on the East Rand, the DP's "battle bus" was attacked by a mob who smashed a window, defaced the bus and threw burning party posters into the vehicle.[27] The inability to reach out to black voters meant that the DP was little known and barely understood in the black community.[28]

De Beer's own efforts to reach out to black voters led to an embarrassing incident. He was promised that in rural northern Transvaal a big group of black supporters had been arranged for him to address. Arriving at the designated meeting place there was no one present. That night the SABC's television news showed him forlornly surveying an empty veld. This image shook Leon and had a lasting effect on him.[29] It certainly influenced the critical way he portrayed De Beer in his memoirs, namely that he had a poor

---

21 *Cape Times*, 14 March 1994.
22 *Cape Times*, 15 March 1994.
23 *Die Burger*, 16 March 1994.
24 *The Natal Mercury*, 13 March 1994.
25 *Beeld*, 11 April 1994.
26 *Cape Times*, 14 April 1994.
27 *The Star*, 15 April 1994.
28 M. Meredith, *South Africa's new era. The 1994 election* (London, 1994), p. 160.
29 Bloom, *Out of step*, p. 49.

campaign as he lacked energy and failed to project himself as a leader. Although he always acted positively to requests to address meetings, however far away or isolated, even driving himself to these destinations, he brought nothing to the meeting. For him De Beer's image of decency and moderation was not enough.[30]

Leon was not the only unhappy Democrat. In a debate with Leon, Dalling raised what the *Sunday Times* (10 April) called a complicitous titter amongst Democrats when he referred to the DP's "Zach-lustre campaign". According to the *Sunday Times* columnist, Hogarth, some DP members called De Beer "Doctor zzzzzzz...." because of his habit to regularly slumber during the day.

For Welsh and Eglin, the reason for his lack of energy during the campaign was the debilitating effects of his cardio-vascular medication, as mentioned earlier.[31] However, Bain is of the opinion that the claims of the effects of his medication is exaggerated as De Beer had run himself ragged in a gruelling campaign.[32] As the SABC's television coverage focused on party leaders, the ANC, NP and IFP dominated the news. De Beer had no choice but to undertake a never-ending succession of public meetings. With the lack of organisational structures, he had little support from the DP. This led to the public disaster in the northern Transvaal with him wandering in an empty veld looking for promised supporters, and his physical state of exhaustion.

Debbie de Beer observed how gruelling the campaign was for her father. In early April she accompanied him for five days on the campaign trail to visit Moria, the Easter gathering of the Zion Christian Church, as well as to dusty and far-and-beyond corners of the northern Transvaal. And yet, despite his poor health, obvious tiredness and the struggle to be continuously buoyant, she realised that he enjoyed the campaign. It was a momentous experience for him to participate in South Africa's first democratic election. To

---

30 Leon, *On the contrary*, pp. 240, 244.
31 Welsh, *The rise and fall of apartheid*, p. 552; Eglin, *Crossing the borders of power*, p. 309.
32 Correspondence with M. Bain, 30 April 2020.

be part of the election was a personal triumph in his opposition to apartheid that had started back in 1950. He uncomplainingly went the extra mile to keep the liberal standard of the DP flying as was evident in his visit to the Modjadji, or Rain Queen, the hereditary queen of the Balobedu. As custom required, he entered her presence on his hands and knees in his expensive suit.[33]

By the beginning of April, De Beer's campaigning made some impact on the electorate. On 3 April, a *Sunday Times* survey found a surge of support for the DP amongst whites and Indians. In the Western Cape between November 1993 and March 1994, the party had doubled its support to 10,5 per cent. This meant that the Democrats could possibly hold the balance of power between the ANC and NP in the provincial parliament and secure a place in the Western Cape government. This was a possibility the *Cape Times* (7 April 1994) welcomed as the Democrats could place a brake on authoritarian tendencies and safeguard the province against corruption and the abuse of power. To maintain this momentum, the party placed newspaper ads with the message: "Vote for the Democratic Party. We might be smaller, but we'll never surrender."[34]

---

33 Interview with Debbie de Beer, 23 April 2020.
34 *Cape Times*, 7 April 1994.

CHAPTER 30
The near annihilation of the Democratic Party
April 1994

On 14 April, the televised debate between Mandela and De Klerk, viewed by what was believed to be the largest television audience in South African history, brought any momentum the DP may have had to an end. Despite their differences and accusations, Mandela took De Klerk's hand at the end of the debate and said: "I am proud to hold your hand, let us go forward together, let us work together to end division and suspicion."[1] The handshake left the perception of two men who would be able to work together for the greater good of the country, and that there was no need for the DP to act as a liberal watchdog. This was evident when Leon addressed a public meeting in Port Elizabeth on 20 April. He could only attract 350 people compared to the busloads of supporters that had come to listen to De Klerk the night before.[2]

The campaign for the Democrats became even more challenging when the NP ran an advertisement campaign "The DP is a little confused – it thinks *we* are their opposition," with a cartoon of De Beer as a diminutive boxer, swinging wildly at De Klerk who is holding him at arms-length, with the SACP wolf in the sheep's clothing of the ANC hovering behind the DP leader.

This cartoon conveyed the message that the Democrats had lost sight of the real threat to South Africa. The NP also managed to plant the information that a significant number of DP MPs and city councillors had joined the ANC.[3] The advertisement effectively

---

1 *Cape Times*, 15 April 1994.
2 *The Argus*, 21 April 1994.
3 See for example *Beeld* and *The Argus*, 21 April 1994.

conveyed the message that a vote for the Democrats was a wasted one, as the NP was the only alternative to the ANC and SACP.

The inability of the DP to gain political momentum reignited criticism that De Beer's leadership was too lethargic. Even Suzman shared this perception. Privately she predicted that the DP could not win more than three or four seats in the new parliament.[4] In an interview with Brian Pottinger of the *Sunday Times* (17 April), De Beer made it clear that he did not take kindly to the claim that he was not active enough: "If they want to get rid of me, they can. They can do that at the National Council meeting after the elections or the congress in September this year."[5] He was more emollient in an interview with *The Cape Times* (19 April): "At 65 I'm not looking to a very long future. But I certainly feel well enough to carry on for some considerable time if that is what the party wants and what appears to be."

"The DP is a little confused – it thinks *we* are their opposition"
From: *The Argus*, 21 April 1994

---

4 Wits, Helen Suzman papers, mb2.33.1.12, H. Suzman – G. Walt, 12 January 1994.
5 *Sunday Times*, 17 April 1994.

Any interest in his leadership or the DP was swept away on 19 April by the announcement that the IFP would participate in the election. As the ballot papers had already been printed, stickers bearing the IFP logo had to be pasted onto the ballot papers. For South Africa's first democratic election it was miraculously good news, but it pushed the DP deeper into the ignored margins. On the 19th De Beer addressed Unisa students in Pretoria. He performed well in the face of hostile questioning, but with the IFP dominating the news not even the local *Pretoria News* reported the meeting. Furthermore, the IFP provided an alternative for those voters who feared a too large ANC majority but did not want to vote for the NP.

However, De Beer's confidence was boosted when six of the mainstream newspapers gave its support to the DP (the ANC and the NP receiving the backing of three each).[6] In Natal, the three leading English-medium newspapers came out for the party. On 15 April, *The Natal Mercury* urged voters to back the Democrats as it was "likely to contribute the most to the building of a true democracy" and that the election of 20 DP MPs would do more for democracy than 200 from the ANC or 80 from the NP. The Pietermaritzburg-based *The Daily News* (22 April) praised the DP as a vexatious watchdog on government excesses, "a whistle-blower on government profligacy, and a potent champion of human rights". The Durban-based *Sunday Tribune* on 24 April highlighted the party's solid track record of liberalism and pointed out that it had a watchdog role to play. It further stated that in an insecure time, a vote for such a party was not a wasted one. In East London, the *Daily Dispatch* gave its full support to the Democrats, while in Johannesburg the *Weekend Star* (23–24 April) made it clear that the DP espoused the principles which the newspaper cherished, and with the proportional system, votes for the party would not be wasted.

On 24 April, Ken Owen, the volatile editor of the influential *Sunday Times*, in a column "Democracy means voting for the least bad

---

6   *The Natal Mercury*, 27 April 1994.

choice", grudgingly expressed his support for the DP as he could not vote for the ANC, NP or IFP. With regard to the ANC, he feared that with a two-thirds majority it could trample over the opposition and rewrite the constitution, while he feared the methods that would be used to achieve its objectives of spreading wealth, educating the masses and housing the poor. The NP was beyond the pale as its main contribution to South Africa was misery, corruption and oppression. The IFP was rejected because of its indefensible record of violence in Natal and that it had retreated into Zulu nationalism which excludes everyone else. Owen acknowledged that the DP was sound and correct in its principles, but that hardly anyone respects its "hand-wringing, shuffle-footed, toffee-nosed leadership". He quipped that the election campaign had shown up the excruciating irony that not even the NP was as remote from "the people", or as uncomfortable in the townships, or as lily white in speech, gesture and style as the leadership of the DP. "It's not that they are racist – they are certainly not – but that they are soulless, isolated in their higher education and higher incomes." According to him the reason why the DP had failed to exploit the new opportunities for democracy was that leadership of the party was in the hands of a clique. He sneeringly concluded that the top of the party's list of candidates was dominated by people on the principal qualification that they know one another, and that they huddled together as comfortable codgers in a club. He concluded: "Anyway, I stuck with the liberals when they were almost extinct; I shall not desert them now simply because they are confused."

Owen was a brilliant journalist, but a cantankerous one who had a tradition of feuding with politicians, and to demolish those with whom he disagreed. Slabbert was savaged by him after his resignation as PFP leader, while he also attacked Leon with a vengeance when he became the DP leader. For De Beer and his record of decades-long opposition to apartheid, Owen's criticism must have been painful, especially as it fuelled the perception that he was a poor leader. A more fulsome declaration of support came from *The Argus* (26 April), praising the DP for its steadfast adherence to human rights and the rule of law, and the paper declared that the party would be a respected and influential broker between the ANC and the NP.

In the last few days before polling day on 27 April, De Beer became more optimistic. He was confident that coloured and Indian communities as victims of apartheid would never vote for the NP, and fearing the size of the ANC's majority, they would vote for the DP,[7] while he felt that the party had won back its white supporters.[8] He was not alone in his optimism as Selfe, based on the numbers provincial leaders had provided to him, predicted that the party would secure at least a million votes.[9] Roger Burrows, the Natal leader, for example claimed that the party would secure more than 10 per cent of the vote in the province, and that support between 15 per cent and 20 per cent was not too idealistic.[10]

De Beer's confidence was furthermore boosted by a succession of successful public meetings. On 20 April, he addressed an enthusiastic meeting in Durban's Exhibition Centre. Greeted with a standing ovation and shouts of "Viva DP", he condemned the ANC and NP as power-hungry and authoritarian parties. He ended his speech on a stirring note: "Let the DP speak loudly for the dissident, for the individualist who does not wish to conform, for those who dare just to be themselves."[11] The next day in the Cape Town City Hall with an enthusiastic foot-stomping-banner-waving crowd of more than 700 people – most of them coloured people – he again proclaimed that the DP was the only party that could effectively guard against the abuse of power by any government.[12] Swept along by the enthusiasm of the crowds, De Beer told *The Daily News* (21 April) that he had taken part in 12 general elections

---

7 The O'Malley Archives, Nelson Mandela Centre of Memory, O'Malley's interview with Zach de Beer, 8 November 1994, https://omalley.nelson mandela.org/omalley/index (accessed 28 August 2019).
8 *Cape Times*, 20 April 1994.
9 Correspondence with J. Selfe, 4 April 2020.
10 *The Natal Mercury*, 20 April 1994.
11 *Cape Times*, 23 April 1994.
12 *The Pretoria News*, 22 April 1994.

and three national referendums and that there was always a swing in the voters' fancy in the last week: "There was a swing now in this election and it was running in the favour of the DP." Two days before election day, De Beer was interviewed by Shaun Johnson and Duncan Guy of *The Star* (26 April). He admitted that the personal attacks on him were hurtful, but that it has not deterred him as he was convinced that he had fought a good campaign and hoped to win at least 40 seats. To the journalists he looked fit and energetic after a hectic campaign; that he was relishing the greatest political battle of his career.

On the 25th De Beer attended a special meeting of parliament. To accommodate the IFP's decision to participate in the election, the interim constitution was amended to make provision for the status of the Zulu king in the parliament of the new KwaZulu-Natal province.[13] De Beer supported the amendment as there was a useful role to be played by the Zulu monarch to provide cultural leadership.[14] That evening he had his final campaign meeting in Johannesburg, a jovial and confident one with a 2000-strong crowd in a balloon-filled marque tent on the lawns of the Houghton Primary School.

De Beer reiterated the campaign message of the DP as a champion of free enterprise and a guardian of democracy:

> Some people make the mistake of thinking that if you have government by an elected majority, you have democracy. You don't. Democracy also requires that people are protected against the abuse of power by government ... we know how to be watchful and determined in checking the abuse of power.[15]

In its final newspaper advertisement on 26 April, the DP splashed the names of all the newspapers that expressed its support for the party: "The Nats claim that we're too small to be a strong opposi-

---

13 *Die Burger*, 26 April 1994.
14 Debates of parliament, 25 April 1994, Col. 16740–16742.
15 *The Pretoria News*, 25 April 1994.

tion to the ANC. If that were true, would all these major newspapers be supporting us?"[16]

On election day an optimistic De Beer voted at the polling station in the Woodstock City Hall, only 200 meters from the house where he was born.[17] Selfe was struck by his excitement. De Beer excitedly told a *Beeld* journalist that at one stage in his life he nearly betted against himself that he would not see the end of apartheid. His optimism of a good result was boosted when he visited polling booths on the Cape flats. Walking past lengthy queues of coloured voters, he was greeted by name in the friendliest way, leg-pulling and good humour, leaving him with the impression that they were all voting for the DP.[18] Jack Bloom, as a candidate for the Gauteng provincial parliament, did not share this optimism as he noticed that with special votes cast at old-age homes, life-long elderly supporters in the Johannesburg northern suburbs were splitting their votes. For the National Assembly many voted NP for the first time in their lives to counterbalance the ANC, but voted DP at the provincial level.[19] The election stretched over three days with numerous irregularities and logistical problems as there was no voters' roll. Early election results made it clear that the DP was doing badly. In Atlantis outside Cape Town where the DP had over 700 members it got fewer than 100 votes.[20] In Natal the Democrats attracted barely one per cent of support. Even in Eglin's stronghold of Sea Point, the NP polled more than 50 per cent against the 29 per cent for the DP.

De Beer was stunned by the results, leaving him, in his own words, more than a little depressed.[21] To journalists he made no attempt to conceal his disappointment: "We are very disappointed. It

---

16 *The Star*, 26 April 1994.
17 *Cape Times*, 28 April 1994.
18 The O'Malley Archives, Nelson Mandela Centre of Memory, O'Malley's interview with Zach de Beer, 8 November 1994, https://omalley.nelson mandela.org/omalley/index (accessed 28 August 2019).
19 Bloom, *Out of step*, p. 49
20 Correspondence with J. Selfe, 4 April 2020.
21 *The Natal Mercury*, 2 May 1994.

is much less than we hoped for ... It seems probable the final result will be worse."[22] And it was much worse when the vote from ANC-voting rural areas were tallied. The DP was all but annihilated as the party secured only seven seats in the National Assembly:

ANC	12 237 600	(62,6 per cent)	252 MPs
NP	3 983 700	(20,4 per cent)	82 MP
IFP	2 058 300	(10,5 per cent)	43 MPs
FF	424 555	(2,2 per cent)	9 MPs
DP	338 426	(1,7 per cent)	7 MPs

DP supporters deserted in droves to vote for the NP, and in a lesser extent for the IFP, as the most hopeful counterweights to the ANC. This was evident in the fact that the party secured 538 655 votes on the provincial level, nearly 200 000 votes more than the parliamentary total, and representation in five of the nine provincial assemblies: Gauteng five seats (5,3 per cent of the vote), Natal two seats (2,2 per cent of the vote), Eastern Cape one seat (2,1 percent of the vote), Northern Cape one seat (1,9 per cent of the vote) and the Western Cape three seats (6,6 per cent of the vote).[23]

---

22 *The Star*, 2 May 1994.
23 *The Star*, 8 May 1994.

CHAPTER 31

Resignation and retirement
1994–1999

For the historian Niall Ferguson the wheel of politics is turned by the god of irony, and De Beer found out that this was indeed the case.[1] Former NP and CP MPs with track records of supporting apartheid, states of emergency and detention without trial returned to parliament, while most of the DP MPs who had opposed apartheid failed to do so. In March 2016, Denis Beckett, a prominent liberal journalist, described the irony that De Beer had led the DP "into the most poignantly bitter success" to get the ANC and the NP to create a nation straight from the liberal manual. His reward was to be slaughtered by the electorate.[2] De Beer himself ruefully pointed out: "The DP saw its policies triumph while its candidates were defeated."[3]

According to Ray Hartley, political editor of the *Sunday Times* (8 May), leading DP figures were shell-shocked and in a dazed state, searching for explanations. De Beer's shock and disbelief are reflected in a letter he wrote to Oppenheimer on 3 May:

> In the forty-odd years of our friendship I've never had a more difficult letter to write to you. We are appalled by the dreadful result we achieved. I feel desperately guilty towards you and other donors for having misled you so grossly. It is one thing to be a little over-optimistic: but this simply bears no relation to anything we

---

1 T. Leon, *The accidental ambassador. From parliament to Patagonia* (Johannesburg, 2013), p. 2.
2 Clipping of *The Star*, March 2016, in the possession of Wendy de Beer Furniss.
3 Fragment of a book De Beer intended to write. (In the possession of Wendy de Beer Furniss.)

discussed. The nearest I can come to an explanation is that, where our traditional supporters are concerned, they fell for the line that the Nats could offer a more effective opposition to the ANC than we could and they found it easy to accept this because the Nats had in effect adopted our policies. As far as the "new" voters are concerned, we made no dent on the blacks, and the coloureds and Indians are even more scared of the ANC than the whites are, and voted accordingly. It is hard to hold one's head up, but I must try. There is still a small nucleus, and it has to be kept alive, at least until some new strategy can develop ... I'm grateful to you as always, and distinctly ashamed of myself too.[4]

Political commentators put the blame for the DP's poor performance squarely on De Beer. For Hartley, the Democrats' old guard leadership was responsible for the catastrophe by insisting on retaining the ailing De Beer as leader even when opinion polls made it clear that amongst voters he was half as popular as the party. In addition, voters were never told what the DP stood for. Instead, they were fed a diet of anti-ANC red baiting.[5] This interpretation was shared by Allister Sparks. For him, the Democrats had waged a disastrous election campaign by demonising the ANC with red peril tactics that would have done justice to P.W. Botha. By bad-mouthing the ANC, the DP cut itself off from any growth potential in the black community and scared whites into the arms of the NP.[6] *Die Burger* (4 May 1994) came to the opposite conclusion, namely that the DP had paid the price for its poisonous attacks on the NP, while the ANC, the real enemy, was ignored.

The harsh reality was that De Beer could not overcome what Andrew described as the "basic forces of history", the perception that the ANC and the NP were the only parties in the election.[7] The party had become a victim of what the political scientist Robert

---

4 The Brenthurst Library, H.F. Oppenheimer papers, OPP/HFO/J1 (100), De Beer – Oppenheimer, 3 May 1994.
5 *Sunday Times*, 8 May 1994.
6 *The Star*, 15 June 1994.
7 *Sunday Times*, 8 May 1994.

Schrire defined as the "don't waste your vote" syndrome. That if you wanted to oppose the ANC, you voted NP.[8] For Leon the debate between De Klerk and Mandela was the watershed moment in dashing the high hopes of the DP:

> We ran a reasonable campaign, but it never made any difference. The FW de Klerk/Nelson Mandela debate was the turning point. Suddenly it boiled down to a choice between the NP and the ANC.[9]

In an interview with Padraig O'Malley on 8 November 1994, De Beer added that the party was handicapped by its lack of an organisational structure. And that crucially, compared to the ANC and NP, the DP got very little television coverage, which may have created the impression that he was a poor leader.[10] For David Welsh, in a liberation election in which race was a decisive factor, the poor showing of the DP had little to do with De Beer's leadership performance.[11] Ultimately, the political die – in the words of Eglin – was loaded against De Beer.[12]

For Leon it was a case that "[w]e had been comprehensively smashed between the hammer of African nationalism and the anvil of minority fears about a new order."[13] He concedes that it is doubtful that the DP would have attracted more votes with any other leader.[14] However, in May 1994, many Democrats were in no mood to accept that De Beer was the victim of appalling circumstances and he became the target of unreasonable blame. His hospitalisation on 3 May with an irregular heartbeat was the final

---

8 *The Natal Mercury*, 19 April 1994.
9 *Sunday Times*, 8 May 1994.
10 The O'Malley Archives, Nelson Mandela Centre of Memory, O'Malley's interview with Zach de Beer, 8 November 1994, https://omalley.nelson mandela.org/omalley/index (accessed 28 August 2019).
11 D. Welsh (ed.), *Hope & fear. Reflections of a democrat. Tony Leon* (Johannesburg, 1998), p. 4.
12 Eglin, *Crossing the borders of power*, p. 309.
13 Leon, *Opposite Mandela*, p. 70.
14 Interview with T. Leon, 1 April 2020.

straw for his critics in the party.[15] Before his hospitalisation De Beer had informed Oppenheimer that there was still the faint hope of a cabinet position in the Mandela government:

> Mandela phoned yesterday. His wording was distinctly Delphic: once I thought he was indicating that he is going to offer me a cabinet place. I may be wrong, and should know within a day or two.[16]

The call that came the next day, 4 May, was not from Mandela but from the chairman of the DP, David Gant. Feeling that the party needed new energy, he had decided that it would be for the best if De Beer resigned. Gant was convinced that for some time he wanted to relieve himself from the leadership, and that only out of loyalty he had stuck it out. He approached Eglin as De Beer's oldest friend and a person with no leadership ambitions for unbiased advice. Eglin in his usual brusque but friendly manner did not encourage or discourage him and responded that he must do whatever he thought was the right thing to do. Gant then met De Beer in his parliamentary office. He listened carefully to Gant and asked whether he had discussed it with anyone else. On being told that Eglin had been consulted, he asked for a few minutes alone. He telephoned Eglin, stating that he knew that he had to go but wanted to do so only in a month or two when things had settled down.[17] His friend's response was that if he was contemplating retirement it was both in his interest, and that of the party, to do so immediately.[18] He also contacted Andrew who concurred that he should stand down.[19] On calling Gant back into his office, he said: "Thank you David, you have lifted a very large cloud from my head." Gant was struck by his honourable and gracious behaviour.[20]

---

15 *Beeld*, 5 May 1994.
16 The Brenthurst Library, H.F. Oppenheimer papers, OPP/HFO/J1 (100), De Beer – Oppenheimer, 3 May 1994.
17 Interview with P. Soal, 11 April 2020.
18 Eglin, *Crossing the borders of power*, p. 309.
19 Correspondence with K. Andrew, 6 April 2020.
20 Correspondence with D. Gant, 4 and 5 April 2020.

The next day De Beer announced that in the light of the DP's poor showing he had decided to retire as party leader and to withdraw from parliament, making a seat available for a younger person who would be able to contribute more to the future of the party than he would be able to do. He made it clear that his resignation had nothing to do with his health as it was in tune with that of any person of his age. On a private note, he added that he had no firm plans for his retirement, but that he wanted to see as much of his family and grandchildren as possible and might write something at some stage. Eglin released a press statement in which he praised his contributions and stated that South Africa and all its people owe a great debt to De Beer, as his career of more than 40 years epitomised decency and sensitivity, and that he had been firm in his opposition to apartheid and steadfast in his commitment to basic liberal values.[21]

The words from his old friend must have been a balm to his political bruises, but even more soothing were the heartfelt letters he received from the De Klerk brothers. Within days of his resignation Willem (Wimpie) wrote him an emotional letter:

> Ek het 'n behoefte om jou 'n saluut te gee. Ek – en baie – het jou ervaar as 'n ryp, opregte mens. Eg in jou liberale waardes. Ernstig in jou politieke verantwoordelikhede. Jou insig, leierskap en politieke kommunikasie het baie vir ons land beteken. Jou rol was dié van 'n onvermoeide saaier en die oes wat gekom het in ons politiek, is ook 'n oes van jou saad. Dis ook 'n vrug van jou bydrae. Ek weet dat jy in die politiek ook blootgestel was aan verguising en rugsteek, want dis die aard van die politiek. Ook dit het jy met waardigheid hanteer. Dis vir my en Nina aangenaam om met 'n kaliber man soos jy te identifiseer. (I wish to salute you. As many others, I have experienced you as a mature and sincere person. True in your liberal principles. Serious in your political responsibilities. Your insights, leadership and political communication meant a lot to our country. Your role was that of a tireless sower, and the harvest that came in our politics

---

21 *The Pretoria News*, 7 May 1994.

is a harvest of your seed. It is also the fruit of your contribution. I know that in politics you have been exposed to vilification and backstabbing, as this is the nature of politics. You also dealt with this with dignity. It is for me and Nina [Mrs De Klerk] a pleasure to associate with a person of your calibre.)[22]

Less emotional, but equally appreciative was F.W. de Klerk, who could commiserate with a fellow leader after defeat:

> Political leadership is mostly a thankless task. Your contribution over the years has been outstanding and it was a privilege to call you a "colleague". As an opponent over the years, I lift my proverbial hat and wish you all the best for the road ahead.[23]

Leon, although feeling sorry for De Beer, had no doubt that he had done the right thing.[24] A few weeks later Leon was duly elected party leader after defeating Andrew. At the party's federal congress in Durban on 23 October 1994, he praised his predecessor for his courage, steadfastness, avoidance of petty bitterness and personal jealousy. He added that De Beer was the rarest phenomenon, a committed politician, and an unusually agreeable and generous man.[25]

After years of opposing apartheid, De Beer was eager to be part of the first fully democratic South African parliament. Up to election day he even anticipated to be part of the Government of National Unity. Although he had had announced more than once that he was willing to stand down as leader, he had hoped to be a member of this parliament. Eglin also anticipated being a member of the new non-racial parliament, enjoying the fruits of more than 30 years of hard work to make it a reality.

---

22 Willem de Klerk – De Beer, 16 May 1994. (In the possession of Wendy de Beer Furniss.)
23 F.W. de Klerk – De Beer, 13 June 1994. (In the possession of Wendy de Beer Furniss.)
24 Leon, *On the contrary*, pp. 243–244.
25 D. Welsh, *Hope & fear*, p. 76.

As the results came in, doubts settled in:

> How unfair would it be if I, who fought for 30 years against apartheid and for a non-racial democracy, was voted out of parliament and those bloody Nats, the architects of apartheid who brought South Africa close to the brink of disaster, would enjoy the pleasure and the honour of being members of South Africa's new democratic parliament – which they had fought against for over forty years.[26]

Eglin would secure a parliamentary seat, but for De Beer as the party leader, the DP's poor performance closed this option. Naturally, he was deeply disappointed by the abrupt end of his political career. Leon was of the opinion that De Beer suffered from a post-election depression.[27] Frances Jowell, Suzman's daughter, also found him in the period after the election "not in a very good state when we met – nothing like the younger Zach, so full of promise and energy".[28] In 2016, Beckett stated that he had his "respectfully distant doubts" whether De Beer ever got over the DP's poor performance and the way his political career had ended.[29] However, De Beer's son, a medical doctor, is of the opinion that although he was deeply disappointed and took some time to get over the result, he was not depressed. He coped with the setback because he knew that he had to take responsibility for the result.[30]

As a veteran of parliamentary politics, De Beer knew that party leaders are measured by their ballot box performances. He was praised for his role in the local elections of 1988 that ended the electoral slide of the Progressives, as well as for the Democrats' good performance in the 1989 parliamentary election. But he was also fully aware that after heavy defeats, political parties need to sacrifice a scapegoat. Strauss as leader of the United Party, as well

---

26 Eglin, *Crossing the borders of power*, p. 309.
27 Leon, *The accidental ambassador*, p. 20.
28 Correspondence with Dr Frances Jowell, 11 August 2021.
29 Clipping of *The Star*, March 2016, in the possession of Wendy Furniss.
30 Interview with Zach de Beer junior, 22 April 2020.

as two of his Progressive predecessors, Steytler and Eglin, were cast aside after dismal election results. He was one of those who felt that his father-in-law had to stand down in 1956, and that Steytler should go after the PP's disastrous performance in the 1966 election. Although bruised by the poor result and the way his political career had come to an end, he made peace with it. He had the consolation that he had done his duty, and the conviction that he had done it to the best of his abilities as he stated in letter to me in response to my expression of appreciation for his leadership of the DP:

> Ek glo nie ek was 'n te slegte leier nie – maar ná so 'n nederlaag moet daar 'n offer wees. Dit is ook so dat ek al 65 is, en die gesondheid minder as volmaak ... (I do not think I was too bad a leader – but after such a defeat there had to be a sacrifice. Also, I am 65 now and my health is less than perfect.)[31]

To Wendy, whom he went to visit in Britain after the election, he did not seem distressed by his resignation.[32] However, he never stopped thinking about the 1994 election and this was observed by Bain in April 1999. As her son was participating in the Two Oceans marathon, she went to stay with De Beer in Clifton. Early in the morning as they were standing outside the building with her son waiting for his ride back to Johannesburg, a waste truck came down the road. All the coloured refuse collectors knew him by name, greeted him, and they had a conversation in Afrikaans. As they left, he ruefully commented on how nice they all were, and that it was a pity he hadn't been able to convince more of them to vote for him.[33]

De Beer's Clifton home, 10 Clifton Breakers, 27 Victoria Road, with its view over the Atlantic Ocean and spectacular sunsets,

---

31 De Beer – FA Mouton, 13 June 1995. (Letter in the possession of the author.)
32 Interview with Wendy de Beer Furniss, 15 April 2020.
33 Correspondence with M. Bain, 7 May 2020.

his beach walks and swimming jaunts when the weather was warm, helped to soothe his political wounds.[34] He had little time to enjoy his sea view as he was offered the ambassadorship to the Netherlands. Leon felt that De Beer's dedicated opposition to apartheid deserved some high recognition and he approached Mandela to offer him a diplomatic position. The President obliged with the embassy in The Hague.

The first time De Beer heard about the offer was when he saw it reported in the *Sunday Times*. To Wendy he expressed his reluctance to move to the Netherlands:

> There is a big yacht anchored in Clifton Bay – rare on Wednesdays – and a splendid sunset developing. I really am very reluctant to leave this place. But my friends are unanimous that I should take the job, Mona is simply madly determined, the President seems to want it – so I shall turn my back on this glory and go sit in the mist and sleet of Holland.[35]

De Beer took his ambassadorial duties seriously, taught himself Dutch, and was viewed as a success. For his children, as well as for Bain who went to visit him, it was obvious that he and Mona enjoyed being in the Netherlands and that he had the respect of the embassy staff.[36] And yet, he told a visiting Leon that being an ambassador was "largely boring; a bit like being the lord mayor".[37] To Gibson he confessed that he would rather sit on his balcony at Clifton and watch the sea.[38] After two years, De Beer resigned, claiming health reasons. According to his son, his health was not that bad, but with his sense of mortality he wanted to be back in

---

34 Correspondence with Wendy de Beer Furniss, 25 October 2021.
35 De Beer – Wendy, 21 September 1994. (Letter in the possession of Wendy de Beer Furniss.)
36 Correspondence with Wendy de Beer Furniss, 28 April 2020; Interview with Debbie de Beer, 23 April 2020 and M. Bain, 30 April 2020.
37 Leon, *The accidental ambassador*, p. 20.
38 Interview with D. Gibson, 1 April 2020.

Clifton.[39] And he did enjoy watching the sunsets and waves rolling in.[40]

Nothing came of his plans to write his memoirs. He was extremely diffident about writing and unsure whether he should provide any account of his life.[41] From the notes that he had made, it seems that after Swart and Suzman had published their memoirs with some success, he felt that his version would be too dull. He instead decided to write a book that disclosed his viewpoints of the period he had lived in and that set out a framework on the issues he wanted to focus on. "The system and the struggle" was first on his list to be addressed. The accusation that he was a collaborator for participating in the apartheid parliamentary system rankled with him in his retirement. In a written fragment, he concluded that credit for the end of apartheid was due to the fighters in the national liberation movement as well as to those who participated in the apartheid system to oppose it, but ruefully concluded that perhaps it was still too soon to evaluate this history. He also wanted to address issues such as political leadership, globalisation and unemployment. Apart from an outline, nothing came of this proposed project.[42]

In his retirement De Beer enjoyed life with his family, grandchildren, and friends such as the Eglins. In August 1997, Eglin's wife, Joyce, died. At her memorial service he paid tribute to her. Afterwards Eglin wrote to him and told him that "I value your friendship very much indeed".[43] He was warmly supportive of Leon as leader of the DP that was gaining significant support, especially in the Western Cape, but he was concerned that his successor was maybe a bit too friendly with the NP. That his buffeting at the hands of the NP had left some scar tissue was evident in a letter he wrote on 29 September 1998 to Leon. He warned him that he

---

39 Interview with Zach de Beer, 22 April 2020.
40 Interview with Debbie de Beer, 23 April 2020.
41 Correspondence with Wendy de Beer Furniss, 24 November 2020.
42 These notes are in the possession of Wendy de Beer Furniss.
43 Eglin – De Beer, 3 September 1997. (In the possession of Wendy de Beer Furniss.)

found the prospect of a DP coalition with the NP in the Western Cape parliament a horrifying prospect, and that he did not think he could live with it.[44]

At the beginning of May 1999, during South Africa's second democratic general election, De Beer experienced some transient ischemic attacks and found it difficult to express himself. This led to an increase of his daily dosage of blood pressure medication, or his "rat poison" as he called it.[45] On 27 May, at about 11:00, he died of a massive stroke in his Clifton home.[46]

Back in 1986, while addressing the Food and Wine Society, he had quoted Chesterton's poem "The rolling English road":

> My friends we will not go again or ape an ancient rage,
> Or stretch the folly of your youth to be the shame of age
> But walk with clearer eyes and ears this path that wandereth
> And see undrugged in evening light the decent inn of death:
> For there is good news yet to hear and finer things to be seen,
> Before we go to Paradise by way of Kensal Green.

He then expressed the following sentiment:

> I first knew and enjoyed that poem when I was seventeen. I formed the hope – which I still cherish – that when my time comes, I will enter death as one would a decent inn – in friendship with everyone and without egocentric fuss.[47]

He had achieved this hope.

Political leaders set aside their differences and across party lines paid tribute to him. Mandela applauded him as a principled opponent of apartheid. Leon praised his decency, humanity and

---

44 Leon, *On the contrary*, p. 302.
45 Mienke Bain – Wendy, 3 May 1999. (In the possession of Wendy de Beer Furniss.)
46 *Cape Times*, 28 May 1999.
47 Z270, Address to the Food and Wine Society, 18 August 1986. (In the possession of Wendy de Beer Furniss.)

principles, and said that his "legacy and memory will be honoured by the DP for all time".[48] In the *Sunday Times* (30 May 1999), Eglin wrote an emotional obituary, "Zach de Beer: Man of integrity". He praised him for keeping liberal values alive in the darkest days of the apartheid state, while he also praised his qualities as a loyal friend and caring person. He ended on an emotional note:

> Well done Zach. You made a difference to the lives of many of your fellow South Africans. You will be remembered with gratitude, affection and respect. Rest in peace.

On the afternoon of Monday 31 May, after the cremation, a memorial service was held in the chapel of Bishops, his former school. In front of almost 400 family members, friends and dignitaries, Eglin listed his old friend's political achievements, and especially his commitment to liberal principles that ran as a golden thread through his political career. He ended his eulogy in Afrikaans: "Dankie, ou maat. Slaap gerus." (Thank you, old friend, sleep peacefully.)

His son Zach gave an intimate account of who his father was. To honour one of his father's last wishes, he decided to delay his visit to Scotland to vote for the DP that Wednesday.[49]

On 3 June there was also a memorial service at the Johannesburg Country Club with tributes by Oppenheimer, Suzman and Godsell. Oppenheimer spoke about what a delightful and entertaining companion De Beer was, and the important influence he had had on his own political thinking. Suzman praised the political abilities of her former parliamentary bench mate saying that he had one of the most brilliant political minds in South Africa. Godsell praised his moral decency and told the audience that he had served as an example that you could be a good white person in the apartheid state. He further highlighted his intellectual integrity that reflected the power of ideas and the strength of reason, his belief

---

48 *Cape Argus*, 28 May 1999.
49 *Cape Times* and *Beeld*, 1 June 1999.

in a just, decent and prosperous South Africa.[50] With the focus on the election campaign, his death was mentioned in passing by South African newspapers praising his gentlemanly qualities. However, it was in British newspapers, the *Guardian* (1 June 1999) and the *Independent* (3 June 1999), that he received lengthy obituaries of praise for his long struggle to bring about democracy in South Africa. Paul Trewhela in the *Independent* was fulsome in his admiration: "Talented, handsome, persuasive, De Beer provided a measure of sanity in South Africa through troubled decades."

Mona received numerous letters of condolences. The most striking ones were those from anti-apartheid activists who were not part of parliamentary politics. Donald Woods, former editor of the East London *Daily Dispatch* who, after being banned and harassed by the apartheid state, had fled South Africa in 1977, expressed his admiration in the following terms:

> Zach was not only a good friend but an inspirational figure in my life – really someone to look up to and be glad of. In those very bad days it meant so much to have someone of his credibility and high intelligence in our national life.[51]

The warmest praise came from Kader Asmal, an anti-apartheid veteran and the Minister of Water Affairs and Forestry:

> He will always be remembered as one of those few whites who was prepared to take risks for non-racialism, and who did so much to prod the business community and other sectors of white opinion into adopting a more realistic attitude towards what was both inevitable and desirable in South Africa. I recall the remarkable work Zach did in the constitutional process, leading to substantial progress in what at times was the most intractable position-taking. He was, in truth,

---

50 Recording of the memorial service at the Johannesburg Country Club, 3 June 1999. (In the possession of Wendy de Beer Furniss.)

51 Donald Woods – Mona de Beer, 19 July 1999. (In the possession of Wendy de Beer Furniss.)

a peace-maker, and the democratic order that has been established bears his mark, too. ... Zach's life was an example to others in steadfastness and courage against the worst possible odds.[52]

---

52 Kader Asmal – Mona de Beer, 28 May 1999. (In the possession of Wendy de Beer Furniss.)

EPILOGUE

On 2 June 1999, South Africa went to the polls. The DP became the official opposition by securing 1 527 337 votes, 9,5 per cent of the national vote, winning 38 National Assembly seats. This was two seats fewer than the 40 De Beer had hoped to secure for the Democrats five years earlier. But then Leon's success was made possible by De Beer's legacy of a party based on a broad and solid liberal foundation. Leon was aware of this and ensured that the former leaders of the party were recognised and honoured where possible.[53] And yet, the Democratic Alliance (DA), the successor to the DP, made no attempt to keep De Beer's legacy alive. For the 2014 election a video on the history of the party, "Know your DA", made no mention of him.[54] A reason for this was the desire of the DA to shed its image as a party for whites. Another crucial factor for him being ignored was that he was seen as a loser. After 1994, many Democrats – hurt, angry and frustrated – held him responsible for the party's poor performance. Those who remembered him were unpleasant. This attitude was reflected in 2004 by R.W. Johnson's unfair attack on him in his *South Africa: The first man, the last nation*:

> With deep unwisdom the DP had elected the hard-drinking Zach de Beer as its leader and he has slumbered his way through the election, nearly sinking South Africa's liberal tradition in the process.[55]

In addition, after April 1994, liberals received no credit in South Africa for the dramatic changes which had taken place. The ANC

---

53 Leon, *Opposite Mandela*, p. 74.
54 E. McKaiser, *DA of nie? 'n Kieser se krisis* (Cape Town, 2014), pp. 133–136.
55 R.W. Johnson, *South Africa. The first man, the last nation* (Johannesburg, 2004), p. 211.

appropriated all the moral capital of the struggle against apartheid. Despite her international reputation as a champion of human rights and the rule of law, Suzman's portrait was removed from a parliamentary corridor, together with those of apartheid politicians, to be placed in a parliamentary cellar.[56] More than a quarter of a century after 1994, the bypassing of the role of liberals, especially those of the Progressive parties, is reflected in the absence of biographies on them. The only one since 1994 to be published on a former Progressive parliamentarian is that by Albert Grundlingh, *Slabbert: Man on a mission*, in 2020.

And yet, De Beer played a significant role in opposing apartheid. His political career was motivated by the ideal of a fair, democratic and prosperous South Africa in which the rights of all its citizens would be protected. His dedication to these principles contributed to the founding of the PP in 1961, the party's durability in the face of numerous defeats and setbacks, and its eventual resurgence in the 1970s. The strength of his character, and his calm and measured approach, combined with his ability to explain the necessity of political reform, helped to lay the groundwork with Colin Eglin for the eventual electoral success of the Progressives by 1974. After the disastrous 1987 election result, he revived a battered and demoralised PFP and played a crucial role in the founding of the DP, as well as in the party's good performance in the 1989 election. This performance was only possible because of his leadership. Through tact and infinite civility, he had kept the newly formed party, of which two of its co-leaders were members of the NP up to 1987, together, while stamping a liberal identity on the DP.

As the DP leader after February 1990, he played a supporting role in bringing about a new constitution, but his main achievement was to keep the party going. With the party trapped between the competing ANC, NP and IFP and with some Democrats eager to join either the ANC or NP, he ensured that the DP survived as an independent liberal voice. Without his unbending leadership,

---

56 M. Shain (ed.), *Opposing voices. Liberalism and opposition in South Africa today* (Cape Town, 2006), pp. 20, 23–24.

there was the possibility that the party would have splintered with the remnants being absorbed by the NP or the ANC. For the Democrats to be able to participate in the April 1994 election, De Beer deserves credit. Then in a state of exhaustion and in poor health, he fought an election against impossible odds. Under these appalling electoral circumstances, the result of winning seven seats was an achievement. A handful of parliamentarians representing a party based on solid liberal foundations enabled possible the electoral breakthrough of 1999, and the eventual founding, growth and durability of the DA.

But more importantly, by 1990 De Beer had helped to convince many whites to accept the end of the apartheid state. He had the satisfaction that in the words of Steytler, he had contributed to help create a democratic South Africa: "Zach, you and I will never be in power; but we will live to see other people applying our policies." The South Africa of today, despite numerous problems and challenges, is a liberal democracy. His career, guided by neither personal ambition nor by party ambition, but by "the long obedience" to the ideal of freedom and equality helped to make this possible. Zach de Beer deserves an honoured place in South African history.

BIBLIOGRAPHY

UNPUBLISHED SOURCES
Archive for Contemporary Affairs, Bloemfontein
P.W. Botha papers
J.G.N. Strauss papers

University of the Witwatersrand Library
Max Borkum papers
Brian Hackland papers
Progressive Federal Party/Democratic Party papers
Helen Suzman papers

University of South Africa
United Party collection
Sir De Villiers Graaff papers
Willem Kleynhans papers
Douglas E. Mitchell papers
Progressive Party papers
Progressive Federal Party papers
Joyce and Frank Waring papers

University of Stellenbosch, Documentation Centre, JS Gericke Library
Frederik van Zyl Slabbert papers

In private possession of Wendy de Beer Furniss
Letters between Zach de Beer and Wendy
Papers of Zach de Beer

University of Cape Town
V.M.L. Ballinger papers

The Brenthurst Library
H.F. Oppenheimer papers

Bishops Diocesan College
De Beer's school record

The O'Malley Archives, Nelson Mandela Centre of Memory
O'Malley's interviews with Zach de Beer and Wynand Malan

OFFICIAL PUBLICATIONS
Debatte van die Volksraad, 1955
House of Assembly debates, 1953–1961, 1977–1980
Debates of parliament, 1989–1994

SECONDARY SOURCES
Books
Barnard, M., *Defining moments* (Cape Town, 2011).
Barnard, S.L. and Marais, A.H., *Die Verenigde Party. Die groot eksperiment* (Durban, 1982).
Basson, J., *Steeds op die parlementêre kolfblad. Met insigte oor die Afrikaner en Afrikaans* (Cape Town, 2008).
Bekker, A., *Eben Dönges. Balansstaat. Historiese perspektief* (Stellenbosch, 2005).
Beukes, W.D. (ed.), *Oor grense heen. Op pad na 'n nasionale pers 1948–1990* (Cape Town, 1992).
Beyers, C.J., Basson, J.L., (eds), *Dictionary of South African Biography*. Vol. V (Pretoria, 1987).
Bloom, J., *Out of step. Life-story of a politician, politics and religion in a world at war* (Johannesburg, 2005).
Boraine, A., *A life in transition* (Cape Town, 2008).
Boraine, A., *What's gone wrong? On the brink of a failed state* (Johannesburg & Cape Town, 2014).
Brooks, E., *A South African pilgrimage* (Johannesburg, 1972).
Brown, H., *A lawyer's odyssey. Apartheid, Mandela and beyond* (Pietermaritzburg, 2021).
Butler, A., *Cyril Ramaphosa. The road to presidential power* (Johannesburg, 2019), pp. 112–113.
Butler, J., Elphick, R., Welsh, D., (eds), *Democratic liberalism in South Africa. Its history and prospects* (Cape Town, 1987).
Callinicos, L., *Oliver Tambo. Beyond the Engeli Mountains* (Cape Town, 2004).
Campbell, J., *Roy Jenkins: A well-rounded life* (London, 2014).
Davenport, T.R.H., *The transfer of power in South Africa* (Cape Town, 1998).
de Klerk, F.W., *The Last Trek – A New Beginning: The Autobiography* (London, 1998).
De Villiers, D. & J., *PW.*, (Cape Town, 1984).
Dommisse, E. Esterhuyse, W. *Anton Rupert. 'n Lewensverhaal* (Cape Town, 2005).
Dubow, S., *Apartheid 1948–1994* (Oxford, 2014).
Du Preez, M., *Louis Luyt. Unauthorised* (Cape Town, 2001).
Eglin, C., *Crossing the borders of power. The memoirs of Colin Eglin* (Johannesburg, 2007).
Ferguson, N., *The square and the tower. Networks, hierarchies and the struggle for global power* (St Ives, 2017).
Friedman, S., *The long journey. South Africa's quest for a negotiated settlement* (Johannesburg, 1993).
Gastrow, S., *Who's who in South African politics*, No. 4 (Johannesburg, 1992).
Giliomee, H., *The last Afrikaner leaders. A supreme test of power* (Cape Town, 2012).

Giliomee, H., *Herman Giliomee: historian. An autobiography* (Cape Town, 2016).
Graaff, D., *Div looks back. The memoirs of Sir De Villiers Graaff* (Cape Town, 1993).
Grundlingh, A., *Slabbert. Man on a mission* (Jeppestown, 2020).
Hancock, W.K., *Professing history* (Sydney, 1976).
Heard, T., *The Cape of Storms. A personal history of the crisis in South Africa*, (Johannesburg, 1991).
Hocking, A., *Oppenheimer and son* (Cape Town, 1973).
Hope, C. *White boy running* (London, 1987).
Jacobs, G., *Beckoning Horizons* (Johannesburg, 1985).
Jenkins, R., *Baldwin* (London, 1987).
Johnson, R.W., *South Africa. The first man, the last nation* (Johannesburg, 2004).
Johnson, R.W., *Foreign native. An African journey* (Johannesburg, 2020).
Kane-Berman, J., *Between two fires. Holding the liberal centre in South African politics* (Johannesburg, 2017).
Kenney, H., *Architect of apartheid: HF Verwoerd. An appraisal* (Johannesburg, 1980).
Kenney, H., *Power, pride & prejudice. The years of Afrikaner nationalist rule in South Africa* (Johannesburg, 1991).
Lawrence, J., *Harry Lawrence* (Cape Town, 1978).
LeMaitre, A., and Savage, M., *The passion for reason. Essays in honour of an Afrikaner African* (Johannesburg, 2010).
Leon, T., *On the contrary. Leading the opposition in a democratic South Africa* (Johannesburg, 2008).
Leon, T., *The accidental ambassador. From parliament to Patagonia* (Johannesburg, 2013).
Leon, T., *Future tense. Reflections on my troubled land* (Johannesburg, 2021).
Louw, L., (ed.), *Dawie 1946–1964.'n Bloemlesing uit die geskrifte van Die Burger se politieke kommentator* (Cape Town, 1965).
Louw, N.P. van Wyk Louw, *Liberale Nasionalisme* (Cape Town, 1958).
Luyt, L., *Walking proud. The Louis Luyt autobiography* (Cape Town, 2003).
Maharaj, M. and Jordan, Z.P., *Breakthrough. The struggles and secret talks that brought apartheid South Africa to the negotiating table* (Cape Town, 2021).
Marks, S., *The Ambiguities of Dependence in South Africa. Class, Nationalism, and the state in twentieth-century Natal* (Johannesburg, 1986).
McKaiser, E., *DA of nie? 'n Kieser se krisis* (Cape Town, 2014).
Meiring, P., *10 politieke leiers. Manne na aan ons premiers* (Cape Town, 1973).
Meleady, D., *John Redmond. The national leader* (Padstow, 2014).
Meredith, M., *South Africa's new era. The 1994 election* (London, 1994).
Mervis, J., *The fourth estate. A newspaper story* (Johannesburg, 1989).
Momberg, J., *From Malan to Mbeki. The memoirs of an Afrikaner with a conscience* (Stellenbosch, 2011).
Mouton, F.A., *Prophet without honour. F.S. Malan: Afrikaner, South African and Cape liberal* (Pretoria, 2011).
O'Meara, D., *Forty lost years. The apartheid state and the politics of the National Party, 1948–1994* (Randburg, 1996).
Owen, K., *These times. A decade of South African politics* (Johannesburg, 1992).

Pakendorf, H., *Stroomop. Herinneringe van 'n koerantman in die apartheidsera* (Cape Town, 2018).
Pallister, D., Stewart, S., Lepper, I., *South Africa Inc. The Oppenheimer empire* (London, 1988).
Pienaar, S., *Getuie van Groot Tye* (Cape Town, 1997).
Reynolds, A., *Election '94 South Africa. The campaigns, results and future prospects* (Claremont, 1994).
Ries, A., Dommisse, E., *Leierstryd* (Cape Town, 1990).
Scher, D., *Donald Molteno. Dilizintaba – he-who-removes-mountains* (Johannesburg, 1979).
Schoeman, B.M., *Van Malan tot Verwoerd* (Cape Town, 1973).
Schoeman, B., *My Lewe in die Politiek* (Johannesburg, 1978).
Shain, M., *Opposing voices. Liberalism and opposition in South Africa today* (Johannesburg, 2006).
Shain, M., *A perfect storm. Antisemitism in South Africa 1930–1948* (Johannesburg, 2015).
Shaw, G., *The Cape Times. An informal history* (Cape Town, 1999).
Van Zyl Slabbert, F., *The last white parliament* (Johannesburg, 1985).
Van Zyl Slabbert, F., *Afrikaner Afrikaan. Anekdotes en analise* (Cape Town, 1999).
Van Zyl Slabbert, F., *Tough choices. Reflections of an Afrikaner African* (Cape Town, 2000).
Van Zyl Slabbert, F., *The other side of history. An anecdotal reflection on political transition in South Africa* (Johannesburg, 2006).
Smuts, D., *Patriots & parasites. South Africa and the struggle to evade history* (Rondebosch, 2016).
Strangwayes-Booth, J., *A cricket in the thorn tree. Helen Suzman and the Progressive Party* (Johannesburg, 1976).
Suzman, H., *In no uncertain terms* (Johannesburg, 1993).
Swart, R., *Progressive odyssey. Towards a democratic South Africa* (Cape Town, 1991).
Taylor, C., *If courage goes: My twenty years in South African politics* (Johannesburg, 1976).
Thompson, L., *The unification of South Africa 1902–1910* (Oxford, 1960).
Treurnicht, A.P., *Noodlottige Hervorming* (Pretoria, nd).
Van Ryneveld, C., *20th century all-rounder. Reminiscences and reflections of Clive van Ryneveld* (Cape Town, 2011).
Van Vuuren, D.J., Schlemmer, L., Marais, H.C., Latakgomo, J. (eds), *South African election 1987* (Pinetown, 1987).
Waldmeir, P., *Anatomy of a miracle. The end of apartheid and the birth of the new South Africa* (London, 1997).
Waring, J., *Sticks and stones* (Johannesburg, 1969).
Welsh, D., (ed.), *Hope & fear. Reflections of a democrat. Tony Leon* (Johannesburg, 1998).
Welsh, D., *The rise and fall of apartheid* (Johannesburg, 2009).
Wilks, T., *Douglas Mitchell* (Durban, 1980).
Wilson, B., *A time of innocence* (Bergvlei, 1991).

Worrall, D., *The independent factor. My personal journey through politics and diplomacy* (Wandsbeck, 2018).

Articles

Barnard, S.L., "Die verkiesing van Sir De Villiers Graaff as leier van die Verenigde Party", *Joernaal vir Eietydse Geskiedenis*, 5 (1) December 1980.

Bell, P., "Changing the guard", *Leadership*, Vol. 7, 3, 1988.

Collie, H., "The man who succeeded Smuts", *The Outspan*, 11 January 1952.

Dubow, S., "Macmillan, Verwoerd, and the 1960 'Wind of change' speech", *The Historical Journal*, December 2011, Vol. 54, No. 4.

Gastrow, P., "Towards a convergence of democrats?", *Die Suid-Afrikaan*, April 1990.

Giliomee, H. "Demokratiese Party se werklike rol", *Die Suid-Afrikaan*, June/July 1988.

Hackland, B., "The economic and political context of the growth of the Progressive Federal Party in South Africa, 1959–1978", *Journal of Southern African Studies*, Vol. 7, No. 1, 1980.

Johnson, R.W., "The DA on the brink", *politicsweb*, 12 October 2011.

Louw, C., "Parlement se man van die daad", *Die Suid-Afrikaan*, June/July 1993

Mattes, B., "The campaign thus far", *Die Suid-Afrikaan*, March/April 1994.

McKensie, E.R., "Its master's voice? The South African "Progressive" parties and business, 1959–1983", *Journal for Contemporary History*, December 1996.

McKenzie, E., "The 1983 referendum: The English press and the Progressive Federal Party campaign", *Kleio*, Vol. 23., 1991.

Scher, D.M., "Louis T. Weichardt and the South African Greyshirt Movement", *Kleio*, Vol. 18, 1986.

Van Zyl Slabbert, F., "Rituals and realities", *Leadership*, Vol. 7, 3, 1988.

Welsh, D., "The Democratic Party. Developing a political culture", *Indicator South Africa*, Vol. 6, No. 3, Winter 1989.

White, W.B., "The United Party and the 1953 general election", *Historia* 36 (2), November 1991.

Unpublished sources

Hackland, B., "The Progressive Party of South Africa, 1959–1981: Political responses to structural change and class struggle" (PhD, Oxford University, 1984).

McKenzie, E.R., "The relationship between the Progressive Federal Party, the English-language press and business with special reference to the 1983 referendum", (MA Unisa, 1992).

Korf, L., "D.F. Malan: A political biography" (D.Phil, University of Stellenbosch, 2010).

McConnachie, A.J., "The 1961 general election in the Republic of South Africa", (MA, University of South Africa, 1999).

Shandler, D., "Structural crisis and liberalism: a history of the Progressive Federal Party, 1981–1989" (MA Thesis, University of Cape Town, 1991).

Scher, D.M., "The disenfranchisement of the Coloured voters, 1948–1956" (D. Litt. et Phil. University of South Africa, 1983).

Newspapers and periodicals
Beeld, Die Burger, Business Day, Cape Argus, Cape Times, The Citizen, The Daily News, Financial Mail, Frontline, The Guardian, Hoofstad, Die Huisgenoot, Impact, Insig, Leadership, The Natal Mercury, The Natal Witness, Oggendblad, Pretoria News, Progress, The Progressive, Rand Daily Mail, Rapport, The Star, Die Suid-Afrikaan, Sunday Express, The Sunday Independent, Sunday Times, Sunday Tribune, Die Transvaler, Die Vaderland, Die Volksblad, Weekly Mail

Interviews
Carlisle, 14 April 2020.
D. Cox, Bain, M., 30 April 2020.
Bain, M., 30 April 2020.
Carlisle, R., 13 April 2020.
De Beer, D., 23 April 2020.
De Beer, Z., 22 September 1986.
De Beer, Z., (son), 22 April 2020.
De Beer Furniss, W., 15, 16, 26 April 2020, 27 August 2021, 2 November 2021, 18 November 2021, 24 May 2022.
Recordings of W. de Beer Furniss's interviews with her mother, Maureen de Beer, 26 April 2020, 1 May 2020, 7 July 2020.
Gastrow, P., 31 March 2022.
Gibson, D., 1 April 1994.
Leon, T., 3 April 2020.
Malan, W., 28 March 2022.
Soal, P., 11 April 2020.
Suzman, H., 2 August 1986.
Viljoen, K., 22 February 2011.

Correspondence
Andrew, K., 6 April 2020.
Bain, M., 7 May 2020.
Carlisle, R., 14 April 2020.
De Beer Furniss, W., 28 April 2020, 29 May 2020, 1, 3 and 16 December 2020, 12 and 13 March 2021, 25 October 2021, 4 November 2021, 3 August 2022.
Gant, D., 4 and 5 April 2020.
Gibson, D., 31 March 2020.
Giliomee, H., 18 November 2021.
Jowell, F., 11 August 2021.
Leon, T., 8 March 2021, 18 November 2021, 4 January 2022.
Malan, W., 29 March and 10 April 2022.
Menell, I., 16, 18 and 21 August 2021.
Mulder, P., 17 March 2021.

Selfe, J., 4 April and 29 May 2020.
Silbert, M., 21 November 2013.
Soal, P., 6 November 2014.
Vigne, G., 6 April 2020.
Worrall, D., 22 March 2022, 27 March 2022.

INDEX

Abraham, J.H. 68
African National Congress (ANC) 7, 90, 122, 180–186, 190–193, 217, 231–249, 253–276, 287–306, 318–320
Afrikaans language 14–16, 23, 36–37, 126, 132, 144, 158, 177, 212, 222, 280, 315
Afrikaner Bond 18
Afrikaners 26–33, 38–39, 42, 45, 58, 79, 97, 136, 141, 156, 166, 192–194, 206–207, 223, 226–228, 274, 290
Afrikaner Weerstandsbeweging (AWB) 179, 192, 237, 256, 274, 290–291
Aggett, Neil 282
Alexander, Ray 21
Allan, Jani 200, 203
Andrew, Ken 10, 221, 249, 258, 261, 264–265, 271, 264–265, 271, 282, 305, 307, 309
apartheid 7–9, 51–68, 79–89, 97–107, 110–114, 131–133, 148, 156–159, 173–191, 210–213, 225–237, 253–261, 270–276, 308–316, 319 *see also* Bantustans, laws & legislation
archival collections 9–11, 16, 35n3, 114n22

Bain, Mienke 10, 200, 288, 294, 311–312
Ballinger, *Dr* Margaret 11, 80–81, 85
Bantustans 64–66, 70, 82, 92, 97, 103, 137, 141, 144, 155, 184, 188, 211, 267, 270–273, 290 *see also* apartheid
Barlow, Arthur 34, 109
Barnard, Marius 202, 216, 224
Basson, Jack 133–134

Basson, Japie 147, 165
Beck, Jaqueline (Jaqui) 72, 114
Beckett, Denis 304, 310
Bekker, Bailey 34, 38
Biko, Steve 148, 156, 282
Bill of Rights 82, 85, 102, 161, 283
Bisho (1992) 267–268
Bishops Diocesan College 11, 15–16, 315
Black Consciousness Movement (BCM) 136
Black People's Convention (BPC) 136
black peril 45, 58–59, 64, 99–100, 111, 118–120
Blackwell, L. 76
Bloom, Jack 205, 302
Bloom, Tony 177, 181
Boesak, Allan 184
Boipatong (1992) 267
Boraine, Alex 139, 167–168, 171, 185, 187
Borkum, Max 10, 142–143
Botha, Louis 18
Botha, Pik 165–166
Botha, P.W. 103, 112, 130–131, 148, 151, 162–163, 176–192, 224, 305
Boyd, Leo 72, 74
Brooks, *Dr* Edgar 21–22, 76
Browde, *Dr* Selma 137
Brown, Henry 105, 106n28
Bunting, Brian 21
Burrows, Roger 208, 300
Buthelezi, *Chief* Mangosuthu 184, 237, 260, 268, 274, 277, 291

Cadman, Radclyffe 146
Cape (Coloured) franchise 18, 24–25,

27, 30, 34, 36, 38, 41–42, 45, 49 *see also* qualified (non-racial) franchise
Carlisle, Robin 78, 187, 195, 256, 279, 281
Carter, Jimmy 152
Cato Manor (1959) 68, 83
Centlivres, A. van der Sandt 76
churches 13, 53, 97, 271, 294
Cillié, Piet ("Dawie" in *Die Burger*) 97, 163, 238
Citizen, The 157, 162 *see also* Information Scandal (1977)
Civil Rights League (CRL) 21, 29, 32
civilisation test 84
Coetzee, Blaar 34, 90
common voters' roll 18, 21n22, 25, 29, 38, 43, 49, 65, 69–70, 76, 82, 84, 146, 175, 219, 302
communism 19, 21, 30, 42, 52, 66, 103, 121, 231
Communist Party *see* South African Communist Party (CPSA/SACP)
Congo *see* Democratic Republic of the Congo (DRC)
Congress of Democrats (COD) 52
Congress of the People 52
Connan, Jack 63
Conservative Party (CP) 11, 177–180, 192, 212–213, 227, 237–241, 248, 262–263, 268, 271–274, 282, 285–286, 290–291
Constitution of the RSA 25–26, 30, 42, 77–78, 140, 177–178, 223, 258–261, 273–274, 281–286, 290, 301, 319
Constitutional Court 273, 283–284
constitutional reform 8, 39, 76, 84, 92, 106, 133, 162, 173, 176, 184, 210, 227–228
Convention for a Democratic South Africa (CODESA) 259–261, 263, 267–269
Cope, J.P. 33, 72
Cottesloe Declaration (1960) 97–98
Cronjé, Pierre 193, 247, 253, 265–266

Dalling, David 246, 256–257, 263–265, 294
Davidson, Ian 195
Davie, *Dr* T.B. (Tom) 20, 23
De Beer, Dan (uncle) 17, 38
De Beer, Debbie (daughter) 10, 23, 294
De Beer, Jean (mother) 13–15
De Beer, Maureen (wife) 10, 22–23, 37, 110, 114, 116, 123–125, 132
De Beer, Mona Vida (wife) 124–125, 202, 225, 312, 316
De Beer, *Dr* Ray (father) 13–15, 17, 22, 27, 32, 51
De Beer, Wendy (daughter) 9–17, 23, 115, 123, 132, 148, 166–169, 216, 219, 221, 237, 264, 280, 311–312
De Beer, *Dr* Zacharias Johannes (Zach) ambassador to the Netherlands 9, 312; business & corporate career 8, 116, 123, 131–133, 139–140, 144–145, 167, 170, 173–175, 188, 199, 287; childhood, school & student years 13–22; conviction liberal 7–8, 13, 17, 21, 61–62, 121, 196, 199, 245–246, 250, 261, 265–266, 308, 315; leadership 51, 78, 115, 130, 135, 166, 187, 197–198, 202, 215–217, 220, 228, 243, 277–283, 307–309, 311; medical practitioner 17, 27, 37, 56–57, 78; personality 27–28, 38, 40, 44, 78, 113, 151, 314; political & parliamentary career 7–10, 18, 27, 56, 62–63, 114–115, 160, 171, 207, 214, 232, 301, 308, 310–311, 315, 320; public speaker 27, 36–37, 44, 58, 63, 160, 173; retirement 16, 216, 232, 280, 287, 291–292, 304, 307–308, 313
De Beer, *Dr* Zach (son) 149, 310, 312, 315
Defiance Campaign 52
De Klerk, F.W. 8, 206, 210, 224–228, 231–235, 239–241, 253–256, 260–264, 270, 272, 286, 296, 306, 309
De Klerk, Jan 57, 102

De Klerk, (Wimpie) Willem 206, 209, 213–214, 308–309
De Kock, Pieter 10, 56, 61
Delimitation Commission (DC) 56
Delius, Anthony 86, 88, 91, 93, 102, 104–107
Delport, Tertius 267
Democratic Alliance (DA) 318, 320
Democratic Party (DP) 8, 10–11, 146, 208, 210–213, 217, 221–307, 311–315, 318–319
Democratic Republic of the Congo (DRC) 93, 103, 112
Democratic Turnhalle Alliance (DTA) 250
Derby-Lewis, Clive 273
De Villiers, Dawie 221
De Villiers, Fleur 191
De Villiers Graaf *see* Graaf, *Sir* De Villiers
De Villiers, René 39, 149
De Villiers, Rocco 149, 153
De Wet Nel, Daan 89, 96
Dhlomo, *Dr* Oscar 271
Dönges, Eben 41, 57
Du Plessis, Barend 211, 226, 262
Du Toit, Stephan 149, 153
Duncan, Patrick 103, 301
Dunlee, Ray 144, 203

Egeland, Leif 134
Eglin, Colin 28, 59, 68, 70–74, 126–130, 133–143, 149–158, 160–170, 185–198, 207–213, 220, 232, 249, 261, 281–284, 307–315, 319
elections: by-elections 43, 54, 80, 95, 99, 103–105, 117–121, 139, 144, 146, 166, 180, 185, 193, 203, 223, 237–239, 241, 247, 256, 262; election campaigns 19, 31, 48, 97–99, 108, 110, 113, 120, 133, 145, 152, 177, 190, 204, 224–226, 262, 287–296, 301, 306; general elections 7, 18, 25, 53, 57, 92, 96, 99, 106, 125, 133, 144–147, 161, 175, 180, 185, 216, 222, 247, 250, 287, 300, 314
English language speakers 26–29, 58, 79, 83, 93, 99, 108–110, 114, 119, 126, 136, 153, 190, 194, 223, 237
Erasmus, Frans 87–90, 103, 106
Erasmus, *Judge* P.R.B. 162

fascism 44, 179
Fenner-Solomon, V.G. 43
Ferguson, Niall 304
Fouché, Jim 105
Fourie, André 225
Fourie, I.S. (Sakkies) 33, 35, 50, 72, 76, 107, 109, 114
Freedom Front (FF) 290, 303
Friedman, *Dr* Bernard 43
Friedman, Steven 225
Fuchs, Lester 246, 279
Furniss, Wendy *see* De Beer, Wendy (daughter)

Gant, David 10, 207, 220, 307
Gastrow, Peter 10, 14, 193, 218, 236, 242, 244, 247, 271
Gevisser, Mark 183
Gibson, Douglas 10, 124, 195, 208, 247, 251, 277, 312
Ginsberg, B. 227
Glasser, Mona *see* De Beer, Mona Vida
Godsell, Bobby 198, 244, 315
Graaf, *Sir* De Villiers 10, 34, 44, 49–64, 67–74, 81, 87–89, 92–94, 96, 98–99, 108, 122, 131, 134, 145–146
Green, Michael 143
Greyling, Paul 158, 160
greyshirts *see* Weichardt, Louis
Group Areas Act *see* laws & legislation
Grundlingh, Albert 319
Guy, Duncan 301

Haak, Jan 65

Hall, Lester 74
Hani, Chris 182, 273
Hartley, Roy 304–305
Herstigte Nasionale Party (HNP) 133–134, 136, 185
Hertzog, Albert 96, 133
Hertzog, J.B.M. (Barry) 15, 68, 70
Heunis, Chris 189
Hickman, Tony 109, 113–114
Higgerty, Jack 48
Hofmeyr, Jannie 194, 207
Hope, Christopher 190
Horak, Bill 48–49
Horwood, Owen 158, 162–163
House of Assembly *see* parliament
Howes, Avril 213
Hulley, Roger 169, 208

Independent Movement (IM) 189, 191, 193–194, 207
Independent Party (IP) 193
influx control 76, 85, 108, 144, 189 *see also* urbanisation
Information Scandal (1977) 157–159
Inkatha Freedom Party (IFP) 8, 184, 236–237, 260, 267–268, 271, 273, 290–291, 294, 298–299, 303, 319 *see also* Zulu monarchy

Jacobs, Gideon 114
Jenkins, Roy 208, 278
Jennings, *Sir* Ivor 47
Johnson, Anthony 245
Johnson, R.W. 120
Johnson, Shaun 301
Jonker, Abraham 34
Jordaan, Kobus 256, 280
Jordan, Pallo 182
Jowell, *Dr* Frances 310

Kahn, Sam 21, 31
Kaunda, Kenneth 139, 181, 224
Kgosane, Philip 88–89
Killian, J.G. 109

Kowarsky, Leo 99–100
Kriel, Hernus 291

land question 64, 68–70, 73, 92, 254–255, 287
Lategan, Esther 189, 191, 193, 207
Lawrence, Harry 10, 40–41, 64, 68, 70, 72–74, 114
laws & legislation 44–48, 62, 66, 79, 84, 106, 122–123, 131, 157, 170–171, 240, 254–255 *see also* apartheid; Group Areas Act (1950) 19, 77, 82, 170, 174, 189, 204, 211, 219, 255; Native Trust and Land Act (1936) 68, 254–255; pass laws 76–77, 85, 87, 89, 91, 108, 174, 182, 187; Population Registration Act (1950) 19, 68, 255; Suppression of Communism Act (1950) 21, 103
Lee-Warden, L.B. 52
Le Grange, Louis 171
Leon, Tony 124, 150, 195, 202, 217, 220, 229, 242–249, 257, 263–265, 279, 283, 292–296, 306, 309–314, 318
Le Roux, P.K. 42
Leutweiler, *Dr* Fritz 186
liberalism 9, 27, 39, 79, 119, 121–122, 130, 135, 161, 190, 202, 220, 245–246, 250, 258, 265–266, 298, 319
Liberal Party (LP) 11, 55, 80, 103, 131–132, 222
Lourens, Frans 241
Louw, Eli 155
Louw, N.P. van Wyk 16, 38
Luthuli, Albert 99
Luttig, P.J. 86
Luyt, Louis 206, 208, 214–215, 222
Luyt, *Sir* Richard 167

Macmillan, Harold 83
Maharaj, Mac 182, 259
Maitland constituency 27–32, 36, 56–59, 71, 74, 94, 98, 109–114, 124, 126, 153, 175, 220, 223, 227

Malan, D.F. 25, 38, 41, 164
Malan, F.S. 17–18, 122, 149
Malan, Wynand 10, 189, 191, 193–194, 198, 202, 206–209, 215–216, 219–221, 226, 228–231, 239–241
Malcomess, John 202
Mamoepa, Ronnie 276
Mandela, Nelson 122, 171, 190, 204, 223, 239, 260, 265, 277, 280, 284, 287–293, 296, 306–307, 312, 314
Mandela, Winnie 191
Mangope, Lucas 290
Marais, J.S. 76
Marais, Kowie 145–146
Matthee, J.C. 238
Mbeki, Thabo 182–183, 185
McHenry, Don 164–166, 211
Menell, Clive & Irene 145, 281
Mervis, Joel 86, 118, 126, 138
Meyer, Roelf 282
minorities 63, 67, 76, 84, 126, 161, 192, 236, 239, 274, 306
Mitchell, Douglas E. 10, 26–27, 35, 43, 49, 51, 60, 64, 68–70, 72, 86–89, 93, 96, 111, 146
Modjadji (Rain Queen of the Balobedu) 295
Mogoba, *Rev.* Stanley 271
Molteno, Donald 10, 21–22, 76–77, 105, 122–123
Momberg, Jannie 207, 214, 229, 235, 242, 253, 258, 262–263, 265
Moorcroft, Errol 194
Moore, P.A. 81
Moss, Sam 256–257
Mulder, Connie 159
Mulder, *Dr* Pieter 10, 213, 233, 278
Muldergate *see* Information Scandal (1977)
Multiparty Negotiating Process (MPNP) 273–274, 277, 281–283
Murray, Hugh 181, 186
Murray, *Dr* Paul 11
Myburgh, Tertius 181

National Democratic Movement (NDM) 193–194, 202, 206–207, 213–214, 221
National Party (NP) 18–26, 29–38, 41, 57–68, 79–81, 86–114, 125, 133–158, 175–180, 184–193, 204–213, 218–248, 249–264, 276–306, 313, 319–320
Natives Representative Council (NRC) 19
Nel, Daan de Wet *see* De Wet Nel, Daan
New Republic Party (NRP) 146–150, 153, 157, 175, 189, 191–192
Nietzsche, Friedrich 7
Norton, Victor 90

Olivier, Nic 176, 210
O'Malley, Padraig 271, 306
Oppenheimer, Ernest 39
Oppenheimer, Harry F. 10, 38–39, 47–50, 54–57, 69, 72–76, 79, 106, 117, 124–125, 132, 145, 149, 154, 167, 177, 181, 198, 259, 317
Oppenheimer, Nicky 289
Owen, David 208, 222
Owen, Ken 121, 298–299

Pakendorf, Harald 181
Pan African Congress (PAC) 7, 9, 85, 87–88, 90–91, 122, 145, 190, 232, 272, 292
parliament: House of Assembly 10, 21, 25, 35–36, 57, 61, 64, 80, 88, 98, 130, 139, 147–149, 155–157, 187, 261, 268; parliamentary caucus 24, 27, 34–35, 48, 80–81, 143, 157, 176, 187, 193–195, 211, 218, 247, 263, 277, 281; Senate 18, 25, 42–43, 47–49, 55–58, 60, 64, 66, 79, 90–91, 176; tricameral parliament 176–178, 188, 210, 273
pass book system *see* laws & legislation
pensions 31, 53, 241
Pienaar, Schalk 36, 79, 83, 97–99, 101, 140

Pistorius, *Prof.* P.V. 124, 128
Potgieter, J.E. 106
Pottinger, Brian 292, 297
Pratt, David 91
President's Council 114, 176, 187, 273
Progressive Federal Party (PFP) 8–11, 16, 147–150, 154–158, 161, 165–172, 175–180, 184–207, 211–217, 221, 227–229, 246, 275, 319
Progressive Party (PP) 7–11, 70, 74, 76–83, 87–96, 99, 103–108, 112, 115–136, 139, 142, 149, 209, 257–259, 286, 292, 319
Progressive Reform Party (PRP) 143–144, 146, 203

qualified (non-racial) franchise 18, 21, 76, 84, 97, 100, 104, 110–112, 140, 143, 161 *see also* Cape (Coloured) franchise

race & racism 13, 17–18, 20, 45, 66, 84, 96, 100–104, 120, 134, 138, 211, 217, 235, 248, 271, 275, 282, 289, 299, 306
racial segregation *see* apartheid
Ramaphosa, Cyril 284
Ramphela, *Prof.* Mamphela 271
Rand Revolt (1922) 20
Rands, Paul 116, 123
Raw, Vause 60–61
Record of Understanding (1992) 268
Reform Party (RP) 142
Relly, Gavin 173, 181–182, 184, 186, 228, 231
republicanism 76, 83, 86, 93–94, 102, 105, 108, 110
Riordan, Rory 238
Rivonia Trial (1963) 122
Rodgers, Bill 208
Ross, Neil 251
Rubin, Neville 105
Rubusana, W.B. 45
Rupert, Anton 145, 181
Russell, Hamilton 90–91, 122

Ryrie, *Prof.* B.J. 22

Sachs, Solly 31
Sauer, Paul 91
Schoeman, Ben 57, 86
Schoeman, Hendrik 166
Schrire, Robert 305–306
Schwarz, Harry 138, 141–143, 202, 213, 218, 230, 246–247
Selfe, James 10, 175, 212, 221, 243, 279, 300, 302
Senate *see* parliament
Senate Plan 47–49, 55–58, 60 *see also* Oppenheimer, Harry F.
Serfontein, Hennie 247–248
Sharpeville (1960) 85, 91, 96–97
Sisulu, Walter 122
Slabbert, Frederick van Zyl 10, 137–143, 147, 161, 167–170, 175–180, 184–187, 190, 200, 206, 225, 271, 275, 299, 319
Smith, Ian 125
Smuts, Dene 7, 261, 283
Smuts, Jan Christian 11, 18, 24, 40, 48, 73, 153
Soal, Peter 10, 28, 137, 149, 150, 218, 241, 278–279
Sobukwe, Robert 122
Social Democratic Party (SDP) 208, 222, 278
Solomon, V.G. Fenner *see* Fenner-Solomon V.G.
Sorour, Peter 181
South African Broadcasting Corporation (SABC) 153, 177, 191, 223, 272, 293–294
South African Communist Party (CPSA/SACP) 7, 21, 232
South African Department of Information 114, 157, 159, 162–163, 175
South African Indian Congress (SAIC) 52
South African Party (SAP) 146

South African Students' Organisation (SASO) 136
Soweto (1976) 144–145, 148, 153
Sparks, Allister 305
Spottiswoode, H.E. 125–126
Stanford, Walter 11, 80, 95
Steel, David 222
Steenkamp, Louis 43
Steyn, F.S. 103
Steyn, Marais 99
Steytler, Jan 11, 33, 57, 59, 63–75, 81–86, 90, 93, 95, 103, 108, 117, 124–131, 134–135, 250–251, 311, 320
Steytler, Willie 72
Strauss, J.G.N. 10, 22, 24–30, 34–38, 41–42, 48–51, 109, 237, 310
Strauss, Maureen *see* De Beer, Maureen (wife)
Strijdom, J.G. 41–42, 45, 58, 61
strike actions 20, 87, 188, 190, 231
Stuart, James 182
Sussens, Aubrey 54
Sutton, Bill 189
Suzman, Arthur 76
Suzman, Helen 10, 35, 43, 61, 72, 76, 81, 88, 109, 113, 122, 129–131, 134–137, 143, 148, 155, 178, 187, 191, 214, 218, 226, 243, 281, 297, 313, 319
Swart, C.R. 105
Swart, Freek 235
Swart, Ray 11, 33, 44, 60, 72, 108, 119–120, 155, 214, 221, 313

Tambo, Oliver 182–183
Tarr, Mike 271
Taylor, Cathy 73, 123
Terblanche, *Col* I.P.S. 88–89
Terre'Blanche, Eugene 179
Thomson, *Prof.* Leonard 76
Timothy, H.M. 27–28
Townley Williams, Owen 33, 106, 119
trade unions 20, 31, 68, 76, 89, 158, 174
traditional leaders 290

Transitional Executive Council (TEC) 281–282
Treurnicht, *Dr* Andries P. 98, 141, 176, 262
tricameral parliament *see* parliament
Trollip, R.A.F. 50
Tsafendas, Demetrio 130
Tutu, *Bishop* Desmond 184

Umkhonto we Sizwe 122
United Democratic Front (UDF) 178–179, 184, 191, 193, 225
United Party (UP) 19, 24–44, 48–68, 71–73, 79–93, 96–103, 107–109, 112–115, 118–123, 126, 131–147, 153, 206, 220, 246, 248
University of Cape Town (UCT) 17, 20–22, 67, 76, 88, 167–168, 173, 220, 271, 277, 289, 293
University of South Africa (UNISA) 8–9, 11, 132, 292, 298
University of the Western Cape (UWC) 292–293
University of the Witwatersrand (WITS) 10–11, 67, 76, 174, 225
Urban Foundation 145, 186
urbanisation 19, 33, 36, 40–41, 53, 57, 65–66, 137, 144–145, 148, 158, 189
see also influx control

Van der Byl, *Maj.* Piet 73
Van der Horst, Sheila 21
Van der Merwe, F.J. 58–59
Van der Merwe, Tian 208, 229–230, 243–246, 255
Van Eck, Jan 193, 218, 242, 247, 253, 263, 265
Van Heerden, Ogies 112
Van Ryneveld, Clive 15, 31, 54, 72–73
Van Schalkwyk, Marthinus 8
Van Zyl, Brand 23
Van Zyl Slabbert *see* Slabbert, Frederik van Zyl
Vermeulen, Piet 137

Verwoerd, H.F. 19, 61–62, 66–67, 80–93, 96–103, 108–114, 130–132
Viljoen, *Gen.* Constand 274, 290–291
Viljoen, Gerrit 225, 234
Viljoen, Klasie 60
Viljoen, Marais 54
Vlok, Adriaan 89
Vorster, B.J (John) 112, 121, 131–136, 145–148, 152, 157, 162, 203
Vosloo, Johan 139
voters' roll *see* common voters' roll

Waddell, Gordon 167, 169, 259
Walus, Janusz 273
Waring, Frank & Joyce 10, 34, 109–110, 113–114
Waterson, Sidney 48, 71–73
Weichardt, Louis 30–32
Welsh, *Prof.* David 232, 273, 294, 306
Wentzel, Tos 209

Wheane, *Prof.* K.C. 47
white supremacy 24, 26, 58, 94, 110, 119, 153, 192
Widman, Alf 100
Williams, Owen Townley *see* Townley Williams, Owen
Williams, Shirley 208
Wilson, Boris 61, 72, 88, 95–96, 258–259, 275
Woods, Donald 316
World War II 17, 19–20, 26, 31, 34, 75, 100
Worrall, Dennis 10, 189, 191–194, 198, 202–203, 206–209, 215–221, 226–231, 237–239, 243, 278–279, 286

Zille, Helen 151
Zion Christian Church 294
Zulu monarchy 274, 290, 301 *see also* Inkatha Freedom Party (IFP)